Wales Unchai...

Writing Wales in Eng...

*CREW (Centre for Research into the English
literature and language of Wales) Series Editor: M. Wynn Thomas (CREW, Swansea
University)*

CREW

CREW series of Critical and Scholarly Studies
General Editor: Professor M. Wynn Thomas (CREW, Swansea University)

This *CREW* series is dedicated to Emyr Humphreys, a major figure in the literary culture of modern Wales, a founding patron of the *Centre for Research into the English Literature and Language of Wales*, and, along with Gillian Clarke and the late Seamus Heaney, one of *CREW*'s original Honorary Associates. Grateful thanks are due to the late Richard Dynevor for making this series possible.

Other titles in the series

Wales Unchained

Literature, Politics and Identity in the American Century

Writing Wales in English

DANIEL G. WILLIAMS

UNIVERSITY OF WALES PRESS
2015

www.uwp.co.uk

British Library Cataloguing-in-Publication Data
A catalogue record for this book is available from the British Library.

ISBN   978-1-78316-211-6 (hardback)
       978-1-78316-212-3 (paperback)
eISBN 978-1-78316-213-0

THE ASSOCIATION FOR
WELSH WRITING IN ENGLISH
CYMDEITHAS LLÊN SAESNEG CYMRU

Typeset by Mark Heslington Ltd, Scarborough, North Yorkshire
Printed by CPI Antony Rowe, Chippenham, Wiltshire

For Stefan Collini

the children will not repeat
the phrases their parents speak

somebody has persuaded them
that it is better to say everything differently

so that they can be admired somewhere
farther and farther away

where nothing that is here is known

W. S. Merwin, from
'Losing a Language' (1988)

CONTENTS

GENERAL EDITOR'S PREFACE

The aim of this series is to produce a body of scholarly and critical work that reflects the richness and variety of the English-language literature of modern Wales. Drawing upon the expertise both of established specialists and of younger scholars, it will seek to take advantage of the concepts, models and discourses current in the best contemporary studies to promote a better understanding of the literature's significance, viewed not only as an expression of Welsh culture but also as an instance of modern literatures in English worldwide. In addition, it will seek to make available the scholarly materials (such as bibliographies) necessary for this kind of advanced, informed study.

M. Wynn Thomas
*CREW (Centre for Research into the English
Literature and Language of Wales)*
Swansea University

ACKNOWLEDGEMENTS

Although sections of each chapter in this book are here appearing in print for the first time and chapter 7 has never been published previously, the greater part of its contents is made up of revised versions and combinations of essays that first appeared in other forms. The earlier versions have been revised, extended and combined so that the volume has a thematic coherence. While readers will inevitably dip in and out of a collection of essays, I hope that some will want to follow the shape of the argument and read the volume, as intended, from beginning to end.

Wales Unchained was conceived during a period of research leave, funded by the Leverhulme Trust, at the department of Celtic Languages and Literatures, Harvard University. I am immensely indebted to Catherine McKenna for her support in making that visit possible, and to Werner Sollors for granting me the privilege of working in his study and devouring his basement library. Among the many pleasures of that research period was the chance to discuss literature and politics with Marc Shell, who gave generously of his time. Many of the ideas in this volume were initially tested on the unwitting members of my MA course on 'Welsh Identities' at the Centre for Research into the English Literature and Language of Wales, Swansea University, and at the stimulating annual conferences of the Association for Welsh Writing in English.

I have incurred the usual range of scholarly, practical and personal debts in writing this book, but am particularly grateful for the chance to thank Yasuo Kawabata, Shintaro Kono, Asako Nakai, Takashi Onuki, Yuzo Yamada and their colleagues contributing to the *Raymond Williams Kenkyu-kai* in Japan for giving debates in Welsh studies a prominent place in their work. Jane Aaron, Kirsti Bohata, Simon Brooks, Jasmine

Donahaye, Katie Gramich, Melinda Gray, Tudur Hallam, Jerry Hunter, Matthew Jarvis, the late and sorely missed Nigel Jenkins, Dai Smith and Andrew Webb have all influenced my thinking on the issues engaged with in this volume. I owe an even greater debt to Tony Brown, M. Wynn Thomas and my father Gareth Williams who read and commented on drafts of the book. Any errors of judgement and dubious assertions are down to my obstinacy rather than any critical failures on their part. It was, as always, a privilege to work with the dedicated team at the University of Wales Press.

Further thanks are due to the editors and publishers of the various publications in which sections of these essays first appeared for allowing me to reproduce this material in revised form. Parts of the introduction appeared as 'Back to a National Future' in *Planet: The Welsh Internationalist* 176 (April/May 2006), pp. 78–85. Chapter 1 is a longer version of 'Withered Roots: Ideas of Race in the Writings of Rhys Davies and D. H. Lawrence' which appeared in Meic Stephens (ed.), *Rhys Davies: Decoding the Hare* (Cardiff: University of Wales Press, 2001), pp. 87–103. Chapter 2 began life as 'Black and White: Writing on Fighting in Wales', in Peter Stead and Gareth Williams (eds), *Wales and its Boxers* (Cardiff: University of Wales Press, 2008), pp. 117–34. I am indebted to fellow literary critic and jazz musician Mark Osteen for his comments on an early draft of Chapter 3 in 2003. Some of this material appeared in a book chapter that I co-wrote with M. Wynn Thomas, '"A Sweet Union"? Dylan Thomas and Post-War American Poetry', in Gilbert Bennett, Eryl Jenkins and Eurwen Price (eds), *I Sang in My Chains: Essays and Poems in Tribute to Dylan Thomas* (Swansea: The Dylan Thomas Society of Great Britain, 2003), pp. 68–79, and in 'Wales-Bird: Dylan Thomas and Charlie Parker', in Hannah Ellis (ed.), *Dylan Thomas a Centenary Celebration* (London: Bloomsbury, 2014), pp. 151–64. The research formed the basis for the 'Dylan Live' show, part of Literature Wales's 'Dylanwad' projects for the centenary of the poet's birth in 2014. It has been a privilege this year to work with poets Martin Daws, Zaru Johnson and Aneirin Karadog and the musicians Ed Holden (Mr Phormula) and Huw V. Williams in bringing 1950s New York to life, while exploring some of the resonances of Thomas's life and work today. The lecture from which the show developed appeared as 'The White Negro?' in *New Welsh Review 104* (summer 2014), 33–42. Chapter 4 develops ideas first presented in Welsh at the Institute of Welsh Affairs Annual Lecture, at the National Eisteddfod in Ebbw Vale, 2010. It was published in a bilingual booklet, *Aneurin Bevan a Paul Robeson: Sosialaeth, Dosbarth a Hunaniaeth/Aneurin Bevan and Paul Robeson:*

Socialism, Class and Identity (Cardiff: Institute of Welsh Affairs, 2010). I am grateful to Paul Robeson's grand-daughter Susan Robeson for her presence at the lecture and comments following its delivery, and for the responses of Leanne Wood AM. Chapter 5 draws on my 'Introduction' to Raymond Williams, *Who Speaks for Wales: Nation, Culture, Identity*, ed. Daniel Williams (Cardiff: University of Wales Press, 2003), pp. xv–liii. The defence of Williams against Gilroy and others was developed in '"Insularly English": Raymond Williams, Nation and Race', *Journal for the Study of British Cultures*, 12, 1 (2005), 55–66. Some of the material on *Border Country* appeared in 'Writing against the Grain: Raymond Williams's *Border Country* and the Defence of Realism', in Katie Gramich (ed.), *Mapping the Territory: Critical Approaches to Welsh Fiction in English* (Cardigan: Parthian, 2010), pp. 217–244. Chapter 6 is a slightly amended version of '"American Freaks": Welsh Poets and the United States', in Daniel G. Williams (ed.), *Slanderous Tongues: Essays on Welsh Poetry in English 1970–2005* (Bridgend: Seren, 2010), pp. 163–97. Chapter 7 is previously unpublished, but began life as 'Problems of Identity: Language and Race in the Literatures of Wales', T. H. Parry-Williams Memorial Lecture, National Library of Wales, Aberystwyth, 4 May 2011. I thank Dafydd Johnston for inviting me to deliver the lecture that year.

The precise details of the quotations used in this book will be found in the notes. For granting permissions I am grateful to the following: Copper Canyon Press for the permission to use (Welsh-)American poet W. S. Merwin's words as the epigraph to this book; Professor Meic Stephens as literary executor for the rights to quote from Leslie Norris, and as secretary of the Rhys Davies Trust for permission to quote from Rhys Davies; Professor John Callahan, literary executor of the Ralph Ellison Estate for the right to quote from the unpublished story 'A Storm of Blizzard Proportions', which exists in several drafts at the Library of Congress, Washington DC; David Higham Associates and New Directions for permission to quote from Dylan Thomas's *Collected Poems*; SLL/Sterling Lord Literistic, Inc., for permission to quote from Jack Kerouac's 'Mexico City Blues'; Gwasg Gomer for the permission to quote from Nigel Jenkins and Jon Dressel; Seren publishers for the poetry of Duncan Bush and Christine Evans; Carcanet Press for the poetry of Gillian Clarke; Gwydion Thomas and the estate of R. S. Thomas for the passages of poetry and prose by R. S. Thomas (© Elodie Thomas, 2014); Merryn Williams for the quotations by Raymond Williams; Menna Elfyn and Bloodaxe Books for Menna Elfyn's poetry; Gwyneth Lewis and Bloodaxe Books for the poetry of Gwyneth Lewis. Every effort has been made to trace the owners of copyright material and the publishers will be pleased to correct any omissions brought to their notice at the earliest convenience.

The dedication is to a model essayist, stimulating PhD supervisor and astute analyst of the Welsh XV, whose friendship and advice are as appreciated today in the year of his retirement as they were almost twenty years ago in Cambridge. Thanks, as always, to my mother Mary and brother Tomos and his family for their emotional, and musical, sustenance and support. There are no sufficient words to thank my wife Sioned, and children Lowri and Dewi. They are unstinting in their love, support and – crucially – commitment to getting me away from the desk. *Diolch o'r galon i chi'ch tri unwaith eto.*

Daniel G. Williams
Alltwen
August 2014

Introduction

The essays collected in this book explore some of the forms taken by Welsh identity, and the ways in which that identity has been made and remade since the early twentieth century by that broad and ill-defined constellation of activities that we call 'culture'. Intellectual historians might come to characterize the last twenty years as the period of 'identity' in cultural studies; a period in which the formation of identities and the problem of subjectivity were dominant themes in the humanities. These have been the years of my evolution as a critic, and the essays collected in this volume contribute to the project of bringing theories of identity to bear on Welsh culture. Among the topics covered are: the racialization of the Welsh in Britain and the United States; the comparative terms in which Welshness has been imagined; the implications of thinking about identity in class, ethnic, gendered and linguistic terms; the problems inherent in creating a Welsh multiculturalism. But this is not simply a matter of choosing Wales as a laboratory for such treatment in a familiar condescending gesture. For if theory may illuminate aspects of Welsh culture, the opposite may also be the case. The Welsh example insistently draws our attention to themes, such as multilingualism and class consciousness, that are often neglected in contemporary anglophone cultural studies. Some chapters deal less with Welsh identity as defined internally than they do with outsiders' images and conceptualizations of Wales. I have tried to draw on comparative materials throughout, for in thinking through the diversity and complexities of Welshness it is helpful to bring as wide a range of examples as possible to the table, theorized in a range of idioms and drawing on insights from other traditions.

To describe the last hundred years as the 'American century', as I do in this volume's subtitle, is to invite controversy. It is a debatable description, one that may seem to unquestioningly accept the contemporary cultural and economic dominance of the United States, and a phrase that reinforces the unfortunate tendency to consider 'America' as equivalent to the 'United States' thus ignoring the histories of Canada, Latin America and the Caribbean islands. Nevertheless, ever since the phrase 'American century' was popularized by the media tycoon Henry Luce, 'America' has functioned as a synonym for 'modernity'.[1] This is certainly the case in Welsh writing and cultural studies, not least in the work of Dai Smith who developed Alfred Zimmern's observation in *My Impressions of Wales* (1921), that industrial south Wales was similar to industrial America, into an approach to modern Welsh history.[2] For Smith,

> if 'American Wales' is metaphor far more than it is a reality, then it is still a profoundly suggestive one, acute in its understanding that what had taken place in Wales was not merely industrialization or urbanization or angliciza-tion but rather a process of discovery as profound for Wales as the making of a specifically American identity in the USA was during the country's own dramatic nineteenth century.[3]

The comparative examples that Smith turns to in his stimulating work are often drawn from that remarkable generation of Jewish intellectuals whose 'entry into the anti-Semitic and patriarchal cultural discourse of the exclu-sivistic institutions of American culture' is described by Cornel West as initiating 'the slow but sure undoing of male WASP cultural hegemony and homogeneity'.[4] A number of these 'New York Intellectuals' – critics such as Irving Howe, Alfred Kazin and Lionel Trilling – were second-generation Americans, children of immigrants from eastern Europe. They became adults during the 1930s Depression, had identified with commu-nism during that period, but had since turned their back on it in the face of Stalinist repression and McCarthyite hysteria. Many were of Jewish descent and fully aware that the most prestigious educational institutions in America had demonized their people and barred them from entering their corridors.[5] Dylan Thomas – whose poem 'Fern Hill' is evoked in the title of this book – was a figure of some importance to this generation.[6] Thomas's impact on America is the subject of a later chapter in this book, but it's worth noting here that according to Alfred Kazin, author of the monumental study *On Native Grounds: An Interpretation of Modern American Prose Literature* (1942), 'Dylan felt a natural affinity with this country, while in Britain, being utterly outside the "Establishment", he was regarded with a certain loving contempt by some of the snobs who so righteously gnashed their teeth after his death'.[7] It seems that for Kazin, the Welsh Dylan had challenged the boundaries of the English literary establishment, and was thus a model for the process initiated in the United States by his generation of Jewish intellectuals as they challenged the hegemony of the white Anglo-Saxon Protestant intelligentsia.

Given their own personal trajectories, Howe, Kazin and others emphasized narratives of assimilation in their explorations of American culture, and in doing so provided Dai Smith with a template for his own analyses of the south Walian industrial melting pot. Smith (a generation removed from the Welsh language) noted that Howe's analysis of 'Jewish-American authors a generation removed from Yiddish' was applicable to the literature of south Wales with its 'yoking of street-raciness and high-culture mandarin', and emphasized that assimilation did not amount to loss for, in Howe's words,

> there were strengths … a rich and complicated ethic … a readiness to live for ideals beyond the clamour of self, a sense of plebeian fraternity, an ability to forge a community of moral order even while remaining subject to a society of social disorder.[8]

Anyone familiar with Dai Smith's work will recognize his influence on the content and, in places, modes of analysis of this book. Smith studied in Lionel Trilling's English department at Columbia in the 1960s and developed a narrative of Welsh history in which the old co-ordinates of language, place and religion were abandoned for class, mobility and secularization.[9] The impact of the Civil Rights and Black Power movements on the academy from the late 1960s onwards led to a rejection of this type of 'assimilationist' narrative in American studies, and whereas the first generation of writers to engage consciously with the immigrant experience had described a process whereby entrance into the republic of letters was granted in exchange for ethnic consciousness, later generations felt that Howe's generation had 'underestimated the degree of cultural persistence' among writers who were credited with achieving 'universal' perspectives in their works.[10]

By the time I was a postgraduate student in the department of African American studies at Harvard, critics who had been educated in the 1970s, such as Henry Louis Gates, Jr., were engaged in defining the distinctive themes, tropes and rhetorical strategies of the Black literary canon. In works such as *The Signifying Monkey: A Theory of African American Literary Criticism* (1988), Gates deconstructed notions of 'race' as they had been perpetuated in imperialist thought, while simultaneously tracing the persistence of African vernacular traditions in African American culture.[11] Similar work, balancing a deconstructive approach to identity alongside an awareness and respect for cultural difference and persistence, was being pursued in other areas of ethnic literature by Marc Shell and Werner Sollors, and by an innovative generation of critics such as Barbara Hillers and Jerry Hunter in Harvard's department of Celtic languages and literatures.[12] If cultural forms could be said to have persisted across centuries, and even to have survived the 'middle passage', then Dai Smith was surely exaggerating when he suggested that the writers of industrial south Wales emanated from a 'major socialist culture' with little relationship 'to the dead hand of a parallel provincial culture' rooted in the Welsh language and religious Nonconformity.[13] The misleading capitalized phrase 'English-speaking South Wales' which is still widely used in anglophone cultural criticism seemed to me an ideological construct designed to marginalize a still living Welsh-language culture, and to ignore the dynamic interrelationships between what Raymond Williams described as 'the residual, dominant and emergent' forces in Welsh society.[14] This was a conviction given a personal charge by the deaths of my grandfathers in the mid-1990s, both brought up Welsh-speaking and working class in industrial south Wales.

If American ethnic studies may be seen to have shifted emphasis from assimilationism to ethnic persistence, many of the most subtle contemporary theorists (often working to varying degrees under the influence of Werner Sollors) tend to explore the tensions between these, not wholly incompatible, tendencies.[15] It seemed to me in the late 1990s that literary criticism, particularly the writings of Jane Aaron and M. Wynn Thomas, offered a space for attending to the genuine differences and the corresponding similarities that existed within the languages, religions and genders that constituted Welsh communities.[16] I attempted to locate myself within this intellectual context, and the essays collected here reflect a decade of engagement with the ways in which the strains of cultural particularism on the one hand, and assimilationism on the other, have manifested themselves within Welsh literature, politics and culture in the last hundred years.

Wales Unchained explores the tensions between these particularistic and assimilationist strains, which are still discernible within contemporary studies of Wales, even if the terms of the debate have been modified in different disciplinary and temporal contexts. The first strain, emphasizing ethnic or cultural difference, may broadly be termed 'nationalist' in that it wishes Wales to unchain itself from what it sees as the unbalanced, unequal and inherently exploitative British state, becoming an independent liberal-democratic nation in Europe. The second strain, a more recent inflection of the 'assimilationist' emphasis, sees nationalism as inherently pernicious and seeks to try and build new forms of 'post-national' or 'cosmopolitan' citizenship based on unchaining the link between liberal-democracy and a national culture. Both strains of thought may be considered responses to what Will Kymlicka describes as the 'nearly-universal reordering of political space from the confusing welter of empires, kingdoms, city-states, protectorates and colonies' into nation states governed by systems of liberal democracy.[17] It is a characteristic of such states that they engage in a process of nation-building aimed at the diffusion of a common national identity, culture and language. This 'liberal nationhood model', argues Kymlicka, has been a 'remarkable success in ensuring democracy, individual rights, peace and security'.[18] But these successes have been achieved at a high cost for the victims of liberal nationhood: immigrants and historic sub-state groups in particular. For minority nationalists (representatives of the first strain of thought described above), Wales has historically been a sub-state region or 'principality' within the British state, the victim of assimilationist cultural practices and extractive economic policies. Their response to this scenario is to argue that Wales should be its own, self-governed, nation. The new Welsh nation would itself, however, be open to the same charges of cultural homogenization with regard to its constituent sub-cultures. The proponents of an independent Wales must believe that the harms of liberal nationalism are not intrinsic to it, and are, in fact, the result of the illiberal chauvinistic intolerance of centralized imperial states. For them, what distinguishes nationalism from chauvinism is a willingness to extend the same rights to other peoples that one claims for oneself. But those (embracing the second strain of thought identified above) who are unconvinced by what they regard as special pleading on behalf of would-be emergent small nations see nationalism itself, in all its forms, as the problem. They seek to transcend the nation by building new forms of 'post-national' or 'cosmopolitan' citizenship that sever the link between liberal-democracy and nationhood, between political values and cultural traditions.

These two strains of thought are given eloquent expression in the opening two chapters of the pioneering volume *Postcolonial Wales* that appeared under the editorship of Jane Aaron and Chris Williams in 2005. Placed, strategically, at the beginning of the book, the chapters by the historian Chris Williams and political scientist Richard Wyn Jones approach the idea of 'postcolonialism' from diametrically opposed positions. In 'Problematizing Wales: An Exploration in Historiography and Postcoloniality', Chris Williams argues that while Wales has not been a colony since at least the Acts of Union, the ideas of postcolonial theory as developed by thinkers such as Edward Said, Gayatri Spivak and Homi Bhabha may be useful in pluralizing, complicating and drawing attention to the inherent ambivalence and hybridity of Wales and of Welshness. For Richard Wyn Jones, on the other hand, the legacy of having been a colony of England from the conquest to the Acts of Union has continued to influence Welsh politics. Unlike Williams, Jones makes little use of postcolonial theory and draws on the earlier 'historical sociology' of *New Left Review* collaborators Perry Anderson and Tom Nairn. While Chris Williams argues that Wales could not be regarded as a colony, given that 'it has been possible for Welsh politicians (such as David Lloyd George, Aneurin Bevan, Jim Griffiths and George Thomas) to rise to positions of high office' and that there was no 'Welsh equivalent of the Amritsar Massacre', Richard Wyn Jones suggests that we should not measure degrees of colonization against a British ideal model, for colonialism has taken different forms in different contexts and periods.[19] In some cases, notes Jones, the colonial relationship was brought to an end not by the granting of constitutional independence but through a process of annexation, and Wales's incorporation into the English state following the Acts of Union bears some resemblance to 'the incorporation of Algeria into the metropolitan French state between 1848 and 1962, and the current status of Martinique, New Caledonia and French Guyana' from this point of view.[20] While Williams is no doubt right to note that 'in terms of Wales's existence within the United Kingdom, the ratio of English or British coercion to Welsh consent has been very low', the ratio of difference and equality varies greatly, as Christopher Clapham has argued, from one type of colonialism to another.[21] Such debates are perhaps ultimately irresolvable, but the nub of the argument between Williams and Jones does not actually lie in their understanding of postcolonialism as such (which, as the editors note, is a vague enough term to cover an eclectic range of approaches), but in their attitude towards nationalism and their views of their nation's future.

Whereas Chris Williams argues that the Welsh should embrace 'post-nationhood' and would do well to avoid an 'anachronistic burst of nation-building, just as the nation-state finally begins to recede from its central position on the world stage', Richard Wyn Jones argues that pronouncements regarding the end of nationalism have proved premature, that the 'nation remains at the core of claims to political legitimacy' and that a fully national future for Wales is 'pregnant with possibilities'.[22] In envisaging Wales as a 'post-nation' Chris Williams draws on the political language of postmodernism, filtered through the work of contemporary postcolonial theorists: a language of marginality, difference, borders, otherness, diversity, ambivalence. For him nationalism is pernicious in that nationalists seek to ignore 'the diversity of those individuals they wish to homogenize as members of the nation' and aim to 'close frontiers both internally and externally'.[23] Williams's 'post-national' Wales

> would be a partially autonomous Wales where that autonomy has a liberating effect for all citizens, and not just for those who subscribe to conventional views of what the characteristics of the nation-state should be. It would be a society that has discarded the notion of a homogeneous nation-state with singular forms of belonging, in favour of inclusivity and cultural diversity.[24]

Williams has embraced a postmodern enthusiasm for margins and minorities, suspecting consensus and solidarity as inherently authoritarian.

Richard Wyn Jones, on the other hand, draws on the political discourse of modernity: a language of rights, justice, exploitation, political legitimacy. Nationalism is the response to colonialism in this world view; it is a child of liberal Enlightenment, an application to collectivities, as well as individuals, of the moral principle that human beings should be self-determining. Jones is a nationalist who has embraced many of the insights of recent historiography, but to assume (as Chris Williams does) that a nationalist should change his views in the light of the fact that Wales sent Members of Parliament to Westminster, that the British state recognized Welsh cultural identity in the Welsh Sunday Closing of 1881, that the Welsh were willing participants in British imperial adventures, or that there was no Welsh equivalent to the Amritsar Massacre, is to misunderstand the nature of radical politics. Feminist demands, as Terry Eagleton notes, are not rendered invalid by the fact that many men throughout history have treated women well, nor is socialism only relevant within the context of child labour and a twelve-hour working day. This is not to suggest that the nationalist principle is always a sound one, or that nothing can count as a criticism of it. It is to argue that nationalism rests upon a moral principle and, in the words of Eagleton,

> cannot be refuted simply by presenting empirical evidence about the nature of the regimes which it opposes, or the character of the movements which

incarnate it ... [I]t is falsifiable only in the way that moral principles generally are, rather than by claiming that, say, the price of bread in Tipperary in 1871 was not as prohibitively high as the Fenians maintained.[25]

In the case of Chris Williams's chapter, what is selected for problematization is, of course, significant. Williams sets his postcolonial ideas against those (unnamed) nationalists who seek to erect 'psychological barriers between peoples, excite unnecessary antagonisms towards others, and render marginal or invisible those whose characteristics do not fit those of the imagined nation'.[26] The resulting sceptical reading of nationalist formulas is both necessary and often convincing, but it would be good to see his theories also applied to the endlessly repeated mantras of Welsh historical revisionism, which are themselves based on a crude and misleading binary opposition between (to quote Chris Williams in 1996) a 'privileged minority' of 'self-blinded visionaries' who espoused a 'linguistically exclusive "Welshness"', and a 'collectivist, universalist' working class who promoted 'an inter-meshing of class and community solidarities whose horizons were truly international'.[27] The essay by the Wales-based African American anthropologist Glenn Jordan in *Postcolonial Wales* may offer a corrective in this respect, for as well as recounting stories such as that of Nora Glasgow Richer, the 'black' Welsh-speaking daughter of a south Walian and West African who was refused membership of Plaid Cymru in the 1950s on the grounds that she was deemed to be insufficiently 'Welsh', Jordan also discusses the ways in which the 'virtual worship of Paul Robeson' has served to obscure the racism of Welsh working-class communities.[28]

The work of critics such as Glenn Jordan and Charlotte Williams on multi-ethnicity and multiculturalism in Wales not only foregrounds the selectivity of Williams's historical narrative, but also exposes Richard Wyn Jones's lack of an engagement with a growing Welsh diversity that is manifest at both political and cultural levels.[29] For Jones, as for Tom Nairn on whom he draws, the primary emphasis is on 'state-form'. While registering that Welsh national difference was largely manifested in the cultural sphere (unlike Ireland and Scotland, where an institutional separation from the British state was maintained in various forms) Jones has little to say about that culture: about shifts in its content, its growing diversity, its linguistic tensions. His claim that a cultural idea of Welshness has been preserved historically by the 'subordinate orders', while Britishness has been the preserve of 'social elites', is an example of the kind of wishful thinking that is characteristic of the nationalist-left at its weakest (and uncharacteristic of his chapter) and is in fact contradicted by his earlier observation that 'the symbolism and ideology of British imperialism permeated Welsh language culture' in the nineteenth century.[30] Chris Williams's very brief engagement with the question of 'cultural imperialism' is, similarly, the weakest section of his chapter. He argues that

> attempts to link Raymond Williams's description of Welsh culture as a 'post-colonial culture, conscious all the time of its own real strengths and potentials, longing only to become its own world but with much too much on its back to be able, consistently, to face its own future', to [Emyr] Humphreys's bizarre assertion that Wales remains in a 'post-colonial situation' in which 'colonial occupation' has become consolidated into a 'settled state of affairs' are strained and unconvincing.[31]

According to Chris Williams, Raymond Williams 'nowhere explains his 1975 "post-colonial" observation'.[32] In the section from my introduction to *Who Speaks for Wales?* (a collection of Raymond Williams's writings on Wales) to which he is referring, I gave several examples of passages where Raymond Williams does indeed substantiate his description of Welsh culture as 'post-colonial'. Far from loosely 'linking' Williams's description to Humphreys's observation, I drew specific attention to the following passage which seems to me a description of the ways in which a power relationship becomes consolidated, and is very close in spirit to Humphreys's allegedly 'bizarre' observation. Raymond Williams is describing a new phase in 'community and nationalist thinking' and notes:

> It is evident also that the hostile and opposing elements to this new kind of politics are ... not only in some distant power centre. This was my saddest discovery: when I found that in myself – and of course by this time I had been away and through a very different experience – in myself that most crucial form of imperialism had happened. That is to say, where parts of your mind are taken over by a system of ideas, a system of feelings, which really do emanate from the power centre. Right back in your own mind, and right back inside the oppressed and deprived community, there are reproduced elements of the thinking and the feeling of that dominating centre. These become the destructive complexities inside what had once seemed a simple affirmative mood.[33]

This strikes me as a characteristically trenchant account of that 'psycho-colonialism' that revisionist historians, apparently hamstrung by their empiricist training, seem particularly anxious to dismiss. The measure of Welsh 'postcoloniality' for Chris Williams is whether 'there is any consensus amongst *historians* as to Wales's colonial status'. Literature does not offer hard empirical evidence, but it is an inevitably limited form of 'problematization' that ignores the pertinent (if peculiar, from the historian's perspective) testimony of art.[34]

This book, then, is intended as a contribution to these debates, from the field of cultural studies. It is written in the belief that 'literature' is a specific activity, but one in which the whole history of a culture is deeply inscribed and which is often ignored by historians and political scientists. No historical event or relationship – as the historians of mentalité have long argued – is finally separable from the way in which it is symbolized in social consciousness. It was Raymond Williams who argued that 'anything as deep as a dominant structure of feeling is only changed by active new experience', and in expanding this insight to the question of national identity he warned us that

> it is a serious misunderstanding … to suppose that the problems of social identity are resolved by formal (merely legal) definitions. For unevenly and at times precariously, but always through long experience substantially, an effective awareness of social identity depends on actual and sustained social relationships. To reduce social identity to formal legal definitions, at the level of the state, is to collude in the alienated superficialities of 'the nation' which are the limited functional terms of the modern ruling class.[35]

Some have suggested that Raymond Williams was an early proponent of the 'post-national' agenda in which 'the idea of a national culture' should be 'decoupled from the civic rights and responsibilities that go with being a citizen of Wales'.[36] This is misleading, for throughout his career Williams consistently argued the very opposite: that political structures can never satisfactorily precede, nor be decoupled from, cultural formations.

Perhaps we currently need the post-nationalist emphasis on hybridity, diversity and ambivalence, alongside the nationalist emphasis on social justice and political legitimacy. On the one hand, if the language of hybridity and diversity is unchained from its material moorings in a national culture it will end up without the political mechanisms necessary for its realization. On the other hand, there is always the danger in the nationalist's desired drive towards full nation-statehood, that the need to acknowledge difference and otherness will be ignored. A joke recalled by Slavoj Žižek may assist us in finally adjudicating between the merits of 'nationalist' and 'post-national' interpretations.

> A man who believes himself to be a grain of seed is taken to the mental institution, where the doctors do their best to finally convince him that he is not a grain but a man; however, when he is cured (convinced that he is not a grain of seed but a man) and allowed to leave the hospital, he immediately comes

back, trembling in fear – there is a chicken outside the door, and he is afraid it will eat him. 'Dear fellow,' says his doctor, 'you know very well that you are not a grain of seed but a man'. 'Of course I know that,' replies the patient, 'but does the chicken know it?'[37]

We might indeed be persuaded that Wales is a post-nation, that this region of 3 million people has managed to bypass national formation and now offers a beacon of post-national citizenship in a wilderness of sovereign states. While acknowledging the appeal of this vision, I am not ultimately convinced by such exceptionalism. Like the paranoid patient and the chicken, the Welsh may be persuaded that they inhabit a post-national polity, but would anyone else recognize this? Tom Nairn argues that those nation-states 'who made it too big, too early, find themselves today unfairly re-dimensioned, struggling to tread water in shallower seas', while

> the survivors can re-group and begin to put things right via 'globalisation' … Common ground-rules and recognition of being 'in the same boat' are one thing; homogeneity is quite another. Or to put it another way: equality of tongues and cultures is one thing, together with translation devices; 'globish' is something else.[38]

Wales's emergence as a political entity out of the moribund husk of the British state is taking place within the context of globalization, a moment where humanity's diversity is establishing itself after 'the phony phase of "nationalisms" that were largely driven by the first-round need to industrialise, on a scale that tended to neutralise variety (and often did obliterate it)'.[39] Culture is likely to play as significant a role as politics in the struggle to create a tolerant, humane and plural Wales within this emergent global context.

Wales Unchained explores the prehistory of our current moment. In this respect it offers a fragmented and incomplete, but hopefully suggestive and illuminating, cultural history of the idea of Welshness. I do not believe, as I hope the comparative materials drawn upon here will make evident, that there is an exceptionalist Welsh tradition of thinking about these ideas. I do believe, however, that there are continuities and patterns in the plural, which have given intellectual life in Wales a distinctiveness in the past, and which continue to inform – though they do not determine – our thinking about these issues in the present. I have attempted to keep in mind, at every stage of the argument, that any identity – however central it may be to people's self-conception – may, in other situations and at other times, simply not be the one that we need. In exploring the cultural and political implications of various forms of identification, the aim has been to draw on the example of Raymond Williams in advancing those ideas 'and ways of thinking, with the seeds of life in them', while undermining and breaking those chains 'perhaps deep in our minds' that connect us to ideas harbouring the 'seeds of a general death'.[40]

The Lure of Race: Rhys Davies
and D. H. Lawrence

I

In reviewing Rhys Davies's 'new style guidebook' *My Wales* in 1937
George Ewart Evans was struck by the fact that the author's analysis of
industrial unrest was based on ideas of race:

> Rhys Davies attempts to take a detached view of the conflict between miners
> and owners since the beginning of the last century. He sees the struggle
> isolated in South Wales, not a world-wide phenomenon. As a result he has
> startling theories of its cause. The strife in South Wales is a natural outcome of
> the presence of mixed breeds in the coalfield. What a notion! Comic of Bill
> Bristol, Mike and Dai working together in the same seam [*sic*]. But is fascist-
> fodder comic?[1]

By 1937 a view of society based upon racial differences was increasingly
being connected with the rise of fascism but, as several critics have argued,
the values that informed fascist ideas of society and culture played a
significant part within European intellectual thought throughout the first
half of the twentieth century.[2] Indeed, one of the most striking, and
disturbing, characteristics of novelist and short-story writer Rhys Davies's
writings is the way in which, throughout his career, he understood and
described the world in racial terms. Individual characteristics, especially
abnormalities, are given racial explanations throughout Davies's writings.
In the early short story 'Arfon' (1931), for instance, Mrs Edwards blames
her husband's racial background for their son's 'idiotic tendencies': 'Gipsy

blood is in you.'[3] Davies was still depicting the world in racial terms in his autobiography of 1969, *Print of a Hare's Foot*, where the Rhondda Valley is depicted as a 'mongrel place' that nevertheless managed to nurture the 'perfection of dark Iberian features' that Davies perceives in his friend Caerphilly whom he decides must be 'a throwback to some more splendid ancestry, a reminder of an old racial sumptuousness'.[4]

While this racial view of the world could, with some justification, be dismissed as 'fascist fodder', an account of Davies's ideas of race is necessary if we are to achieve a full understanding of the social and political values informing his fictions. Furthermore, his racial conception of the world is indicative of a significant strain within Welsh writing in the first half of the twentieth century. The issue of race also throws an illuminating light on Rhys Davies's, by now well-known, relationship with D. H. Lawrence. Society in the fictions of Davies and Lawrence is made up of distinctive racial groups, and their writings are indicative of a significant shift that occurred in the discourse on race between the late nineteenth and early twentieth centuries. This shift has been described as the replacement of a nineteenth-century universal concept of 'Culture' with a modernist, pluralist, definition of lower case 'cultures'. The characteristic nineteenth-century commitment to a universal culture to which all people should aspire is seen to give way to the twentieth-century's anthropologically informed awareness of cultural difference and pluralism.[5] This shift in ideas of race can be traced by comparing the commitment to plural racial cultures that we encounter in the writings of Davies and Lawrence, with the desire to forge a single homogeneous common culture that we encounter in the writings of the leading Victorian social critic, Matthew Arnold. The argument that follows is informed by the writings of the critic Werner Sollors, who bases his analyses of ethnicity on a distinction between consent (the bonds of culture) and descent (the bonds of heredity and blood).[6] Consent and descent are not mutually incompatible terms, but adopting these terms will allow me to isolate, within a varied and complex field, two divergent strains that are characteristic of racial thought in the late nineteenth and early twentieth centuries. My goal in what follows is to trace some of the roots of Davies's and Lawrence's racial ideas, and to explore the impact that their ideas of race had on their writings. Their racial understanding of the world has far-reaching consequences for their depictions of Wales and the Welsh.

II

The Welsh in Rhys Davies's writings are represented in racial, primitivist, terms. Welshness is not defined by a consensual engagement in an histori- cally developing culture, but rather is pre-programmed 'into the blood' of characters.[7] The Welsh are thus defined according to a set of eternal, immutable and primitivist characteristics that are passed down through the generations; they 'at heart are still bucolic and simple' notes Davies in *My Wales*, 'they still have their priceless Celtic sense of wonder, they are still beautifully child-like'.[8] The 'individual Welsh spirit' is 'poetic' and 'imag- inative', and the Welsh 'seldom worry themselves with the weighty problems of modern civilisation'.[9] 'There is still a primitive shine on Wales' he notes later, 'one can smell the old world there still'.[10] In Davies's first novel *The Withered Root* (1927) the Welsh are described as 'a race of mystical poets who have gone awry in some way', and it is the fact that Reuben Daniels's mother is of 'the old pure Welsh blood' that gives the preacher his poetic imagination, for 'he of her descent would in other days have sung poems and carried his harp from village to village, a bard bred of the rough hills and wild people'.[11] Reuben and his mother inhabit a valley described in the novel's opening as 'a community to itself' in which 'its rock-crowned hills imprisoned hardly any but the native Welsh, and in their bleak isolation the people lived with all the primitive force of the Welsh'.[12]

Davies's primitivist depiction of the Welsh is most pronounced in the novel *The Black Venus* (1944) in which the 'black Venus' of the title is a statue owned by the 'fiercely independent' Lizzie Pugh. It stands as an incarnation of an uninhibited sexuality and a primitive resistance to industrialized society. The story is set in the rural village of Ayron, a place where 'streams ran pellucid as in the dawn of time', that feels 'a thousand miles from the railway station' and where, beyond the machinery of surveillance developed in industrial settlements, old Welsh customs such as 'courting in bed' – where, in cold houses with few rooms, couples would get to know each other in bed with a bolster laid between them – continue unabated.[13] The racial difference represented by the black Venus mirrors the difference that Davies constructs between the native Welsh and the English who dismiss the indigenous population as 'savages' who go 'prowling about in the night'.[14] The black Venus of Rhys Davies's novel is thus a symbol of both the Welsh self and the Other, of the Welsh people's complicity in colonialism and their subjugation as colonized subjects, and of a primitivized rural past that the author – a native of the industrialized

Rhondda – simultaneously longs for and disowns. These ambivalences constitute a key tension in much of Davies's work. In *My Wales*, he tells his reader that a visitor to south Wales 'will come across a distinct species of short and sturdy people with long, dark, curly heads and black eyes'.[15] These 'are probably descendants of those Silures of Iberian aspect whom Tacitus describes as being in possession of South-West Britain'. The Silurian is significant for Davies because he 'is the oldest Welshman known to us by characteristic and feature'. These 'characteristics' are brought into focus on a train ride where the narrator witnesses an encounter between a Silurian and an American who 'was bright as the morning, sharp as an arrow, and as full of swift lean strength'. But

> when the Silurian entered at Brecon, and sat beside him, his brightness thinned, his movements appeared jerky, squirmy, controlled by nerves damaged in a civilisation that could not really touch the Silurian's core. The Silurian's vitality was warm, deep and shrewd; the mobility of his expression had a soothing beauty, he was perceptive of the earth and the things around him, from a source deep within him; he would know how to touch things. The American was living outside himself; I could see now that he was scarcely ever a part of his body; he jumped and careered about and jerked out questions about the land, brightly using his mind and storing information away in it, like a card-index.[16]

The American represents modernity, and is a man whose 'nerves' have been 'damaged' by modern civilization and whose mind works 'like a card index'. The Silurian, in stark contrast, represents the 'warmth, depth and shrewdness' of a previous, and in some ways superior, civilization. The very presence of the Silurian forces the narrator to revise his views of the American, and results in a change both in the behaviour and consciousness of those present: the American's 'brightness thinned' and the narrator becomes aware that the American 'was living outside himself' in a rationalized world where the functions of the mind are wholly disconnected from the experiences of the body. The collision between America and Wales is depicted as the collision of two racial types with fundamentally different instincts.

Tony Brown has noted that Davies, in developing his racial conception of Welshness, was drawing on the ideas of H. J. Fleure, professor of geography and anthropology at the University College of Wales, Aberystwyth.[17] From the 1910s onwards Fleure dedicated himself to the exploration of racial types in Wales. Though Fleure was an outspoken critic of racism, he nevertheless based his analyses of British racial types on a distinction between 'Nordic', 'Alpine' and 'Mediterranean' stocks.

While explicitly noting the dangers of applying the linguistic designation 'Celtic' to physical anthropology, he nevertheless believed that the 'little dark people' – the fundamental 'Mediterranean' type found in mid Wales – were ill disposed to industrialism and had cultivated religion, music and poetry while leaving commercial enterprises to the Nordic types. Born in Guernsey and concerned about the alienation bred by urban industrial societies, Fleure argued for the retention of those rural values that he believed persisted among the racial remnants in the more remote western areas of Wales. He viewed Wales as the 'ultimate refuge' of 'old thoughts and visions that had been lost to the world' and hoped that once the 'fever of industrialism' had subsided, the riches of the Celtic tradition would be rediscovered.[18]

In addition to Fleure's influence, Davies was also indebted to his major literary influence and friend D. H. Lawrence for his conceptualization of the Welsh as a primitivist, anti-materialist and poetic people. In *Print of a Hare's Foot,* Davies recalls that he 'listened carefully' to Lawrence's argument that

> What the Celts have to learn and cherish in themselves is that sense of myste-rious magic that is born with them, the sense of mystery, the dark magic that comes with the night, especially when the moon is due, so that they start and quiver, seeing her rise over their hills, and get their magic into their blood. They want to keep that sense of the magic mystery of the world, a moony magic. That will shove all their chapel Nonconformity out of them.[19]

This 'mysterious ... moony magic' that is associated with the Celts is embodied fictionally in the character of Morgan Lewis in Lawrence's novella of 1924, *St Mawr*. Lewis, the groom from Merioneth, occupies a position in the novel 'half-way' between the coldly rational world of humans and the warm, instinctive world of animals.[20] Lou notes that when she speaks to Lewis 'I'm not sure whether I'm speaking to a man or to a horse', and this animalistic primitivism is reflected in the fact that Lewis is made the spokesman for a mystical and magical view of life:[21]

> If you didn't go near the fire all day, and if you didn't eat any cooked food nor anything that had been in the sun, but only things like turnips or radishes or pig-nuts, and then went without any clothes on, in the full moon, then you could see the people in the moon, and go with them.[22]

The emphasis on the moon and on primitive beliefs reinforce the image of the Celts that informed Lawrence's advice to Rhys Davies. For both Davies and Lawrence the Welsh are perceived in racial terms as embod-ying a number of unchanging and eternal characteristics – imagination, a belief in the supernatural, a poetic temperament – and both authors thus continue a tradition of thought that extends back to the late eighteenth century. Walter Scott popularized such ideas in the contrast between the Gaelic culture of a feudal Highland society and the hard-headed commercial ethos of Lowland life in his novel *Waverley* (1814), a contrast which itself derived from the visions and fabrications of early romantics such as Thomas Gray and James Macpherson.[23] However, the idea of the Celt received its most influential formulation, especially with regards to Wales, in Matthew Arnold's lectures of 1866 *On the Study of Celtic Literature*.

Arnold begins his study of Celtic literature with a somewhat melancholy description of attending an eisteddfod in Llandudno, where, on an 'unfortunate' day of 'storms of wind, clouds of dust and an angry, dirty sea', he listens to the last representatives of a once proud tradition reciting verse in a language that Arnold admits he does not understand.[24] Upon leaving the festival pavilion he meets

> an acquaintance fresh from London and the parliamentary session. In a moment, the spell of the Celtic genius was forgotten, the Philistinism of our Anglo-Saxon nature made itself felt, and my friend and I walked up and down by the roaring waves, talking not of ovates and bards, and triads and englyns, but of the sewage question, and the glories of our local self government, and the mysterious perfections of the Metropolitan Board of Works.[25]

The English philistine's world of material affairs, of instrumental activity, of the 'machinery' of industrial society, is juxtaposed to the creative, imaginative, poetic world of the Celt. As the contrast between English philistinism and Celtic creativity suggests, Arnold's lectures were not primarily directed at the Celts themselves, but were concerned with exposing certain deficiencies within the emerging culture of England. Wales is thus presented, in contrast to England, as a place

> where the past still lives, where every place has its traditions, every name its poetry, and where the people, the genuine people, still knows this past, this tradition, this poetry and lives with it, and clings to it; while, alas, the prosperous Saxon on the other side, the invader from Liverpool and Birkenhead, has long ago forgotten his.[26]

Arnold's lectures were based on the belief that the withering, poetical and magical cultures of the Celtic race should now feed into, and revitalize the emergent, progressive, yet rather drab and Philistine, culture of the English nation. The distinction between the English nation and the Celtic race is significant, for whereas the English in Arnold's analysis are an emergent people, a product of history and subject to further development, the Welsh and the Irish are conceived of in visualized terms, demonstrating certain eternal racial characteristics, atemporal, static and destined for both cultural and racial absorption. Arnold thus produces a Celt characterized by certain enduring visible traits which inevitably, and crucially, make the Celts 'ineffectual in politics'.[27] 'The Celtic genius' he notes has 'sentiment as its main basis, with love of beauty, charm, spirituality for its excellence … ineffectualness and self-will for its deficit'.[28] The Celt is 'always ready to react against despotism of fact', is 'sensual', and is 'particularly disposed to feel the spell of the feminine idiosyncrasy; he has an affinity to it; he is not far from its secret'.[29] These are the Celtic characteristics that we also encounter in the writings of Rhys Davies and D. H. Lawrence, and while this does not necessarily suggest a direct influence, it testifies to the fact that the Arnoldian criteria had become part of the very language in which the Welsh conceived of themselves, and in which they were conceived of by others.

Arnold's conceptualization of the Celt also relates to the writings of Davies and Lawrence in that all three authors invoke primitive Celtic characteristics as the basis for mounting a critique of the materialism and philistinism of contemporary, industrial society. Matthew Arnold was one of the pivotal figures in Raymond Williams's analysis of *Culture and Society* (1958) which influentially explored the ways in which nineteenth-century critics of industrialism adopted the term 'culture' to denote a sense of how the creative life of the mind could be set in opposition to a declining, increasingly regimented, social order. The more the actual social reality of industrial capitalism was seen to be debased and exploitative, the more the idea of 'culture' developed as a term of critique. 'Culture' in the new industrial landscape came to mean

> first, the recognition of the practical separation of certain moral and intellec-
> tual activities from the driven impetus of a new kind of society; second, the
> emphasis of these activities as a court of human appeal, to be set over the
> process of practical social judgement and yet to offer itself as a mitigating and
> rallying alternative.[30]

In later life Williams came to regret the fact that issues of race and national identity were missing from his discussion of *Culture and Society*. Indeed, what is striking in Arnold's Celtic essays is the fact that the critique of English industrial and materialist society is developed in terms of the alleged cultural traits and characteristics of nations.[31] The division between a narrow Philistine society and a humanizing Culture that Arnold famously developed in *Culture and Anarchy* (1869) finds its precursor in the distinction between the instrumental materialism of the English and the poetic sensibility of the Celts in the essays on Celtic literature.

The structure of Arnold's argument, where Celtic traits are invoked as a means of critiquing the values and aspirations of contemporary society, is mirrored in the writings of both Rhys Davies and D. H. Lawrence. If Arnold begins his Celtic essays standing in Llandudno where he looks eastwards towards the 'Saxon hive' in Liverpool, and westwards towards Anglesey 'where the past still lives', the characters in Lawrence's *St Mawr* also encounter a landscape that is divided along lines of nationhood:[32]

> The Needle's Eye was a hole in the ancient grey rock, like a window, looking to England; England at the moment in shadow. A stream wound and glinted in the flat shadow, and beyond that the flat, insignificant hills heaped in mounds of shade. Cloud was coming – the English side was in shadow. Wales was still in the sun, but the shadow was spreading.[33]

The spreading shadow is symbolic, for this is a tale in which an anti-materialist primitivism – embodied in the Welsh horse St Mawr, its groom Lewis and the Native American Phoenix – is juxtaposed against the materialism of an exhausted Western civilization embodied in the figure of Mrs Witt and her daughter Lou. Lawrence follows Arnold in utilizing a primitive Celticism, embodied in both animal and man in the following passage, as a means of highlighting the deficiencies of his own culture.

> But now where is the flame of dangerous, forward-pressing nobility in men? Dead, dead, guttering out in a stink of self-sacrifice whose feeble light is a light of exhaustion and *laissez-faire*.
>
> And the horse, is he to go on carrying man forward into this? – this gutter? No! Man wisely invents motor-cars and other machines, automobile and locomotive. The horse is superannuated, for man. But alas, man is even more superannuated, for the horse.[34]

If the Welsh groom and his horse stand as the last bastions of nobility in Britain, the laissez-faire values of contemporary society will soon drive them to extinction; the shadow that lies over England in *St Mawr* 'is spreading' and will soon encroach upon Wales.

Rhys Davies also invokes a primitive Celticism as a means of critiquing the dominant values of a materialist society. Pugh Jibbons in the short story 'Blodwen' (1931), for instance, is represented as one 'of the Welsh who have never submitted to industrialism', and it is he who ends the tale in the arms of Blodwen whose eyes hold 'the memory of lost countries'.[35] Both characters represent a set of values that stand in opposition to those of the industrial society which they inhabit. In *The Withered Root*, Reuben

Daniels, whose 'soul' is 'sick', seeks solace in religion from the 'rows and rows of dirty-grey dwellings' which are 'like galleries sunk in some murky, deserted inferno'.[36] Reuben seeks transcendence by turning to God, and becomes a revivalist preacher. He ultimately comes to regard his religion as a symptom of, rather than an answer to, the forces of industrialism however, and Davies powerfully conveys this moment of realization as the preacher begins to think of himself and his social role in the mechanized terms of an industrial society:

> He would see himself as a mechanical doll, lifting one arm in suitable gesture, then the other, while, forcing himself to go on, his voice sang out brokenly until the glittering machine in him ran down. And all the time the rapt, staring faces before him would exude a sweat of gratified pleasure and their bodies would pant and their breasts heave as that pleasure sank into their very bowels.[37]

Reuben, who is 'of the old pure Welsh blood' and would 'in other days have sung poems and carried his harp from village to village', ultimately turns his back on religion and finds transcendence from the industrial world only in death.[38] It can therefore be seen that Lawrence and Davies are to a considerable extent continuing a Victorian tradition of social criticism in their use of Celticism as a vehicle for critiquing those aspects of their contemporary society that they disliked.

III

However, if Davies and Lawrence follow Arnold in invoking a Celtic primitivism as a means of exposing the narrow materialism of their contemporary societies, the twentieth-century writers' social vision is ultimately considerably more pessimistic than that of their Victorian predecessor. Arnold's social criticism is directed not so much at the 'industrial community' itself, as at the 'common tide of men's thoughts' within such a community. He states explicitly in *Culture and Anarchy* that culture 'admits the necessity of the movement towards fortune-making and exaggerated industrialism' and 'readily allows that the future may derive benefit from it'.[39] His views on the Welsh language are particularly illuminating with regard to this dimension of his thought. Arnold calls for the eradication of Welsh as a living language in his essays *On the Study of Celtic Literature*, and presents his argument in the following terms:

I must say I quite share the opinion of my brother Saxons as to the practical inconvenience of perpetuating the speaking of Welsh ... Cornwall is the better for adopting English, for becoming more thoroughly one with the rest of the country. The fusion of all the inhabitants of these islands into one homogeneous, English-speaking whole, the breaking down of barriers between us, the swallowing up of separate provincial nationalities, is a consummation to which the natural course of things irresistibly tends; it is a necessity of what is called modern civilisation, and modern civilisation is a real, legitimate force.[40]

If Arnold often invokes culture as an alternative source of values to industrial society, here he deems 'modern civilisation' to be a 'real, legitimate force' and the source of welcome changes in society. Culture is not opposed to modern civilization, for the latter creates the context for the dissemination of the former. Arnold's vision is democratic in the sense that his goal is to construct a shareable, accessible, common culture in Britain that makes the 'best knowledge and thought of the time' relevant to all. That common culture is ultimately based, however, on the belief that society's 'best knowledge' can only be disseminated through the medium of English. The Welsh language is thus seen to represent a hindrance to the man of culture's project of diffusing 'the best knowledge ... from one end of society to the other'.[41] The deepest desire in Arnold's writings is towards reconciliation: the reconciliation of classes, races and religious sects in the formation of a common participatory culture. That culture is not defined along lines of racial descent. Arnold does not advocate that the Welsh be excluded from the national culture because of their race, but argues that their current linguistic practices must change if they are to participate fully in that common English culture. If, at times, Arnold emphasizes the pervasive influence of race and heredity, this strain in his thought is always tempered by his belief that a 'community of practice is more telling than a community of origin'.[42]

If race, for Arnold, is ultimately determined by culture not blood, culture for Rhys Davies and D. H. Lawrence is ultimately determined by race. What we witness in the shift from Arnold to Davies and Lawrence is a shift from the idea of a single common culture to the idea of plural cultures. Whereas Arnold desired 'the fusion of all the inhabitants of these islands into one homogeneous ... whole', Lawrence's plea to society was to 'give me differences'.[43] This shift from a commitment to the idea of a common culture of consent to an emphasis on a plurality of ultimately irreconcilable cultures of descent can be traced in Lawrence's *St Mawr* where Mrs Witt observes that 'Europe was organic, like the helpless particles of one sprawling body. And the great body in a state of incipient decay.'[44] Her daughter Lou is described as 'one of these nervous white women with lots of money' who wants to 'escape from the friction which is the whole stimulus in modern social life'.[45] She complains to her mother that 'she can't live', and would be 'dead if there weren't St Mawr and Phoenix and Lewis in the world'.[46] This primitivist threesome stand in opposition to the dominant values of society, but have no future role to play within it. We are told, for instance, that the horse St Mawr was 'raised for stud purposes – but he didn't answer', and this inability or unwillingness to procreate is mirrored in its groom Lewis, who when asked why St Mawr 'doesn't get any foals', answers 'Doesn't want to I should think. Same as me.'[47] Far from representing an Arnoldian source of primitivist revitalization for a materialist European culture, the horse and its groom are represented as a dying breed, the last of their kind. Whereas Arnold felt that the philistinism of the English could be alleviated by an infusion of Celticism, Lawrence's Welsh groom Morgan Lewis argues that 'There's too many people in the world for me to help anything.'[48] Similarly Reuben Daniels in Davies's *The Withered Root* wastes his poetic sensibility in the cause of a nonconformist revival, is sexually frigid, never marries and finds his only solace at the hands of a prostitute before dying with 'the face of one for whom life had not yet begun'.[49] Whilst there is a sense that civilization is in a state of decay, the primitive races offer no source of revitalization for their roots are withering in an industrializing world. In contrast then to Arnold's desire to see an infusion of poetic Celticism transform the philistinism of English life, the primitive characters in Lawrence's and Davies's fictions offer no such hope for regeneration for they are essentially impotent. The fact that the representatives of primitive cultures – St Mawr, Morgan Lewis, Reuben Daniels – do not procreate underlines that these are the last representatives of their kind, and also preserves their symbolic racial purity.[50]

This notion of unsurmountable racial difference informs Davies's description of the Silurian and the American discussed earlier, a scene that shares some similarities with Lawrence's description, in his essay 'On Being a Man', of an encounter between a white European and a 'negro' aboard a train. Just as the presence of the Silurian affected the American's behaviour in Davies's *My Wales*, making his 'brightness dim' and making it seem as though he were 'living outside himself', the 'negro' forces a change in the narrator's consciousness.

> The thought-adventure starts in the blood, not in the mind. If an Arab or a negro or even a Jew sits down next to me in the train, I cannot proceed so glibly with my knowing. It is not enough for me to glance at a black face and

say: He is a negro. As he sits next to me, there is a faint uneasy movement in
my blood. A strange vibration comes from him, which causes a slight disturbance in my own vibration. There is a slight odour in my nostrils ... I now can
no longer proceed from what I am and what I know I am, to what I know him
to be. I am not a nigger and so I can't quite know a nigger, and I can never
fully 'understand' him.

What then? ... I can admit that my blood is disturbed, that something comes
from him and interferes with my normal vibration. Admitting so much, I can
either put up a resistance, and insulate myself. Or I can allow the disturbance
to continue, because, after all, there is some peculiar alien sympathy between
us.[51]

Lawrence is clearly drawing here on a racist discourse that views individuals of other cultures as not only sensuous, but also as odorous and
disturbing. The shift in the passage from 'negro' to the disparaging 'nigger'
reflects the narrator's attempts at maintaining his racial superiority when it
is being threatened by the presence of the 'other'. Nevertheless, the initial
dismissal gives way to a desired connection as the opening 'glance'
develops into an emotional and psychological engagement. Despite the
alleged 'alien sympathy', the predominant impression is that we are
dealing here with fundamental differences. Lawrence does not universalize his own sense of identity but is forced into a 'disturbing' awareness
of his own limited subjectivity. This encounter between races on a train
represents the broader process of geographical mobility made possible in
the modern era by technological advances, and leads to a new awareness
of cultural relativization.

A similar scene is depicted in fictional form in Rhys Davies's short story
'Fear'. The tale is narrated in the third person but the events are seen from
the perspective of a young boy.

As soon as the boy got into the compartment he felt there was something
queer in it. The only other occupant was a slight, dusky man who sat in a
corner with that air of propriety and unassertiveness which his race – he
looked like an Indian – tend to display in England. There was also a faint
sickly scent.[52]

Davies proceeds to depict the Indian in wholly racialized terms. Not only
is he odorous, his 'puckered face' communicates a sense of 'childish
stupidity' and he begins to 'utter a low humming chant' which engenders a
response in the boy which is very similar to Lawrence's description of a
'movement' in his 'blood': 'They faced each other across the compartment's length. Something coiled up in the boy. It was as if his soul took
primitive fear and crouched to hide.'[53] The word 'coiled' is significant, for

it transpires that the Indian chants in order to placate a cobra that he carries in his basket. The 'archaic chant' has much the same effect on the boy as it does upon the snake, suggesting a common response to such stimuli from people of many races and from animals. The Indian explains the art of chanting and offers the boy a free entrance to the fair in Newport where he is to perform. But despite these gestures of fraternity across the racial divide, the child remains fearful and escapes from the carriage at the first opportunity, suddenly aware of the 'colossal dangers of the open world'. As in Lawrence, the abiding impression is one of incommensurate racial difference.

Thus rather than advocating a fruitful amalgamation of races, the characters in the fictions of Lawrence and Davies inhabit societies where racial differences are preserved. One result of this shift from the Arnoldian belief in a common culture to the commitment in Davies and Lawrence to the preservation of racial differences is that primitivism ceases to be a stage in a process of historical development, but rather becomes a criterion for racial and cultural authenticity. Thus, as the individual 'Celt' or 'Negro' become less 'primitive' he or she is also regarded as being less racially authentic. An example of this racial belief at work occurs in Davies's *Print of a Hare's Foot* where he recalls Lawrence's 'deep dislike' for a 'young Negro waiter'.

> To see Lawrence's eyes gleam with watchful revulsion as the waiter laid a dish on the table seemed grotesque to me – why be so stirred over the young man? It was his hands Lawrence watched: thin, dusky, nervous hands laying very, very carefully a plate of *vol au vent* on the table. I watched too, as I had been bade.
>
> 'You saw his hands, how uncertain they were, no *feeling* in them! No Feeling. It's quite sickening, he can't even place a plate down properly, he fumbles, hesitates, it's like a dead hand moving, every moment I expect to see the plate go to the floor'. And the denunciation came: 'All his movements are so *mental*, he doesn't trust to his blood, he's afraid. Look at him walking down the room, look at his legs, look how they hang together and cower, pushed forward only by his mind! Ugh!' And he ended with a hiss of absolute revulsion. It was true, as I looked at the waiter's legs, that they were rather soft and dejected-looking, clinging together as if for company as he took his short, gliding kind of steps down the room. Yes, his gait was vaguely unpleasant – that hesitating glide, as if practised, and the subjected look of the legs. There was little that was spontaneous about the youth, certainly. But this fierce antipathy![54]

Although Davies is surprised at Lawrence's revulsion, his own primitivist values are also exposed as he expects the Negro waiter to be 'spontaneous' and admits, in sympathy with Lawrence, that the waiter's 'hesitating glide' looked 'practised'. Lawrence's wrath results from his perception that the 'Negro' is not behaving according to a set of racial expectations. In the racial thought of Lawrence and Davies modernization is understood to be a racial betrayal.

This primitivist view of the individual and of the community results in the separation of ideas of the primitive and the modern from the actual social history that produced them. I have already discussed the range of eternal primitivist attributes that Davies ascribed to the Celts, and the more closely that primitivism is equated with Welshness in Davies's writings the less that these primitive characteristics are seen to represent a stage in the development of society, and the more they are seen to be the inevitable expressions of a racial identity. Thus any modern transformations in the cultural practices of Welshmen are deemed to be fundamentally un-Welsh. In *My Wales*, for example, we witness the rise of working-class militancy being dismissed in racial terms:

> Outside the chapels another section of the industrialized race grizzled and let loose moans and complaints. These noises were intrinsically of the same nature as the groans inside the chapels – sighs of longing, panting and yearnings for a blessed and perhaps impossible land where idealistic justice was maintained with a nice regard for one and all. The outside section, some said and still say, was composed of rootless ruffians and barbarous aliens, particularly Irishmen, who were merely stirring up trouble for its own sake, loving a fight, bored with the monotony of work. Any excuse served to call a strike, which might develop into rioting, arson, plundering.[55]

This is not all that Rhys Davies has to say about 'The South Wales Workers' in the longest chapter of *My Wales*, but the passage is indicative of a structure of argument that reappears at several points in his work. The use of animalistic terms – grizzle, moan – conveys a pervasive sense of otherness as the reasons for industrial strife are placed at the feet of those who are deemed to be 'aliens' in a Welsh culture that Davies has already defined in largely primitivist, Arnoldian, terms. Ultimately, industrialism is itself a profoundly un-Welsh development for Davies. The industrialized valley is described as 'a slatternly woman abandoned to wretchedness' in *The Withered Root* and Davies hopes in *My Wales* that 'After the ugly hundred and fifty years' interruption from the outside world, perhaps Wales can now return to its former pastoral unison.'[56]

IV

The ideas of race that inform the writings of Rhys Davies and D. H. Lawrence carry significant consequences for their approach to history and their understanding of human communities. In the October 1943 edition of the journal *Wales* that included articles advocating the rise of 'An Emergent National Literature' by George Ewart Evans, the reconstruction of Welsh politics 'From the Foundations' by Gwynfor Evans, and an editorial in which Keidrych Rhys 'sincerely' hoped that Anglo-Welsh literature was simply 'a stage on the way back to the use of Welsh for literature', Rhys Davies's excerpts 'From My Notebook' struck a somewhat discordant note.

> If asked (in the offensive suspicious way!), I always say I am not Welsh to the Welsh, just as I say that I am not English to the English. The scorn of my Welsh interrogator is my delight, and when he begins to insult me I know that here is an impure Welshman and an inferior man who needs a prop of nationality. As soon as I am asked or am expected to show my 'Welshness' I know that Satan is tempting me to make a pretty fool of myself.[57]

There seems to be a contradiction here, for whilst rejecting the idea of national identity, the above passage relies on a distinction between 'pure' and 'impure' Welshmen. In the same article Davies also recommends that the artist should 'Live out of Wales for a time' but then goes on to suggest that 'you will be a purer Welshman for it', and while he urges the artist to 'Never carry a flag' he goes on to note that 'self-conscious nationalists, earnest students and "protectors" of the culture' will always fail to 'bring the essence of Wales before one'.[58] Davies seems to be taking away with one hand what he is then re-introducing with the other. The idea of a distinctive Welsh culture is rejected whilst the ideas of a 'pure' and 'unself-conscious' Welshness are maintained. The emphasis in Davies's 'From My Notebook' is on the individual consciousness. 'A man is greater than his country' he argues, 'as a human being you have no need of a flag'.[59] This emphasis on the individual is complicated, however, by the references to a Welshness that is inevitably a collective identity.

This tension between a simultaneous commitment to 'individualism' and to the sense of a national community is reflected in D. H. Lawrence's meditations on national identity in his *Studies in Classic American Literature* (1923). Lawrence insists on the 'isolate' character of the 'essential American soul', but complicates this insistence with respect to national identity by making it a general characteristic of life: 'The central

law of all organic life is that each organism is intrinsically isolate and
single in itself.'[60] This tension is replicated in Lawrence's discussion of
Herman Melville where he considers Moby Dick to be 'isolate' whilst also
being 'the deepest blood-being of the white race'.[61] It is a tension that also
manifests itself in the opening pages of Lawrence's study where he argues
on the one hand that 'men are only free when they are doing what the
deepest self likes', whilst claiming on the other that men are only 'free
when they belong to a living, organic, believing community'.[62]

While clearly believing in some kind of national distinctiveness, both
Davies and Lawrence perceive that there's a danger for the autonomy of
the individual artist if he or she subscribes to any collective manifestations
of identity. Davies dismisses all culturally institutionalized embodiments
of Welshness – be they the 'Eisteddfod, the Nationalist Party, Welsh M.P.s,
all Welsh writers' – as 'fundamentally useless'.[63] Similarly Lawrence,
whilst encouraging American artists to foster their distinctiveness,
perceives a danger for the individual consciousness in what he calls 'the
social' for it leads to a 'merge' that results in a failure to 'listen in isolation
to the isolate Holy Ghost' who 'speaks as individually inside each
individual' and never to 'the general world'.[64]

The danger to individual autonomy posed by collective identities is
addressed in the writings of Rhys Davies and D. H. Lawrence by their
conceiving of the national community as a 'race' rather than as a 'culture'.
They conceive of the group in terms of descent rather than consent. It
seems that, for both Davies and Lawrence, the individual may be forced
away from his or her individuality by a consensual idea of a communal
identity which calls for an active participation within the culture of a civil
society. The individual's autonomy is not seen to be threatened in the same
way, or to the same extent, if one bases one's sense of community in race,
for whilst the idea of race does inevitably refer to people outside the
individual it is not dependent on any social relation to them; membership
of the group is predetermined by blood. Thus Lawrence can read James
Fenimoore Cooper's *The Deerslayer* as an 'isolate' who is nevertheless a
representative of the 'pure white'.[65] In *St Mawr*, Morgan Lewis represents
a noble primitivism and is identified as an 'aristocrat … in his own way',
but 'it was an aristocracy of the invisible powers, the greater influences,
nothing to do with human society'.[66]

Similarly, for Rhys Davies the 'purer' Welshmen are those who live in
isolation:

> There are several Welsh people in Wales, on remote farms, in dreamy chapels,
> tending sheep on hill-tops. But they have never heard of Wales. If you ask

them 'Welsh you are?' they will look at you in a puzzled way. These are the only Welsh; they will always exist if left alone.[67]

Welshness does not derive from participation in a Welsh culture and society for Davies, for the real Welsh are unconscious of their identity; it is already predetermined. Whilst the notion of racially distinct communities has generally been regarded as the preserve of nationalists, Davies's racial view of the world derives from his commitment to individualism. Indeed, the dominant strain within Welsh cultural nationalism in the twentieth century has been based on the idea of a linguistic, as opposed to a racial, continuity. Rhys Davies dismissed the Welsh language as 'an unnecessary though charming accomplishment for petty use' and ridiculed the idea that 'Welsh nationality – or any other – is a matter of knowledge of the language, place of residence, accent, absorption in the culture'.[68] He thus rejects a consensual conception of identity based in culture, and subscribes to a view of identity based in race. The idea of race in the writings of Davies and Lawrence embodies a collective entity that does not jeopardize the integrity of the individual, for membership of the group is predetermined. This, ultimately, is the advantage of race in the constitution of a community for both Davies and Lawrence.

V

If Rhys Davies and D. H. Lawrence follow an Arnoldian tradition of Victorian social criticism in utilizing a primitivistic conception of the poetic and anti-materialist Celt as a means of mounting a critique of the rationalism and materialism of contemporary society, they diverge fundamentally from that tradition in their conception of the relationship between race and society. Racial differences, for Matthew Arnold, can ultimately be transcended through common cultural practices. Cultural practices, for Davies and Lawrence, are determined by race. This results in a commitment in their writings to unassimilable racial differences, and in an ahistorical view of racial identity in which primitivist behaviour becomes a criterion for racial and cultural authenticity. The replacement of the cultural by the racial in the writings of Rhys Davies and D. H. Lawrence is an attempt at making it possible for the individual to be part of a predetermined community of descent, without that posing a threat to his or her autonomy.

Black and White: Boxing,
Race and Modernity

In Owen Martell's acclaimed novel *Dyn yr Eiliad* (Man of the Moment, 2003), the main characters walk to a

> hen dafarn y tu ôl i City Road a mynd i eistedd mewn cornel yn y bar ... Roedd gyda nhw luniau o boxers lleol ar y waliau ac un poster yn hysbysebu fight rhwng 'Whites and Blacks'.[1]

> [old pub behind City Road and sit in a corner in the bar ... The walls were lined with photos of local boxers, with one poster advertising a fight between 'Whites and Blacks'].

Martell concentrates on the personal, individual, thoughts of his main characters, but suggestive references to Welsh history, culture and folklore appear between the novel's interior monologues. The narrator does not go on to explore the meaning and significance of the poster, but the reference is a suggestive one. The 'old pub' is the Tavistock Arms on Bedford Street, Cardiff, where the poster, dating from 1934, is still on the wall.[2] The bout being described in stark racial terms is between Jack McKnight (welter-weight champion of Ireland) and Herbie Nurse (coloured welterweight, Cardiff). The poster at once testifies to the crude racial terms in which boxing fights were described in the 1930s, while simultaneously alerting us to the complexities and contradictions inherent in the relationships between race, ethnicity and national identity in that period. For 'white vs. black' on this poster also happens to involve, from another perspective, the white Irishman, McKnight, fighting the black Welshman, Nurse. This chapter aims to explore the tensions and contradictions embodied in this poster, and does so by looking at the ways in which the 'black and white' of the boxing ring has often found itself reflected in the 'black and white' of the printed page.

From Mark Twain to Ernest Hemingway, Norman Mailer to Joyce Carol Oates, American writers in particular have been fascinated by the metaphorical and symbolic resonances of the boxing ring.[3] Perhaps the most insightful American commentator on boxing, however, is the African American novelist and essayist Ralph Ellison, whose seminal novel *Invisible Man* (1952) contains a number of allusions and references to prize fighting. A famous reference to boxing in the novel occurs when the narrator recalls seeing a 'prize fighter boxing a yokel':

> The fighter was swift and amazingly scientific. His body was one violent flow of rapid rhythmic action. He hit the yokel a hundred times while the yokel held up his arms in stunned surprise. But suddenly the yokel, rolling about in the gale of boxing gloves, struck one blow and knocked science, speed and footwork as cold as a well-digger's posterior. The smart money hit the canvas. The long shot got the nod. The yokel had simply stepped inside his opponent's sense of time.[4]

In his discussion of boxing and literature in *The Culture of Bruising*, Gerald Early uses this passage as a basis for exploring the uneasy relationship between white and black boxers in American culture. He notes that with the exception of Jack Dempsey and Gene Tunney, 'virtually every white champion has been, despite his style, a yokel: Sharkey, Braddock, Schmeling, Baer, Carnera, Marciano'. In contrast, black prize fighters have been regarded as 'Tricksters of style: Jack Johnson, Muhammad Ali, Sugar Ray Robinson, and Sugar Ray Leonard'. Against black opponents, states Early, 'white yokels were not even really fighters; they were more like preservers of the white public's need to see Tricksters pay the price for their disorder'.[5]

The most well-known account of a white 'yokel' taking on a black 'trickster' is Sylvester Stallone's Oscar-winning movie *Rocky* (1976). Rocky Balboa, an inarticulate Italian-American, is plucked from obscurity to take on and defeat the quick-witted and agile African American, Apollo Creed. Creed is clearly moulded on Muhammad Ali (even down to his rivalry with Joe Frazier). If Ali, in later life, would become an all-American hero lighting the Olympic torch at Atlanta in 1996, during the 1960s – when he embraced Islam, changed his name from Cassius Clay, and resisted the draft – he was widely disliked, distrusted and vilified by many Americans.[6] Thus if the real Ali seemed invincible in the ring, the Hollywood dream factory could simulate his defeat at the hands of a white unknown. Balboa is improbably brought into fighting shape by Mickey, a weathered trainer played by an ageing Burgess Meredith. In advising his white protégé on how to deal with a threatening African American, Meredith was actually repeating a role that he'd played – in a rather different context and for different ends – thirty years earlier.

A Welcome to Britain was a film made in 1943 by the British Ministry of Information with the support of the American Office of War Information. In it, Burgess Meredith is a GI guide who introduces American soldiers to some of the embarrassing situations that they might encounter while stationed in wartime Britain. A white GI is shown flirting with a barmaid, throwing his money around and making disparaging remarks about a Scotsman's kilt. Having outraged the locals, he boards a train and gets into a compartment with an African American GI. An elderly British lady invites them both back to her house for tea, and Burgess Meredith confides to the camera that while this sort of thing wouldn't happen at home in the United States, it is not unusual in Britain.[7] The message is clearly directed primarily at white GIs, suggesting that they should adopt a veneer of ethnic tolerance – whether encountering kilted Scots or Black members of their own nation – while in Britain.

Among the more notable GIs to have been stationed in Wales during the Second World War was the novelist Ralph Ellison himself. (Rocky Marciano was another, who fought future Welsh rugby international Jack Matthews in a bout at St Athan.[8]) In his short story of 1944 'In a Strange Country', Ellison offers a fictional account of his time in Swansea and Morriston. It begins with the central character Parker, an African American GI, sitting in a Welsh pub recalling events that have happened earlier that evening.

> Coming ashore from the ship he had felt the excited expectancy of entering a strange land. Moving along the road in the dark he had planned to stay ashore all night, and in the morning he would see the country with fresh eyes … Someone had cried 'Jesus H. Christ,' and he had thought, He's from home, and grinned and apologized into the light they flashed in his eyes. He had felt the blow coming when they yelled, 'It's a goddamn nigger,' but it struck him anyway. He was having a time of it when some of Mr Catti's countrymen stepped in and Mr Catti had guided him into the pub …
>
> At first he had included them in his blind rage. But they had seemed so genuinely and uncondescendingly polite that he was disarmed. Now the anger and resentment had slowly ebbed, and he felt only a smouldering sense of self-hate and ineffectiveness. Why should he blame them when they had helped him? *He* had been the one so glad to hear an American voice. You can't take it out on them, they're a different breed; even from the English.[9]

The passage traces a shift in Parker's perception of the Welsh, from initially including them in his 'blind rage' to his increasing awareness of their ethnic difference. Following an encounter with white GIs, Parker has a literal black eye that functions as a suggestive metaphor in a story preoccupied with issues of sight and self-perception. Upon entering the club with his Welsh hosts the light strikes Parker's injured eye – 'it was as though it were being peeled by an invisible hand' – and the story proceeds to explore the layers of identity that constitute the African American self – the black 'I'.[10]

In an earlier draft of a story based on his experiences in Wales, Ellison's main character tries to establish a sense of his identity by evoking the boxers whom he clearly admires. Sitting in an American Red Cross Club attached to Libanus Chapel in Morriston he finds himself 'obsessed' by the first black heavyweight champion of the world, Jack Johnson:

> They didn't praise him as they do Joe Louis, but what I like is that he went where he wanted to go and did what he wanted to do … Old Jack Johnson had something Joe Louis doesn't have. Have I? Dog beneath Joe's skin. All chained up inside. In the ring Joe's a controlled explosion. From containing himself. Joe's fight is a machine, Jack's was a dance. Those silent movies … Old Jack reached out for life … Fought them with his fists, fought them with his grin, fought them with his high-powered car. [11]

While Ellison doesn't make the connection, it is of course somewhat appropriate that his central character should be thinking about Johnson and Louis while stationed in Wales. For on the 30 August 1937, Jack Johnson had a ringside seat at Yankee Stadium to watch the Welshman Tommy Farr last the full fifteen rounds, only to lose on points to Joe Louis.[12] Louis, for Ellison, despite his reputation as a heavy hitter, was really a stylist, 'as elegant as the finest of ballet dancers'.[13] Tommy Farr was thus another white 'yokel' defeated by a black stylist. From a Welsh perspective, however, that yokel's journey from Blaen Clydach to Yankee Stadium embodied, as Dai Smith has argued, the cultural trajectory of industrial Wales itself.[14]

The centrality of the Louis vs. Farr fight in the Welsh imagination is captured in Selwyn Griffith's sequence of poems *Arwyr* (Heroes) of 1989 in which the poet recalls being woken as a child to hear the fight 'yn clecian fel cesair / o berfedd y Phillips' ['spitting like hailstones / from the innards of the Phillips'].

> Y gwyn a'r du
> yn colbio'i gilydd

> yn Saesneg,
>   a'r dyrfa'n genllysg o sŵn.
>
> [Black and White
> pummelling each other
> in English,
>   and the crowd a hailstorm of sound.][15]

The English being emitted from the radio is part of the unusual thrill of the fight for the Welsh-speaking child, and those who argue that the dominant Welsh experience of the twentieth century has only been captured in English would do well to consider the fact that the most powerful literary account of the Farr vs. Louis bout in Welsh literature, in either language, appears in this sequence of poems.

This is a fact that would also pose a challenge to those who, throughout much of the twentieth century, sought to defend a Welsh language and culture imagined to be rooted in organic rural communities against the encroachments of modern, mobile, 'industrial civilization'. In describing the *Culture and Civilization of Wales* to an English-speaking audience in 1927, T. Gwynn Jones illustrates his observation that 'among those brought up in a Welsh atmosphere, intellectual interest is general' by recalling 'a number of agricultural labourers discussing the subject of divine immanence, forming their own terminology with astonishing exactitude, and displaying wonderful originality of thought'. Even Flintshire miners, notes Jones, are able to discuss Welsh epigrams, 'appealing, as to an authority on the rules of alliteration, to a man whose name – Murphy – was not the only evidence of Irish extraction. This was some five miles from the English border, on the other side of which I hear discussions on boxing.'[16] The point is blatantly clear: a valuable Welsh-language culture is sufficiently strong to even acculturate an Irishman into the ways of Welsh poetry, while the philistine English are the victims of a crass popular culture symbolized by that most exploitative and demeaning of sports, boxing.

This use of boxing to make a distinction between Wales and England is repeated in a more complex and ambiguous form in Raymond Williams's celebrated autobiographical novel *Border Country* (1960; discussed in detail in chapter 5). 'Several men from Glynmawr' cross the border from 'dry' Wales into England to drink on a Sunday. The bar is empty, but the owner expects 'a few more after chapel' to the feigned astonishment of the business-minded Morgan Rosser who admires the freedom to drink granted by English law: 'Go, what a country'. Morgan proceeds to encourage his friend Lippy to 'do us a bit of boxing'.

'Righto then,' Lippy said, and took off his jacket. He walked to the open stone floor by the window. He raised his hands and began squaring and hunching his shoulders ... With a sudden intense concentration, he scuffed his boots along the stone floor, and began to dance backward and forward, his thin body weaving, his fists leading and guarding, his face grim.

'Warm her up,' Morgan shouted ...

Lippy seemed to respond to the call, although by now he was so closely shut in by the imaginary circle of his boxing, his eyes half-closed with the effort, that he seemed beyond reach. Faster and faster came the flurry of blows on the air; faster and faster the weaving of the frail body; fiercer the expression of the weak, blurred, sweating face. The other men watched stolidly, while the furious exhibition continued.

'That's enough now,' Harry said at last, but Lippy was past stopping.[17]

England offers a release from the intense communal restrictions on the Welsh side of the border. It is a country in which one can drink on a Sunday, and engage in the pleasures of popular culture. Lippy recalls being described as a 'promising flyweight' in his youth, and, in keeping with the novel's broader meditations on pasts, memories and belonging, the imaginary bout seems to be an act of revisiting an earlier self. The scene also serves to foreground the tensions and differences between the novel's two father figures: the entrepreneur Morgan Rosser, and Harry Price, the signalman who embodies the communitarian values of Glynmawr in his benign, if somewhat repressed, being. Morgan feels liberated away from Glynmawr, and celebrates English drinking laws while goading Lippy into his boxing exhibition. Harry says little throughout the scene until he steps in to tell Lippy when to stop, and encourages the increasingly fractious group of men back to the rhythms and structures of their everyday lives across the border.

If T. Gwynn Jones and Raymond Williams foregrounded the distinctions between Wales and England in their fighting scenes, others drew on boxing to explore internal Welsh differences. In his appropriately titled novel *The Heyday in the Blood* (1936), Geraint Goodwin conceives of the border country in the intensely racial terms that I explored earlier in the work of Rhys Davies. When the young man Llew fights Mathias, the keeper of the King's Head tavern, Goodwin draws on the distinction, made by anthropologists such as H. J. Fleure, between the Iberian and Celtic racial types thought to constitute the Welsh population:[18]

They stood there, man and lad, with the breadth, not of age but of race – the 'little dark people' and the full loose-limbed Celt – between them; a knowledgeless enmity which neither of them knew. They stood there, toe to toe like the powers of light and darkness, watching one another with the instinctive watch of animals. The man's was the provoked courage of the baited, of the turned on, unyielding and passive, with no life in it, but life-defying in its still-ness, its oriental depthlessness. But the lad had the exultant, leaping courage of his race, flame-like and pure. It was the adventure, the battle that brought joy to his nostrils.[19]

The complex tale of treachery and jealousy which leads to the fight is deemed largely irrelevant here, as each man draws on the unconscious, 'knowledgeless', enmities of race. The Celt's flared nostrils ultimately triumph over the 'oriental' immobility of the 'little dark' man, reflecting the assumed triumph of the Celts in early Welsh history. If, as in the stories of Rhys Davies, race functions for Goodwin as a means of locating social tensions in an autonomous realm beyond the understanding of history or the scope of politics, their contemporary W. J. Gruffydd drew on boxing to comment on the cultural shifts that he discerned in his contemporary Wales. While he could remember a time when 'who was the best preacher, who had won the chair, what choir had won' would be the questions exer-cising Welsh minds,

> today – in Glamorgan at least – what is of over-riding significance for us as Welshmen are the prospects of Jack Petersen or Tommy Farr, or some other Englishman born in Wales to overcome with his fists an Englishman born in England or a black man from America.[20]

Tommy Farr was, in fact, like T. Gwynn Jones's 'Murphy', a Welshman of Irish extraction, and if he was unlikely to be caught discussing the Welsh bardic measures, Farr had some knowledge of the Welsh language. He recalls in his autobiography *Thus Farr* that his trainer Joby Churchill – 'a little Welsh-speaking man straight from the mountain' – would yell instructions in Welsh so that the opposing fighter and his team wouldn't understand him.[21]

Fictional characters such as Goodwin's Llew, and historical figures such as Joby Churchill, indicate that Welsh-language culture has been far more diverse in its structures of feeling and forms of expression than the words of some of its culturally conservative spokespersons would wish. Boxing had already been portrayed in Welsh literature well before the 1930s. In his fourth novel *Gwen Tomos* (1894), Daniel Owen, a lacerating commentator on religious hypocrisy and Victorian mores, depicted a brutal fight between Harri'r Wernddu and Ernest y Plas (who has been trained to box at Oxford and is a representative of Anglican conservatism).[22] Boxing also appears as theme and metaphor in what is perhaps the most celebrated Welsh-language novel of all, Caradog Pritchard's *Un Nos Ola Leuad* (One

Moonlit Night, 1961), where the north Walian Now receives a battering from the experienced 'Hwntw' Joni Sowth.[23] The south Walian Congregationalist minister, poet and short-story writer William Thomas Davies changed his name first to Davies Aberpennar, and secondly to Pennar Davies (after his birthplace Aberpennar/Mountain Ash), and in doing so was following the example of his father's cousin, Frederick Hall Thomas. While William Davies adopted Pennar, his forebear Frederick Thomas initially wished to call himself 'Fred Cymry' before being persuaded to use the anglicized term for his nationality. It was as 'Freddie Welsh' that he became the first boxer to win an official world championship for Wales in 1914.[24] In the short story 'Pencampwr' (The Champion), Pennar Davies explores the personal, religious and political tensions of south Walian society as two Communist 'comrades' – Boio Bifan and Nic Mog – engage in a bitter bout in which sexual rivalries and physical jealousies come to the fore. The tale has an unlikely ending as Boio seems to experience a religious conversion and – while pleading, inwardly, to Jesus to bring both the bout and his life to an end – allows Nic to knock him out.[25] Changing his name was an act of cultural and political significance for Pennar Davies, who learned Welsh, wrote in that language and embraced nationalist politics. His was a prophetic stand against the social pressure towards anglicization, which was followed in the 1960s by Cymdeithas yr Iaith Gymraeg (The Welsh Language Society) as it campaigned for Welsh names to be included on road signs, for a television channel in Welsh and for official status for the Welsh language. The philosophy of civil disobedience adopted by the society was influenced by the Civil Rights movement in the United States, and it is to this period that Myrddin ap Dafydd returned in his poem 'Newid Enw' (Changing a Name). Here, the strict metre rules of *cynghanedd* create the formal ring in which Muhammad Ali is evoked, dancing like a butterfly. But it is the transcendence of a brutal history symbolized in the transformation of Cassius Clay into Muhammad Ali that is the poet's main concern:

> *boy* oeddet ti yn y bôn,
> yn Gassius, un o'r gweision.
>
> A'r enw fu'n crynhoi
> yn haearn tân arnat ti'n
> serio o hyd; ond o'r sarhau
> o lynges o gaethlongau,
> o gleisiau'r dyddiau pris da
> a'r chwil, daeth pili-pala.
>
> [You were still for them a boy
> A Cassius, one of the slaves.

And the name became an intense
metallic heat branding
persistently; from that oppression
from the fleet of slave ships,
from the bruises of the pay day
and the whip, emerged a butterfly.][26]

Clay's transformation into Ali is an allegory for his people's struggle for civil rights since slavery, but ap Dafydd also intends us to trace the allegorical logic of the poem back to political acts of revolutionary re-naming in Wales itself.

I have discussed the political and cultural implications of this kind of allegorical dramatization elsewhere, suffice here to note that there was nothing particularly unusual, then, in the fact that Selwyn Griffith should have commemorated the Tommy Farr vs. Joe Louis fight in Welsh – a language that was, after all, heard in the ring at Yankee Stadium in August 1937. If 'Arwyr' won Selwyn Griffith the Crown at the 1989 Eisteddfod, he aspired as a child towards the culture of bruising rather than versifying, and in doing so offered a rather different account of the struggle, that had proved so disturbing for W. J. Gruffydd, between a Welshman and a 'black man from America':

dan fy wyneb blac-led,
    fi oedd Louis;
a Huw Cefn Rhyd
oedd yr arwr o Donypandy;
    erys craith dan fy llygad hyd heddiw
    yn farc o fuddugoliaeth Farr.

[under my black-leaded face
    I was Louis
while Huw Cefn Rhyd
was the hero from Tonypandy;
    a scar beneath my eye today
    attests to Farr's victory.][27]

If Hollywood could concoct a white heavyweight champion in the shape of Sylvester Stallone in 1976, then the boys in the yard replay the fight while reversing the judges' decision. But the poet, significantly, is Louis: the black lead transforms the white Welsh writer into a black American boxer. Here, the racial and ethnic tensions encountered in the responses of writers such as T. Gwynn Jones, W. J. Gruffydd and Geraint Goodwin to boxing is represented in terms of the stark differences of black and white. But here, the distinction is complicated by the fact that it is the Welsh writer who identifies with the black boxer. This connection between Welshmen and African Americans recurs with a surprising regularity in Welsh literature on boxing, and calls for further analysis.

It is in the underrated writings of Jack Jones that we encounter the most sustained use of the tropes of whiteness and blackness in Welsh literature. Racial impersonation is central to both the form and content of Jones's suggestively titled *Black Parade* (1935) which attempts to offer a fictional account of the industrialization of his native Merthyr. During the course of the novel the central character, Saran (based on the author's mother), makes several visits to the theatre, and amongst the performances mentioned in the text we find *Uncle Tom's Cabin*, *The Octoroon* and, when the theatre is converted into a cinema, *The Singing Fool*.[28] *Uncle Tom's Cabin* refers to the hugely popular stage production of Harriet Beecher Stowe's anti-slavery novel of 1852; *The Octoroon* was also an abolitionist work, written by Irish American Dion Boucicault and first performed in the 1850s, while *The Singing Fool* was the most successful talkie ever upon its release in 1928, and was blackface performer Al Jolson's sequel to *The Jazz Singer*. In fact, all these performances relied on 'blackface' performances in which facial greasepaint or burnt cork was used to darken the skin, a tradition that can be traced back to early nineteenth-century American minstrelsy and that continued well into the twentieth century. In aiming to trace the cultural forms that industrialization bred in south Wales, Jones's fictional evocation of blackface performances offers a suggestive metaphor for the ethnic, linguistic and cultural changes occurring in Welsh society in the later decades of the nineteenth century and the opening decades of the twentieth century in which his panoramic novel is set.

The ways in which Jack Jones (influenced as he was by American novelists John Dos Passos and James T. Farrell) employed the racial imagery of American popular culture to comment obliquely on the changing ethnic composition of Welsh society can be usefully illustrated with reference to two boxing scenes that occur in *Black Parade*. The first presents the Welshman Harry plastering the Irishman Flannery's 'mug until the nose, moustache and lips were pounded into one piece of blood-soaked hairy flesh'. Glyn, the character from whose perspective we view the fight, is reduced to vomiting violently by the sight. The tone in which the other fight is described is rather different:

'I'll knock that bloody smile off your chops,' muttered Harry as he went for the nigger bald-headed. But when he got to where the nigger had been a split second before the nigger wasn't there. But he soon learnt where he was when a stinging left came from somewhere to almost flatten his nose. 'Damn you,' he muttered, turning and charging in the direction the blow had come from, only to receive a stinger from another direction. And so it went on throughout the round, a round during which Harry saw but little of the coloured man who smiled ... 'Science, that is,' murmured Billy Samuels proudly as the smiling untouched negro returned to his corner at the end of the second round, by which time Harry was in a very bad way indeed ... He was carried to his corner, where he was washed and brought to his senses, and after that was done Billy Samuels shook him by the hand and said that never had he seen a gamer chap than Harry had that night proved himself, and the negro boxer also shook Harry by the hand and said that he was the stiffest proposition he had met in any part of the United States of America or here in this country ...[29]

The black boxer is merely a 'nigger' when the fight begins, but is slowly elevated into the more respectable 'coloured man' and 'negro' in the face of the pounding that Harry receives. The African American is introduced as Joe Wills before the fight, a name that implicitly evokes a widely covered American boxing controversy of the 1920s. The main challenger for the title of heavyweight champion, held by the white Jack Dempsey, was the African American Harry Wills. A fight between the two men was never arranged, partly because Dempsey's promoter didn't believe in interracial fights, and partly due to a fear of race riots of the kind that had accompanied Jack Johnson's victories in the previous decade.[30] Jack Jones splits Harry Wills's name between the Welshman Harry and the African American Wills, a suggestive identification of both the Welshman and African American with the boxer famously denied his chance to fight for the heavyweight title.

The difference between the two fights in Jones's novel reflects a difference in the social, and fictional, status of the Irish and African Americans. Ethnic tensions between the Irish and Welsh, as Paul O'Leary has noted, were common in nineteenth-century south Wales, a reality reflected in the visceral violence of the bout between Harry and Flannery.[31] African Americans posed no such threat and the way in which Jones depicts the scene seems to evoke – to adopt Gerald Early – a culture of clowning more than a 'culture of bruising'. Wills's perpetual smile and ability to disappear whenever Harry tries to land a punch is reminiscent of the trickster figure in African American culture, and the clowning 'coon' of minstrel shows. The black boxer plays the kind of minstrel role that the grandfather describes in Ralph Ellison's *Invisible Man*: 'I want you to overcome 'em with yeses, undermine 'em with grins, agree 'em to death and destruction, let 'em swoller you till they vomit or bust wide open'.[32]

The minstrel mask is used to hide a submerged hatred and the smiling boxer destroys Harry before patronizing him by claiming that he has never met stiffer opposition. This seems unlikely as, according to Jones's account, Harry never manages to land a punch during the whole fight. While Jones utilizes a heightened realism to depict Harry's bout with the Irishman Flannery, the fight with the African American Wills seems to belong to the realm of symbol and metaphor rather than reality. Eric Lott, in his suggestive account of blackface minstrelsy, argues that to

> put on the cultural forms of 'blackness' was to engage in a complex affair of manly mimicry ... To wear or even enjoy blackface was literally, for a time, to become black, to inherit the cool, virility, humility, abandon ... that were the prime components of white ideologies of black manhood.[33]

In Jack Jones's *Black Parade* Joe Wills embodies the 'cool, virility' and 'abandon' described by Lott, and the ambivalence of Welsh responses to African American masculinity is captured in the connection that Jones implies between the two fighters: the Welsh Harry, and African American Wills.

Returning to the terms of the Ralph Ellison passage quoted earlier, while Wills is the 'trickster', Harry in this scene is the 'yokel' taking on the black prizefighter, and while he fails to land the one devastating blow, he is arguably stepping into the prizefighter's 'sense of time' by getting into the ring in the first place. For the yokel to step into the boxing ring was to climb from rural provincialism into modernity. To be modern, as Marshall Berman memorably argues

> Is to find ourselves in an environment that promises us adventure, power, joy, growth, transformation of ourselves and the world – and, at the same time, that threatens to destroy everything we have, everything we know, everything we are. Modern environments and experiences cut across all boundaries of geography and ethnicity, of class and nationality, of religion and ideology: in this sense, modernity can be said to unite all mankind. But it is a paradoxical unity, a unity of disunity: it pours all into a maelstrom of perpetual disintegration and renewal, of struggle and contradiction, of ambiguity and anguish. To be modern is to be part of a universe in which, as Marx said, 'All that is solid melts into air'.[34]

In Welsh literature the boxing ring represents this experience of modernity. In Louise Walsh's recent *Fighting Pretty*, boxing offers a context in which to shatter stereotypes and to blur the distinctions of gender as the narrator learns to fight with her sparring partner Alanna who 'started when she was eight' and whose mother confesses that 'she looked like a boy , so we didn't tell nobody, not even the trainer'.[35] The ring is a rapidly transforming society in microcosm, and in twentieth-century literature offered an allegorical representation of the transformations in Welsh society. It is a space where gender boundaries may be challenged, in the work of Louise Walsh, and for an earlier generation of writers a place where rural 'yokels' could be transformed into industrialized modern men. Between 1861 and 1911, as a result of the explosive growth of the coal industry, the population of the county of Glamorgan grew by 253 per cent, and in the decade preceding the First World War Wales was ranked second to the United States as a centre for immigration. Wales, an agricultural land of about 500,000 people in 1800, was transformed into an urban nation of 2,500,000 by 1911.[36] In a society that saw major changes in the make-up of its ethnic composition the question of who was native and who was foreign, brother and other, became a question of some concern. Within this context, a tradition of blackface minstrelsy, as Susan Gubar has noted, 'assures its audience that difference is visible, always encoded in the same way, skin deep'.[37] While, as Kevin Gaines notes, minstrelsy in America reflected white anxieties over urbanizing trends amongst black people, Susan Gubar argues that racechanging conventions also 'enabled artists from manifold traditions to relate nuanced comparative stories about various modes and gradations of othering'.[38]

Alexander Cordell contributes to one of those 'manifold traditions' by exploring 'modes and gradations of othering' in his typically vivid and sweeping historical fiction based on the life of Jim Driscoll, *Peerless Jim* (1984).[39] Cordell makes it clear that the Cardiff boxer's Irish background makes him representative of the cultural melting pot of early twentieth-century Cardiff.

> Tiger Bay, formed between the canal and Bute Street was an enclave that was neither Welsh nor Irish, but of its own; a melting-pot of every nationality from Greece to China and Arabia to Spain ... I walked slowly along the streets of Tiger Bay, savouring its humanity. For me these people were mine; neither English, Irish nor Welsh, yet identifiably of my blood. The rouged and powdered faces of the prostitutes, the slant-eyed Chinese, the stunted features of the starved and ill, of whatever creed or colour, these I counted as my own.[40]

This early process of ethnic identification forms a basis for Driscoll's later relationship with the African American boxer Rastus. Described initially in stereotypical terms as 'the big black man' who speaks in a 'velvet, Negro spiritual voice', Rastus becomes Driscoll's trusted guide and companion when fighting in the United States. When Driscoll decides to leave America and return to his native land,

[t]he only one who might have persuaded me to think again was Rastus, for there had been built between us, within an orbit of mutual pain, a masculine understanding, which comes from taking punches on the chin. And my pity for my new friend increased when I suspected that he was going blind. The culmination punching of two hundred fights had built tell-tale layers above his shaggy brows; the retinas of his eyeballs were intermediately displaced so that clear sight came and went, making oscillations of static objects: Rastus lived, I knew, in a kaleidoscopic world of phantom colours: sometimes, like me, he entered a dim, after-lit land where reigned nothingness.[41]

Rastus is less a character here than an alter ego for Driscoll – as the phrase 'like me' suggests in the final sentence above. The African American represents 'nothingness', and is therefore a canvas on which Driscoll can project his fantasies. The process of identification here connects symboli-cally with the earlier description of Tiger Bay which is itself 'a dim, after-lit land' in Cordell's description of it. In a society structured along the racial lines of black and white, binaries are broken and dissolved in the dim, after-lit land of the boxer's imagination.

The possibility, or indeed probability, of being maimed physically in the ring, present as a sub-theme in Cordell's nostalgically evocative story, is made central in Leslie Norris's writings on boxing. The brutality of the boxing ring is captured in his poem 'The Ballad of Billy Rose' (1967), where an encounter with a blinded beggar drives the narrator's memory back to 'the hub / Of Saturday violence' where he witnessed the boxer Billy Rose being 'Ripped across both his eyes', ending a career in the ring and condemning the poem's subject to a life of penury.[42] Maiming and brutality are also the key words in Norris's short story 'A Big Night' (1976), which has a racial subtext. Disturbed and apparently brutalized by having sneaked in one Saturday to witness a professional fight between Cuthbert Fletcher and Ginger Thomas, the narrator, in the story's final scene, returns for Tuesday's session in the gym:

Everything began to feel fine. It wasn't until I put the gloves on to spar with Charlie Nolan that I realised that something was wrong. I kept on seeing Ginger Thomas, destructive and graceful, his hands cocked, moving into Cuthbert, as he had on the Saturday night. I could see his face, relaxed and faintly curious, the sudden blur as he released three or four short punches before sliding away. I knew too that I was doing this to Charlie, but I couldn't stop. Charlie was bleeding from the mouth and nose and he was pawing away with his gloves open. I could tell he was frightened. Yet I kept on ripping punches at him, my hands suddenly hard and urgent and the huge, muffling gloves we used no longer clumsy.[43]

We are told earlier that Cuthbert Fletcher (based on the real-life black Merthyr boxer Cuth Taylor) 'would have been featherweight champion of Wales except that he was coloured'.[44] While the Welsh crowd cheer 'with relief and pride' when Cuthbert wins on points, it is the 'lack of emotion' as much as the 'precise fury and venom' of Ginger Thomas's attacks that captures the narrator's imagination.[45] Norris does not explore the possible meanings of this identification as the fight is replayed in reverse with Charlie Nolan/Cuthbert Fletcher receiving a pummelling at the hands of the narrator/Ginger Thomas. Having reduced Nolan to tears the narrator leaves the gym, never to return, just as Norris closes the door on the event, omitting any explanatory commentary and thus forcing his readers to consider the multiple meanings and significances of the two friends' repeat performance of an original contest between white and black.

The implicit connection that, as I hope to have demonstrated, so many writers make between black and white in Welsh boxing literature, becomes explicit in Jack Jones's dramatic narrative *The Black Welshman*, that was serialized in *The Empire News* in 1957. Jones writes in the first person as an African American boxer who escapes to Wales having killed a white assailant. Known as Tom Ross, but actually named Abraham Dowling, born free in Chicago to a father who had been a slave, the narrator becomes known as 'the black Welshman (*y Cymro Du*) because in time I spoke the language better than most Welsh people'.[46] The erudite, racially conscious, African American narrator recalls his early career in Chicago:

> I trained for my fights in a bit of a gym my employer had fixed up in a corner of the large warehouse in which I still worked as a packer. My trainer and seconds, all coloured men, also worked there. The work itself was good training for one who did not smoke or drink but I was not tied to my work now that I was making a name for myself in the ring. My trainer had for a time had the handling of Sam Langford, the coloured heavyweight whose lack of inches alone prevented him from going right to the top. I refused to be matched with a coloured man for the entertainment of crowds composed in the main of white men, few women watched fights in those days. White hopes I would take on at the rate of a couple per month but I would not use my fists on a black brother whatever the inducement offered. Later I did, but not until I landed in Wales.[47]

Having evoked the conventions of black minstrelsy as a vehicle for exploring the social changes that he observed in his family's life in *Black Parade*, Jack Jones ultimately donned the black mask himself in portraying a Welsh-speaking, African American ex-boxer who bears witness to the cultural shifts taking place in the Rhondda. The tale ends wistfully with the black Welshman turning for solace to a bilingual Bible as he recalls the Rhondda of the past and the Welsh-speaking girl who was once the love of his life.

> Let's … leave my story just as it is, then I shall have more time for this Book of ours and all who are in it including our Saviour. But here am I talking to you when I should be reading, and fancy me, the black Welshman, turning first to the English side. That's how it is, the Welsh language is on the wane here in Mid-Rhondda, where no-one ever spoke it so sweetly as you … Yes, a great change has come over the Rhondda in my time, it is now a Borough … The new Rhondda reads more than it boxes. I can't think of one professional boxer in the whole of the Rhondda these days, yet I remember when there were at least a dozen and another hundred trying to fight their way into the ranks of professionals.[48]

Jones's 'Black Welshman' witnesses and offers a commentary on the industrialization of Wales, and sees the early effects of deindustrialization manifested in the story by the fact that boxers are becoming a dying breed.

Neither Jack Jones, nor his 'black Welshman', lived to see the Rhondda depicted in the most experimental and successful of all Welsh boxing novels, Ron Berry's *So Long Hector Bebb* (1970). The novel's landscape is quite literally postmodern: it is a world, as several characters testify, in which industrial mobility has become post-industrial stagnation:

> 'This Wales of ours is going to rack and ruin. I tell you, brawd, what's wanted is a bloody revolution. Wipe the slate clean, start all over again as if we'd just lost our bloody tails.'
> 'Back to the caves? He-he-he, not in our time, mister'.[49]

The novel opens with Bebb planning a boxing comeback having been banned for a year. He has already regained the British title by the time we get a third of the way through the novel, but things then take a turn for the worse when he kills a man for fondling his wife. In the crass, brutal, misogynistic, but at times linguistically dazzling, world of the boxing fraternity Bebb gains some sympathy:

> You had to cross Hector first to send him into one of his non-stop fits. What Millie Bebb does is fling her what's-it at him for Em to touch up her clout. Em sticks his hand there in open public! Like I say, God stone me cold, the man isn't born who'll take such. He was always on about Mel Carpenter's bad luck. Luck, by Christ. They reckon you could hear Emlyn's head smacking the counter from outside the Transport Café. LUCK! Em's mouth spilling the old tomato juice. No wonder they took Millie away for a couple of weeks … Mind, speaking for myself I hope they don't find Hector. Never find him, that's what I hope.[50]

While some characters compensate for material deprivation with linguistic bravura, Hector Bebb achieves a measure of freedom in leaving the ring to live a primitive life in the forests above the valley towns of Tosteg and Blaenddu. In Berry's novel the narrative trajectory from yokel provincialism to prizefighting modernity embodied in the Ralph Ellison passage quoted at the beginning of this chapter is reversed. Rather than stepping into modernity, Hector Bebb steps out of modern time and returns to the mountains: the prizefighter becomes a yokel. The history of Wales as reflected in its boxing literature seems to have come full circle. But I'll conclude this chapter by noting that, in his return to primitive life, Bebb carries with him an image of his better self and an embodiment of the world that had given his life purpose and meaning: a copy of *Ring* magazine where 'another shiny Negro posed on the cover'.[51]

Blood Jumps: Dylan Thomas, Charlie Parker and 1950s America

I

In 'El perseguidor' (The Pursuer, 1959), a short story by the celebrated Argentine novelist Julio Cortázar, a groundbreaking jazz musician named Johnny Carter is pursued by Bruno, a critic who is increasingly anxious about his inability to capture the essence of jazz in prose. According to Doris Sommer, Cortázar's original Spanish conveys Bruno's unease and self-doubt about his vocation as a critic, an anxiety intensified by the fact that 'Johnny's capacity for intellectual speculation' is 'more than equal to Bruno's'.[1] Johnny quotes Dylan Thomas's 'O make me a mask' and proceeds to offer an interpretation of the poem which develops into a meditation on the arbitrariness of words and signs. Cortázar uses Thomas's words as the epigraph to his work, which is dedicated in memoriam to the musician on whom the story is so clearly based: African American alto saxophonist Charlie Parker. There's no evidence that Parker himself ever offered an interpretation of lines by Dylan Thomas, but Cortázar is drawing on the fact that many likened Parker to Thomas, not least in the fact that their remarkable creative exploits were seen to 'be matched by equally extraordinary acts of personal dissolution'. Parker died in New York, aged thirty-five, in 1955. Thomas had died two years earlier in the same city, aged thirty-nine. Both deaths offered themselves to romanticization and mythologization. Rather like Thomas's character Samuel Bennett who was destined to shed 'seven skins' in the original plans for the story 'Adventures in the Skin Trade', Cortázar's Carter performs many roles, wears many masks, and is continually eluding the pursuit of critics and coroners alike. The saxophonist and his art form cannot be captured in prose. The problem for Carter is that Bruno's biography of his life contains the bare facts, 'but what you forgot to put in is me'.[2]

The fictional saxophonist's critique of Bruno's work may be levelled, with some justification, at this chapter. For I am less concerned with the actual, historical, figures of Charlie 'Bird' Parker (1920–55) and Dylan Thomas (1914–53), than I am with what they came to represent in 1950s America. As will become clear, they were very widely compared, most influentially so in poet Kenneth Rexroth's celebrated essay 'Disengagement', which attempted to construct a genealogy for the 1950s 'Beat movement':

> Like the pillars of Hercules, like two ruined Titans guarding the entrance to one of Dante's circles, stand two great juvenile delinquents – the heroes of the post-war generation: the saxophonist, Charlie Parker, and Dylan Thomas. If the word 'deliberate' means anything, both of them certainly deliberately destroyed themselves.
>
> Both of them were overcome by the horror of the world in which they found themselves, because at last they could no longer overcome that world with the weapon of a purely lyrical art ... Dylan Thomas's verse had to find endurance in a world of burning cities and burning Jews. He was able to find a meaning in his art as long as it was the answer to air raids and gas ovens ... I think all this could apply to Parker just as well, although, because of the nature of music, it is not demonstrable – at least not conclusively.[3]

Rexroth's placement of Dylan Thomas and Charlie 'Bird' Parker in the context of wartime atrocity and destruction implicitly raises the question of the function of art during, and following, a period of frightening barbarity. It is clear from the opening quotation that for Rexroth – who never developed his comparison beyond a few vague references to both artists' 'lucidity' and 'fluency' – Charlie Parker and Dylan Thomas were responding to a crisis in post-war culture: that of how, in the aftermath of the death camps and the atomic bomb, could art endure at all. There is evidence throughout Thomas's letters and poems that he was haunted by the atrocities of war, testifying to the truth of Rexroth's dramatic observation that his 'verse had to find endurance in a world of burning cities and burning Jews'. In a letter to the poet and sometime actress Julian Orde written in May 1945, Thomas evokes 'the throbbing of tractors, the squealing of rats and rabbits in the traps, the surging of seagulls, thrushes, blackbirds, finches, cuckooing of cuckoos, cooing of doves, discussion of works, blinding of wives, sputtering of saucepans and kettles' outside his window in New Quay before noting that it is an 'ordinary day, nature serene as Fats Waller in Belsen'.[4] The discrepancy, in this essentially humorous anti-pastoral scene, between the trivial every-day goings on of a Welsh coastal town and the atrocities recently perpetuated and disclosed on mainland Europe is disconcerting, as is the way in which Thomas heightens that discrepancy by juxtaposing the Harlem stride-pianist Fats Waller (who had died in 1943) with Belsen. Fats Waller is made to represent a natural life force that is seemingly unaffected and oblivious to the barbarism of war. The tendency manifested in this letter, to represent African Americans as sources of natural primitivism in a hostile and alienating world, has a long history, but was given a new lease of life in the writings of 1950s America, and is a characteristic of the racial thought of that period. The comparison made between Dylan Thomas and Charlie Parker was informed by this romanticizing and mythologizing primitivism.

II

Thomas's four visits to the United States occurred when the Cold War was at its iciest, with McCarthyism at its height before the slow thaw that occurred following the death of Stalin who, like Thomas, died in 1953. It was a period of American military dominance, consumer craving and political conservatism in which a new generation of American writers bared the dark side of national affluence. The post-war economic boom had supposedly landed Americans in a placid valley of consumer goods: pastel pedal pushers, self-cleaning ovens and cheeseburgers delivered by waitresses on roller skates. For many writers and artists, society seemed to be a massive supermarket designed to fulfil the needs of consumers. Randall Jarrell's witty essay 'A Sad Heart at the Super-market' offered a plaintive diagnosis of the future of culture in a consumerist society, and the same note was echoed by Allen Ginsberg 'shopping for images' in his poem 'A Supermarket in California' and by Lawrence Ferlinghetti in 'The Pennycandystore beyond the El'.[5] Theodore Roethke captures the spirit of the age when he describes the 'frigidaires snoring the sleep of plenty' in 'Last Words', and the need to choose between newly available goods runs through the poetry of the 1950s as a diffuse but insistent voice.[6] In Karl Shapiro's 'Drugstore',

> every nook and cranny of flesh
> Is spoken to by packages and wiles.
> 'Buy me, buy me' they whisper and cajole.[7]

Gregory Corso's 'In the Fleeting Hand of Time' describes a man

> led 100 mph o'er the
> vast market of choice
> what to choose? what to choose?[8]

Alan Dugan decides 'Not to Choose' in a poem of that name:

> goods, deeds, credits, debts.
> Have it your own way, life:
> I'm just here to die, but I
> would rather live it out as a fool
> and have a short life in contempt
> and idle graces, but, instead,
> the office telephone goes off
> and voices out of its dark night
> command me, 'Choose, Choose ...'[9]

Saul Bellow warns us in his novel *Seize the Day* of 1956 – 'You want to avoid catching the money fever. This type of activity is filled with hostile feeling and lust. You should see what it does to some of these fellows.'[10] Unfortunately, Tommy Wilhelm, Bellow's main character, does catch the money fever, and the novel's final scene shows him weeping at a stranger's funeral, mourning the death of genuine human connections in a harsh and alienating world. Tommy's grief and isolation ennoble him, since 1950s novelists agreed that those who succeeded in the mercenary culture were, in the words of *Catcher in the Rye*'s Holden Caulfield, 'phony bastards'.[11]

This was the context for the rise of the 'hipster', described by Norman Mailer in his essay of 1957, 'The White Negro':

> A totalitarian society makes enormous demands on the courage of men, and a partially totalitarian society makes even greater demands, for the general anxiety is greater. Indeed if one is to be a man, almost any kind of unconventional action often takes disproportionate courage. So it is no accident that the source of Hip is the Negro for he has been living on the margin between totalitarianism and democracy for two centuries.[12]

The hipsters represented a counterculture in formation, and had their world view expressed and dissected by the writers of the 'Beat era' such as Jack Kerouac, Allen Ginsberg and William Burroughs. If Norman Mailer suggests that one source of 'the hip' was the Negro (a problematic assumption to which I shall return), then another source was Dylan Thomas. Part of the appeal of Dylan Thomas and Charlie Parker to the writers of 1950s America was that their early deaths and obsessive, consuming, commitment to their art proved that they were no 'phony bastards'. They were perceived to be that which the Beats most admired: artists who dedicated their lives to writing, and whose lives were characterized by excess. Whereas Salinger's Holden Caulfield, like many other 1950s 'misfits', is ushered into the analyst's office, tranquilized and made to adapt, the early deaths of Dylan Thomas and Charlie Parker had enabled them to avoid such enforced conformity.

In an essay written following Thomas's death in 1953 his friend and fellow poet Karl Shapiro began to lay bare the process by which Thomas was being translated into American cultural terms:

> The animal to Thomas is everything and we listen because he calls it animal, not spirit or essence or potentiality or something else. It is the authentic symbol for a poet who believes in the greatness of the individual and the sacredness of the masses. It is Whitman's symbol when he says he thinks he could turn and live with animals ... And there are suggestions of Druidism (which I know nothing about) and primitive fertility rites, apparently still extant in Wales, all mixed up with Henry Miller, Freud and American street slang ... Thomas was outside the orbit of the English poets, who succeeded Eliot and cannot easily be placed in their tradition. He was anti-tradition by nature, by place, by inclination. Certainly Thomas's love for America can also be seen in this light: America is the untraditional place, the Romantic country *par excellence.*[13]

Shapiro is clearly emphasizing the primitive, the animal and the druidic in Thomas, and his essay as a whole is an example of a tradition of thought that has been described as 'romantic primitivism': the belief in the spiritual superiority of pre-industrial societies and peoples.[14] For the Beat writers, African Americans were the primary group to be envisaged in such terms. In his long poem *Howl*, Allen Ginsberg witnesses 'the best minds of my generation destroyed by madness, starving hysterical naked / dragging themselves through the negro streets at dawn / looking for an angry fix', and in his cult novel *On the Road*, Jack Kerouac had his narrator Sal Paradise walk

> At lilac evening ... among the lights of 27th and Welton in the Denver colored section, wishing I were a Negro, feeling that the best the white world had offered was not enough ecstasy for me, not enough life, joy, kicks, darkness, music, not enough night.[15]

This view of the African American as offering a source of revitalization for a corrupt, alienating, materialist society was given its most powerful and influential expression in Mailer's essay on the White Negro:

> So no wonder in certain cities of America, in New York of course, and New Orleans, in Chicago and San Francisco and Los Angeles ... this particular part

of a generation was attracted to what the Negro had to offer. In such places as Greenwich Village, a ménage-à-trois was completed – the bohemian and the juvenile delinquent came face-to-face with the Negro, and the hipster was a fact in American life. If marijuana was the wedding ring, the child was the language of Hip for its argot gave expression to abstract states of feeling which all could share, at least all who were Hip. And in this wedding of the white and the black it was the Negro who brought the cultural dowry.[16]

This notion of the 'dowry', of a marriage between the masculine white and feminine black, is significant. For if African Americans were imagined to be a source of folkish wisdom and spiritual reinvigoration, the Celts were also imagined in similar terms. The leading Beat era writer Jack Kerouac took a particular pride in his Breton ancestry and in a letter of June 1949 stated:

> Recently, also, I read Matthew Arnold's Study of Celtic Literature, and every-thing in my intention seems to begin to focus. I found a name in Celtic lore, Keinvarvawc. Pretty close hey? From things like Celtic literature it's possible to pluck up perfect golden bones of images … such as the Doors of Bran, who told his lieutenants they would be happy only if they refrained from opening certain doors. This like telling oneself not to open the horror-doors the dark-doors of futile melancholy …[17]

The reference to Matthew Arnold's lectures is intriguing, and suggests something of the nature of racial thinking within the Beat movement.

In his essay 'Democracy' (1861) Arnold, the Victorian man of letters, asked 'what influence may help us to prevent the English people from becoming, with the growth of democracy, "Americanised"'?[18] Arnold's words suggest that by the 1860s 'Americanization' was already being used as a concise way of referring to the sweeping changes occurring as a result of the social movement towards democracy, as manifested in the decline of the aristocracy's influence on the political and cultural life of the nation. This process left the middle class to determine the future tone of the national life, a prospect which could not be welcomed, for Arnold believed that the middle class in England was characterized by its narrow, uncultured and 'philistine' conception of what that life should be. In Arnold's lectures *On the Study of Celtic Literature*, to which Kerouac refers (and which I discussed in chapter 1), solutions for the problems engendered by a process of 'Americanization' are sought in the ethnic hybridity that Arnold believes characterizes the 'English' nation:

> Let me notice in passing, however, that there is, in truth, a Celtic air about the extravagance of chivalry, its reaction against the despotism of fact, its straining human nature further than it will stand. But putting all this question of

chivalry and its origin on one side, no doubt the sensibility of the Celtic nature, its nervous exaltation, have something feminine in them, and the Celt is thus peculiarly disposed to feel the spell of the feminine idiosyncrasy; he has an affinity to it; he is not far from its secret. Again, his sensibility gives him a peculiarly near and intimate feeling of nature and the life of nature; here, too, he seems in a special way attracted by the secret before him, the secret of natural beauty and natural magic, and to be close to it, to half-divine it ... The Celt, indisciplined, anarchical, and turbulent by nature, but out of affection and admiration giving himself body and soul to some leader, this is not a promising political temperament, it is just the opposite of the Anglo-Saxon temperament, disciplinable and steadily obedient within certain limits, but retaining an inalienable part of freedom and self-dependence; but it is a temperament for which one has a kind of sympathy notwithstanding.[19]

For Arnold, then, the counter-force to Saxon philistinism, is a Celtic resistance to industrialization manifested in that race's sensitivity, femininity and attraction to 'natural magic'.

Arnold was an English Unionist who believed that these valuable Celtic attributes of 'femininity' and 'natural magic' would reach their full maturity when combined with masculine Saxon rationality, in the making of the hybrid, superior, Englishman. Arnold's essays, however, as R. F. Foster notes, ultimately 'reinforced an interpretation of Celticism that strengthened irreconcilable ideas of separatism'. W. B. Yeats, like many members of the Irish Renaissance, evoked Arnold's lectures in support of his view that 'the flood-gates of materialism are only half-open among us as yet in Ireland; perhaps the new age may close them before the tide is quite upon us'.[20] As the twentieth century proceeded, and America emerged as the leading capitalist super power, a wide range of writers and thinkers, from a variety of political and cultural persuasions, tended increasingly to equate America with a rampant individualist capitalism, while the imaginative, poetic and communitarian Celtic countries were seen to offer a valuable counter-force.[21] The narrative whereby the Celtic race feeds into and revitalizes the emergent, yet rather drab and philistine, culture of the English nation, is structurally identical to that offered by Norman Mailer in relation to African Americans in the United States almost a century later. It is also manifest in Kerouac's attitude towards African Americans, and informs his attitude towards his Celtic ancestry. This strain of thought has been described as 'contributionism', where a minority people are encouraged to think that their primitive folksiness and spirituality will make a significant contribution to the life of the dominant society.[22] These contributionist narratives imposed upon African American

and Celtic peoples informed the reception of the works of Thomas and
Parker during their lives and posthumously.

III

If the alleged 'primitivism' of Parker and Thomas could be turned to as a
source of cultural revitalization for an 'over-civilized' society, it could also
be perceived as a threat. Both saxophonist and poet were sources of admiration and anxiety due to their ability to transgress and break the boundaries
of society, decency and art. In his study of jazz as myth and religion, Neil
Leonard analyses the tendency to view Charlie Parker as a 'trickster', that
'complicated figure, part human, part animal' who

> is an ambivalent, ambiguous figure full of contradiction and irony – in one
> moment charming, altruistic, intelligent, and creative, and in the next gross,
> stupid and deceptive, a liar, thief, or seducer. He may have uncertain sexual
> status or outlandish appetites symbolized sometimes by outsize genitals ... He
> may combine black and white symbolism in clever chicanery, marked by a
> childishness that can be his undoing.[23]

Leonard proceeds to discuss a whole range of outlandish stories concerning
Parker, such as the following account by Ross Russell of a night in 1948 at
the Argyle Lounge, an expensive Chicago club.

> Charlie finished a set and placed his horn on the top of the piano. Then he
> stepped off the bandstand, walked past the tables on the main floor, into the
> foyer, entered the pay telephone booth, closed the door and proceeded to
> urinate on the floor. The yellow stream gushing forth as from a stallion, its
> pool dark and foaming as it spread under the door of the telephone booth and
> into the foyer. He came from the booth laughing. There was no explanation or
> apology.[24]

There are also stories of Parker's insatiable sexual appetites – such as
Miles Davis's recollection of sitting in the back of a taxi while Bird,
already 'shot up' on heroin, drinks whisky, eats chicken and tells his
female companion for that night 'to get down and suck his dick'.[25]

Tales of Dylan Thomas's behaviour tend to be less explicit, but he is
similarly represented as a figure who openly breaks the conventions of
respectability. Thomas was willing, at times, to live up to and to reinforce
some expectations of him. In 'After the Funeral', a poem written in
memory of his aunt Ann Jones and set in that largely Welsh-speaking west
Wales where many of his relatives lived, Thomas can be seen to be

'wrestling verbally' with the local Nonconformist minister.[26] In M. Wynn Thomas's powerful reading, the poem returns to the natural world and turns nature into an alternative religion: '[I] Bow down the walls of the ferned and foxy woods / That her love sing and swing through a brown chapel, / Bless her bent spirit with four, crossing birds.'[27] Thus when, in a letter about his aunt's funeral, Thomas confessed to feeling 'utterly unmoved, apart, as I said, from the pleasant death-reek at my negroid nostrils', he is in a sense defining himself as a racial primitive, and rooting that primitivist oneness with nature in the rural Wales of his ancestors.[28]

If religious Nonconformity was an early target for his subversive imagination at home, it seems that Dylan Thomas found social conventions and expectations to be exasperatingly repressive during his visits to America. John Berryman recalled Thomas's 'social savagery' at a post-reading party in Seattle:

> We had about ninety seconds' talk when our hostess, an affected and impe-
> rious lady known locally as the Duchess of Utah, crashed into and between us
> with 'Well! Literary gossip, eh?' in a tone both injured and superior, meaning
> that we had no right (after thirteen years) to seclude ourselves from the avid
> professors and professors' wives for one minute, or rather two. Thomas had
> already greeted everyone, incidentally; I kept out of the way until his chores
> were done. He was still on his first drink. Now he looked at our short hostess
> with resentment and contempt, and said slowly, 'We were just discussing
> Hitler's methods of dealing with the Jews, and we have decided that he was
> quite right'.[29]

Berryman proceeds to defend Thomas as no anti-Semite, and is anxious to note that they had in fact been discussing the poems of Alun Lewis whose work Thomas has just performed. But the story is a particularly unpleasant example of Thomas's role as an outrageous taboo breaker, and Berryman is deliberately reinforcing that dimension of his character. There are many stories of this kind in John Malcolm Brinnin's *Dylan Thomas in America*, where the Welsh poet's primitivistic, child-like and subversive nature are consistently foregrounded:

> The sexual life of Dylan Thomas was already as much a source of legend as
> was his fabulous capacity for alcohol. Reports from Boston to Los Angeles
> suggested he lived by lechery, fondling girl sophomores and the wives of
> deans with an obsessive disregard for anything but his own insatiable desires.
> The tumescence of his poems fed such rumours and supported them; uncov-
> ering sexual imagery in the poems of Dylan Thomas had already become a
> national undergraduate pastime. The precise, obscene references and the four-
> letter ejaculations of his drunken talk, his often lascivious retorts to civil

questions, and his lewd attentions to details of the female anatomy were repeated and embellished. In California, it was reported, he had suffered through an intolerably long and dull dinner party with a group of male professors. When cigars were passed around, Dylan, refusing to sink into the general stupor, addressed the company: 'Gentleman, I wish we were all hermaphrodites!' 'Why,' said one of the professors politely, 'why do you wish that Mr. Thomas?' 'Because, gentlemen, then we could all **** ourselves.' Similar stories cropped up everywhere, along with rumours of a sexual prowess and a sexual preoccupation indicating satyriasis.[30]

Both Thomas and Parker were thus constructed in terms that correspond closely to the figure of the 'trickster', that 'liminal figure' in whom we see, according to Victor Turner, 'naked, unaccomodated man, whose nonlogical character issues in various modes of behavior: destructive, creative, farcical, ironic, energetic, suffering, lecherous, submissive, defiant, but always unpredictable'.[31] In the cultural imagination of 1950s America, Parker and Thomas embodied certain, perhaps necessary, ideals of the transgressive artist.

Transgression was appealing in a post-war America where mass production required mass consumption by 'a mass middle class – a prosperous working class with a bourgeois identity'.[32] The African American philosopher Cornel West notes that this process co-existed with, and was to some extent countered by, 'the first major emergence of subcultures of American non-WASP intellectuals'. West draws particular attention to 'the so-called New York intellectuals in criticism' and 'the bebop artists in jazz music'.[33] As I noted in the introduction to this book, 'The New York Intellectuals' were the first generation of critics of Jewish descent to have a profound influence on American culture through the journal *Partisan Review* in the first instance and, in due course, by entering the higher echelons of the academy. Despite their being linked by West, there would be very little relationship between the 'bepoppers' and the 'New York Intellectuals'. Indeed, Lionel Trilling, Irving Howe and Alfred Kazin, among others, sought to defend serious and highbrow art against mass culture. They venerated the high, elitist, modernists – Eliot, Pound, Yeats – and considered art a judgement on what they saw as the crass materialism of mass society. This generation of Jewish intellectuals challenged the hegemony of the WASPs, but did not change the basic cultural values of American academe. Lionel Trilling's great achievement, for example, was to reinterpret the tradition of Matthew Arnold so that it could now include people like himself.[34] It was, however, one of this generation, Alfred Kazin, who wrote the most perceptive analysis of Dylan

Thomas's influence on America. Kazin identified with the anti-establishmentarian nature of Thomas's work and life, noting that the Welshman was 'utterly outside the Establishment' in Britain and was thus 'regarded with a certain loving contempt by some of the snobs who so righteously gnashed their teeth after his death'.[35] If the way in which Thomas had challenged the establishment was a source of admiration, and indeed inspiration, for Kazin and his fellow second-generation Jewish intellectuals, he was also a cause for concern in that he threatened to blur the boundary between high art and popular art. His recordings and incredibly popular readings challenged the highbrow cultural values of an American bourgeoisie seeking to retain its cultural authority in the face of an increasingly prosperous working class. 'Dylan's records are fancied by the same people who admire the new jazz' noted Kazin, 'his impending appeal, winsome and raking, [is] similar to that of a Frank Sinatra'.[36] Charlie Parker was the source of similar concerns. Ted Gioia notes that the 1940s saw the first generation of jazz musicians who wished to be 'coequals with the purveyors of highbrow culture', rejecting their status as entertainers.[37] Bebop drew, simultaneously, on the 'pungent roots and rhythms of Kansas city', and the 'rarefied atmosphere of high art'.[38] Parker seemed to embody these forces, as a musician who drew on the blues traditions of his native Kansas, but who would also call his musicians to the stage by playing a few bars by Stravinsky or Hindemith.[39] While Thomas popularized poetry, Parker forced jazz to transcend its squalid origins to become 'America's classical music'. 'Highbrow' and 'lowbrow' were becoming imprecise categories, and part of the explanation for the comparisons made between Thomas and Parker in the 1950s related to their location between 'high' and 'low', and their contemporaneous roles in breaking these cultural hierarchies.[40]

If the view of Thomas and Parker as transgressive tricksters was reinforced by their roles in blurring cultural boundaries, this view of them also derived from the boundary-breaking nature of their art. Parker's biographer and record producer Ross Russell suggested that there might be an aesthetic similarity between poet and musician in the following terms:

> Like Dylan Thomas, Charlie Parker had boldly crossed a well-defined fron-
> tier and freed the language of his art from dross and cliché, investing it with
> a new intensity, color, and significance. The magnificent openings of
> 'Parker's Mood', 'Slam Slam Blues', and 'Bird of Paradise' were, for those
> responsive to black music, as charged and as evocative as Dylan's poetry.
> There was the same impression of a molten vocabulary cooled and fused
> into a new idiom.[41]

Both Thomas and Parker are seen to have crossed well-defined frontiers, and it might be worth pursuing this idea as a means of indicating, provisionally, some of the possible bases for comparing their works. Given that bebop was regarded as a revolutionary turn in the history of jazz it is surprising that Parker's pieces are usually based on a limited number of traditional harmonic frameworks: the 12-bar blues, 'I Got Rhythm', and a small number of other popular songs such as 'Cherokee', 'How High the Moon' and 'All the Things You Are'. Quite central to Parker's music, as Max Harrison notes, 'is a two-way, and even contradictory, process whereby he rooted his music in the constraints of commonplace 12- and 32-bar chord sequences and in the rhythm section's regular pulse, and then did everything to challenge, even subvert, these'.[42] Similarly in Thomas's poetry there is also a tension between his linguistic and imagistic risk-taking, and formal conservatism. His explorations of emotional and physical states of being, of psychic and social fragmentation, and of the limits of poetic language are expressed in traditional poetic forms and procedures; sonnet, villanelle, terza rima, precise syllable counts and consistent, if often subtle, rhyme schemes. James A. Davies relates this characteristic of Thomas's work to a 'bourgeois or middle-class impulse towards order and authority', but it is also the case that the tension between form and content, between the subjective and constructive, becomes part of the very meaning of Thomas's poems and Parker's compositions.[43] If 'free jazz' and various forms of avant-garde poetry would attempt to eschew form altogether form the late 1950s onwards, Thomas and Parker belonged to the generation that created the foundations for later experiments. Their reliance on form, coupled with a desire to transcend it, foregrounded and seemed to enact the boundary-breaking and transgressive nature of their art.

In the work of the anthropologist Claude Levi-Strauss, the tension between the subjective and constructive dimensions of artistic practice are explored in relation to music, which he believes allows access to the 'primitive terrain' within cultures, posing a challenge to modern, measured concepts of time. For Levi-Strauss music functions as a model for his ideas of myth, for both music and myth show an ability to capture the diachronic movement of time in the synchronic texture of the moment:

> Below the level of sounds and rhythms, music acts upon a primitive terrain, which is the physiological time of the listener; this time is irreversible and therefore irredeemably diachronic, yet music transmutes the segment devoted to listening to it into a synchronic totality, enclosed within itself. Because of the internal organization of the musical work, the act of listening to it

immobilizes passing time; it catches it and enfolds it as one catches and enfolds a cloth flapping in the wind.[44]

This illusion of 'immobilizing passing time' is a common element in the works of Dylan Thomas and Charlie Parker, as both are artists engaged in a process of confronting, challenging, and meditating upon the meaning of, time. The title of Charlie Parker's composition 'Now's the Time', for example, may be read as an oblique commentary on the poetics of bebop itself, for the piece is a musical meditation on temporal possibility.[45] Structurally, 'Now's the Time' is a basic 12 bar blues, with the addition of a diminished chord on the last two beats of bar 8 and of a G minor in bar 9 delaying the expected dominant C7 chord until bar ten. The variety in accentuation, in length of notes and attack and in range throughout Parker's three remarkable choruses suggest that time can be organized intentionally through the use of accent and stress, pulse and phrasing. Parker's choruses offer a series of similar, yet evolving, experiments with our experience of time.

All three choruses follow a very similar pattern, which can be divided into groupings of four bars. The opening four bars of each chorus contain powerful but fairly conventional blues phrases which evoke Parker's Kansas City roots. Bars 5–8 are the busiest in each chorus, where the arrival of the subdominant in bar 5 gives way to eight and sixteenth note chromatic patterns. The final four bars of each chorus take us back to an emphasis on quarter and eighth notes (or quavers and semi-quavers) and to the F minor harmony, with each chorus ending with the C or F of the tune's defining opening cadence. There is a tension within the piece between blues and non-blues materials, with each chorus moving from a grounding in the blues outwards towards greater abstraction before returning to the minor harmony and blues sensibility. It thus occupies a liminal space between 'African American' and 'European' sensibilities, between highbrow and lowbrow, and thus blurs the boundaries of cultural identity. This impression is intensified by the way in which 'Now's the Time' oscillates between movement and stasis. Following the busiest eight bars in the whole solo, for instance, Parker ends his second chorus by stating the theme's tonic (F) to dominant (C) cadence before choosing to stay on the dominant, thickening his tone with vibrato in the process as if momentarily enjoying a respite of peace before slowly evolving his final chorus through a series of fragmented phrases.

Time itself seems to stand still at this moment in the improvisation. Music critic Simon Frith argues that music's ability to frame time offers an experience that is essentially similar to sex, for it is a means not only for 'releasing physical urges' but also for 'expanding the time in which we can, as it were, live in the present tense'.[46] Parker's 'Now's the Time' evokes the past by way of the blues, within the context of a bebop performance that is a meditation on what it means to live in the present. Within the structure of a conventional blues Parker plays across the choruses, blurring the rigidity of the form, and in the held notes at the end of the second chorus in particular seems to be attempting to halt the passing of time itself.

If language is consistently 'uninhibited', an 'incorrigible contortionist and shameless shape-changer', in Dylan Thomas's poems, his works are also informed by a profound awareness of poetry's temporal dimension.[47] Thomas described his intentions as a poet as follows:

> Out of the inevitable conflict of images – inevitable, because of the creative, recreative, destructive and contradictory nature of the motivating centre, the womb of war – I try to make that momentary peace which is a poem. I do not want a poem of mine to be, nor can it be, a circular piece of experience placed neatly outside the living stream of time from which it came; a poem of mine is, or should be, a watertight section of the stream that is flowing all ways; all warring images within it should be reconciled for that small stop of time.[48]

As with Levi-Strauss's argument regarding the similarities between music and myth, Thomas's description above seems to suggest that the lyric utterance can be simultaneously synchronic and diachronic. The poem amounts to a distillation of the forces interacting within a single synchronic moment, which is under continual threat of disintegration from the diachronic movement of time's 'living stream'. Indeed, time often features as a destructive force in Thomas's poetry, wielding a scythe that 'kills me terribly' in 'Then was My Neophyte'.[49] In 'Once Below a Time' the hands of a grandfather clock merge with a pair of threatening scissor-blades in the image of 'clock-faced tailors' and in 'When I Woke' we encounter a 'man outside with a billhook'.

> Up to his head in blood,
> Cutting the morning off,
> The warm-veined double of Time.[50]

Against the threat posed by time, Thomas seeks moments of stasis. 'Should lanterns shine' ends with a moment of perpetual stasis with 'The ball I threw while playing in the park' having 'not yet reached the ground', and the related earlier poem 'Light breaks where no sun shines' ends on a similar note as 'Above the waste allotments the dawn halts'.[51] *Under Milk Wood* in Thomas's late 'play for voices' is a utopian village where 'it is always opening time in the Sailor's Arms' where the clock's hands are permanently stuck 'at half past eleven'.[52] Childhood can only be recalled whilst 'time allows' it in 'Fern Hill', and the poem's opening word 'Now' signals the poem's meditation on time and memory whilst also establishing the immediacy of childhood experience.[53]

It is perhaps 'Now', described by Vernon Watkins as Thomas's most 'unwarrant[ably] obscure' poem, that enacts the poet's desire to reconcile the 'warring images' of his work within a 'small stop of time'.[53] It may be considered a self-reflexive avant-gardist poem, and to juxtapose it against the temporal experience of Charlie Parker's 'Now's the Time' (discussed above) may offer a useful entrance into its potential meanings. In its 'insistence on form' 'Now' is described by Walford Davies and Ralph Maud as Thomas's 'greatest tribute to words in themselves, paying such fanatical attention to them in the way they weight a line that referential meaning is ultimately lost in the presentational'.[55] Thomas is seen to have 'reached the extremity of one direction of his poetry' with this poem, and indeed 'Now' can be read as a realization of Theodor Adorno's desire for a lyric poem

> in which the subject, without a trace of his material being, intones in language until the voice of language itself is heard. The subject's forgetting himself, his abandoning himself to language as if devoting himself completely to an object – this and the direct intimacy and spontaneity of his expression are the same.[56]

In its use of puns, double-entendres, alliteration and repetition, 'Now' creates the sense of language intoning in its own voice. Thomas spoke of his concern for the sound of words, which were 'as the notes of bells, the sounds of musical instruments, the noises of wind, sea and rain'.[57] If Parker's 'Now's the Time' is a 12-bar blues, Thomas's 'Now' is constructed of formally consistent stanzas which gives the poem a similarly circular, repetitive structure. As John Goodby notes, despite the strange stanza shape, 'the first four lines make a single iambic pentameter, yielding a regular quatrain of alternate ten and eleven-syllable lines'.[58] Thomas, like Parker, is playing creatively with formal conventions, drawing on the reader's formal expectations while simultaneously challenging them. The opening of every stanza in Thomas's poem involves an aural and semantic play between 'Now' and 'nay', which then opens up into a series of more developed images in the last three lines of each stanza. The poem begins as follows:

Now
Say nay,
Man dry man,
Dry lover mine
The deadrock base and blow the flowered anchor,
Should he, for centre sake, hop in the dust,
Forsake, the fool, the hardiness of anger.

Now
Say nay,
Sir no say,
Death to the yes,
The yes to death, the yesman and the answer,
Should he who split his children with a cure
Have brotherless his sister on the handsaw.

Now
Say nay,
No say sir
Yea the dead stir,
And this, nor this, is shade, the landed crow,
He lying low with ruin in his ear,
The cockerel's tide upcasting from the fire.[59]

It is a poem, as its title suggests, that attempts to arrest the living stream, that attempts to capture the moment, to organize time. Ralph Maud has suggested that the key to the poem lies in ascertaining what 'Thomas would be saying no to so emphatically' and suggests that the poem enacts a rejection of the poet's own suicidal impulses.[60] John Goodby reads the poem as the 'soliloquy of a Hamlet-like figure', who in the form of a parodic avant-garde poem, tries 'to argue himself into turning his suicidal anger outwards against the world'.[61] Death is clearly a theme in the poem from the image of one about to 'hop in the dust' in the first stanza to the Shakespearean resonances of one 'lying low with ruin in his ear'. However, the stanzas do not begin with 'No', but rather with 'Now'. The series of repeated 'Nows' at the opening of each stanza illustrates the impossibility of achieving a moment of peace in the inevitable progression of a poem, and the dominant emotion communicated is thus frustration. We may identify three primary sources of frustration within the poem. There is the frustration deriving from the poet's own inability to capture a moment of time, to stop the inevitable passing of history. Secondly, and related to this, the poem enacts a frustration with language itself as the poet struggles to create meaning from letters on a page. In this respect 'Now' is a characteristically late modernist poem that seems to reject all conventional connections between word and referent. The poem ends with the word 'cloud' obscuring the view thus denying the reader any keys for unlocking the poem's meaning, and subtly suggesting Thomas's parodic intent.[62] Thirdly, the poem may also enact a process of increasing sexual frustration, with each stanza representing a failed attempt at reaching climax. From the 'boys' limbs' being 'whack[ed]' in 'Our Eunuch Dreams', to the 'leaden bud / shot through the leaf ... wrenched by my fingerman' in 'A Grief Ago', masturbatory images abound in Thomas's early writings, and references to the 'yesman', the 'handsaw' and the 'hardiness of anger' may also suggest masturbation.[63] This is a thematic preoccupation noted primarily by detractors of Thomas's early poetry, but here the sexual imagery is wholly appropriate to the poem's wider meditations on time, death and language itself. John Goodby celebrates the centrality of the 'sexual body' in Thomas's work, and notes that in general it can be said that the early works collected in Thomas's first collection *18 Poems* associate 'masturbation with narcissism and deathliness'.[64] 'Now' may be read as an example of this. There is a growing intensity in the three stanzas quoted above. The lover is 'dry' in the opening stanza for he seems to be impotent, but the repeated 'yesses' in the second stanza may be read – as the repeated 'Yesses' in Molly Bloom's final soliloquy in Joyce's *Ulysses* – as an aural representation of the masturbatory act. Whereas Ralph Maud suggests that the brother is imagining killing himself, thus leaving his sister 'brotherless', in the final line of the second stanza, these lines may also suggest an incestuous fantasy where the speaker denies kinship in order to fantasize about his sibling.[65] He comes close to sexual fulfilment in the third stanza where we witness the 'cockerel's tide upcasting from the fire', which as William York Tindall notes, 'is a brilliant concentrate of Lawrence's escaped cock (Christian and phallic), the phoenix, and the water of life'.[66] Climax is never achieved, however, as the 'ball fail[s]' in the fourth stanza, and the speaker describes himself as the 'come-a-cropper rider of the flower'. The theme and imagery of sexual frustration is appropriate in that 'Now' is a poem that dwells and plays on the medium in which it is written. The repeated 'Now' at the beginning of each stanza may therefore be seen to express a simultaneous sexual and linguistic frustration. Simon Frith's equation of music, sex and time seems appropriate in discussing Thomas's poem, for 'Now' approximates the unrepresentability of music.

Parker's 'Now's the Time' and Thomas's 'Now' are compositions about time and temporality. Both poem and jazz performance indicate that time can be consciously organized and manipulated through accent, stress, pulse and phrasing. Rather than affirming the alienations that the high modernists argued were bred by modern society (Pound, Eliot on the right, Adorno on the left), both poem and jazz performance gesture towards the possibility of attaining an ideal described by Simon Frith in relation to pop music: 'an ideal defined by the integration of what is routinely kept separate – the individual and the social, the mind and body, change and stillness, the different and the same, the already past and the still to come, desire and fulfilment'.[67] To hear Thomas read his poems on the Caedmon gramophone recordings heightens this impression. Whilst a poetry reading inevitably takes place in time, the duration of the track seems to frame time, to give it structure. Oscillating between uniqueness and repetition, Thomas's poetry readings and Parker's visceral saxophone performances represent a convergence between stage and audience, saying and being, body and voice. In listening to Thomas reading his work we may detect a growing concern with the location and exploitation of the musical rather than semantic potential of the voice. This concern with 'voice' was fully reflected by Parker, who abandoned the warm vibrato of swing-era players such as Benny Carter and Johnny Hodges for a sharpness of attack and piercing clarity of articulation. Thomas and Parker were innovators, drawing on the formal traditions of their respective arts while blurring the boundaries between form and content, the subjective and constructive, the annotated and the aural. A boundary-breaking impulse was a constitutive element of Parker's improvisations and Thomas's poems, and this informed the ways in which they were imagined to be artists who broke the bounds of artistic and social conventions. If mainstream culture would regard them as transgressive primitives, the complexity of their creations and dedication to their art challenged those stereotypes even as they were being formulated.

IV

If a lascivious sexual appetite, outrageous behaviour and willingness to break boundaries and taboos were among the signs of authentic, sponta-neous, primitive genius in the 1950s, these alleged characteristics could also lead to the mythicization of artists. During their lives, and particularly following their deaths, Thomas and Parker became symbolic figures, removed from actual history and recreated as deified, religious, types representing broader spiritual and cultural forces. Karl Shapiro was discomfited by the way in which Dylan Thomas's perceived 'childishness' and 'innocence' caused him to be seen as a victim of capitalism and 'the signal for a verbal massacre of the bourgeoisie, reminiscent of the early decades of our century'.[68] Shapiro was responding to works such as Kenneth Rexroth's lengthy poetic 'massacre of the bourgeoisie', 'Thou Shalt Not Kill' – a response to Thomas's death on 9 November 1953.

> He is dead.
> The canary of Swansea.
> Who killed him?
> Who killed the bright-headed bird?
> You did, you son of a bitch.
> You drowned him in your cocktail brain.
> ...
> You killed him,
> Benign Lady on the postage stamp.
> ...
> In your lonely crowd you swept over him.
> Your custom built brogans and your ballet slippers
> Pummelled him to death in the gritty street.[69]

It was at Rexroth's weekly seminars in his apartment at 250 Scott Street, San Francisco, that Allen Ginsberg heard him read his elegy to Dylan Thomas, and the poem's claim that the values of a capitalist society destroy human creativity would reverberate through Ginsberg's celebrated poem *Howl* a few years later. If Ginsberg, in that poem, observed 'angel headed hipsters contemplating jazz', Jack Kerouac attempted to fuse music with poetry in his recordings with pianist Steve Allen, and saxophonists Al Cohn and Zoot Sims.[70] In a letter to Ginsberg, Kerouac boasted that his jazz-accompanied readings were the 'greatest poetry records since Dylan Thomas'.[71] In the '239th chorus' of his *Mexico City Blues*, featured on the first of his albums, Kerouac captured the process by which Charlie Parker became mythicized as a transcendent being lying beyond the realities of material life:

> Charley [*sic*] Parker looked like Buddha
> Charley Parker, who recently died
> Laughing at a juggler on the TV
> after weeks of strain and sickness,
> was called the Perfect Musician.
> And his expression on his face
> Was as calm, beautiful and profound
> As the image of the Buddha
> Represented in East, the lidded eyes,

The expression that 'All is Well'
  – This is what Charley Parker
Said when he played, All is Well
You had the feeling of early-in-the-morning
Like a hermit's joy, or like
    the perfect cry
Of some wild gang at a jam session
'Wail, Wop' – Charley burst
His lungs to reach the speed
Of what the speedsters wanted
And what they wanted
Was his Eternal Slowdown.
A great musician and a great
    creator of forms
That ultimately find expression
In mores and what have you.[72]

David Yaffe notes that as a good friend of Williams Burroughs ('Old Bull Lee' in *On the Road*), Kerouac would recognize the lidded eyes 'not as mere Chinoiserie but the nodding out of a junkie'.[73] But the bitter reality lying behind Parker's breakneck solos – fuelled as they were by heroin addiction – is of no real interest to Kerouac who sees in the founder of bebop the visage of the Buddha himself.

It was passages such as this, and the famous scene from *On the Road* (quoted earlier) where Sal Paradise walks 'At lilac evening … among the lights of 27th and Welton in the Denver colored section, wishing I were a Negro', that African American novelist James Baldwin criticized as 'absolute nonsense and offensive nonsense at that'.[74] He objected to the crass primitivism of the Beat image of African Americans, and the blindness of Beat writers to the social realities of African American lives in a racially divided society. Somewhat surprisingly, the black nationalist Eldridge Cleaver defended the Beats, and admired the fact that 'they dared to do in the light of day what America had long been doing in the sneak-thief anonymity of night – consorted on a human level with blacks'.[75] However, despite the Beat borrowings from the clothing, lifestyles and attitudes of jazz musicians generally, and black beboppers such as Charlie Parker specifically, African American Beat writers, as A. Robert Lee noted, 'might well be thought to have gone missing in action'.[76]

Nevertheless, there were a few significant 'black beats', most notably Ted Joans who daubed Greenwich Village with 'Bird Lives' graffiti following the saxophonist's death, and Bob Kaufman whose poem to Bird, 'Walking Parker Home', in his collection *Solitudes Crowded with*

Loneliness is followed by a poem entitled 'Afterwards They Shall Dance' that portrays some of the key artists deemed to have influenced the Beat movement, ranging from Poe to Baudelaire to Billie Holiday. A stanza is dedicated to Dylan Thomas:

> Dylan took the stone cat's nap at St. Vincent's, vaticaned
>   beer, no defense;
> That poem shouted from his nun-filled room, an insult to the
>   brain, nerves,
> Save now from Swansea, white horses, beer birds, snore
>   poems, Wales-Bird.[77]

A great deal of biographical information is packed allusively into a stanza which follows the Beat tendency to celebrate Thomas as a romantic who dedicated himself to poetry and drink. St. Vincent's is the Roman Catholic hospital in New York where Thomas died, the white horses suggest the waves off the Welsh coast whilst also referring to the poet's favourite bar in Greenwich Village, and the African American poet's reference to Thomas as 'Wales-Bird' links Thomas with Charlie 'Bird' Parker while also invoking images of transcendence.

Charlie Parker and Dylan Thomas also appear in the writings of the most celebrated 'Black Beat', LeRoi Jones. Jones is a particularly interesting figure as he began as a Beat poet in 1950s Greenwich Village, before abandoning his Beat bohemianism for black nationalism, his home downtown in Greenwich Village for an apartment uptown in Harlem, and his slave (and partly Welsh) name LeRoi Jones for the African Imamu Amiri Baraka. Baraka's character Clay in the play *Dutchman* undergoes a similar conversion as the drama develops, and towards the end he seeks to destroy the white, beat, image of black musicians:

> Charlie Parker? Charlie Parker. All the hip white boys scream for Bird. And Bird saying, 'Up your ass, feeble-minded ofay! Up your ass.' And they sit there talking about the tortured genius of Charlie Parker. Bird would've played not a note of music if he just walked up to East Sixty-seventh Street and killed the first ten white people he saw. Not a note![78]

The black Buddha of Kerouac's poem, who tells us that all's well with the world, becomes the vengeful militant of Baraka's play whose art is a sublimation of murder. Baraka traces the development of his thought, from Beat to black nationalist in his autobiography of 1984, and includes a passage on his responses to Dylan Thomas.

> There were writers too in that circle. One I remember, Clyde Hamlet, who imitated Dylan Thomas. But many people did then. [Steve] Korret's work at

this time was connected very consistently with Thomas, who was roaring around the Village, especially the White Horse Tavern ... Hamlet was suave and sophisticated, I thought, he was hip to me. That's why I couldn't understand his poetry sounding so exactly like Dylan Thomas's when it seemed to me, once I'd read Thomas, that anyone reading him would realize immediately that his poems were simply Thomas imitations and little else.

What I'd said before about how my reading was taking me into something and away from something at the same time is relevant here. Because this circle of Korret's and indeed his influence, to a certain extent, was merely a continuation of the other 'whitening' influences I had been submitting to enthusiastically under the guise of information, education ... So that Europe as intellectual center was yet another stone to the weight of 'alienation' from black (if that is not too strong a word) that was building up in me. Exiting from one world and entering another. That's the way this learning I'd committed myself to had taken shape ... And I learned quickly that the Cages and Cunninghams were very highly esteemed in that circle. Almost mythological beings, and ditto 'Dylan,' as Korret called him, like they were cutbuddies. So I was heavily into Dylan.[79]

LeRoi Jones's shift from 'Beat poet' to 'black nationalist' can be traced in these responses to Charlie Parker and Dylan Thomas. Baraka's autobiography testifies to the centrality of Thomas's work for the Beat writers of 1950s Greenwich Village, but what is most noteworthy here is the way in which Thomas is made to represent the domination of European literary models and values on the black artist. Writing from the black-nationalist standpoint that he adopted in the 1960s, Baraka is dismissive of his own literary activities as a Beat writer and considers his 1950s works as the products of a false-consciousness in which his primary literary influences were contributing to his alienation from 'blackness'. Far from being Shapiro's marginal Welsh writer whose surrealistic and anarchic poems placed him at odds with American consumerist culture and mainstream English poetic practices, Thomas, for Baraka, is a representative of the 'intellectual worship of Europe' which is 'the remnant of colonialism, still pushed by the rulers through their "English Departments and concert halls!"'[80]

Notwithstanding the power of Baraka's nationalist rejection of Thomas, there are other, alternative, responses to the Welshman's work within the African American literary tradition. Richard Wright, for example, used lines from 'Light Breaks Where No Sun Shines' as an epigraph to his controversial *White Man, Listen!* Wright drew on Thomas's lines

> When logics die,
> The secret of the soil grows through the eye
> And blood jumps in the sun ...

to reinforce his rejection of 'blood and soil' as the basis for political action. He called on 'the White man' to turn to the 'precious heritage – the freedom of speech, the secular state, the independent personality, the autonomy of science – which is not Western or Eastern, but human'.[81] In Wright's work (as in that of Edward Said more recently), exilic outsiderness is the vehicle for enacting a humanist tradition that builds on the most valuable strains in Western and Eastern thought, and Thomas is seen to embody a poetic expression of this universalist belief. Novelist Ishmael Reed, who has always walked a tightrope between universalism and nationalism in his novels and political writings, recalls visiting the White Horse Tavern because of its connection with Dylan Thomas, while his fellow Californian, poet Al Young, views Dylan Thomas as a figure who can testify to poetry's ability to speak across lines of nationality and ethnicity, and to transcend the often highly charged debates on culture, race and identity in which it occasionally becomes embroiled.[82] When asked, in the late 1990s, to introduce his favourite poet for an anthology, Young chose Dylan Thomas. The editors asked him to reconsider – they wanted him, a contemporary African American poet, to pick a black poet. He ended up introducing Langston Hughes, but in a gesture of protest at having been racially pigeonholed in this way, Young wrote his introduction to Thomas in any case, and published it on the web.

> I had clipped this black and white publicity likeness of Welsh poet Dylan Thomas from a New Directions catalog and Scotch-taped it next to a cut-out from Down Beat of Bird: jazz genius Charlie Parker. One of my outspoken buddies who visited my attic digs would always stare at those two pictures and comment: 'Who did you say this poet dude was? He looks like he's more tore up than Bird.' ... The Dylan Thomas of whom I speak with such runaway affection was not only a poet; for a literate chunk of the English-speaking world, he seemed the epitome of a poet. That he died at 39 in 1953 was important to my generation. Parker, who died two years later, only made it to 35 ... The whole point, we thought, was to make a statement, make a splash, and then die early enough to let people know you really meant what you stood for
> ...
> It was love of Dylan Thomas' art that led me to learn about things Welsh just as my love of Charlie Parker's music led me back to Kansas City with its wide-open gambling, prostitution, political corruption and graft, and all that plentiful, beautiful music. Each of them keeps leading me back to my own origins and pre-natal origins through the light-years time takes to fill the sky of one mind, one heart. 'The common wages / Of their most secret heart,' was one way Dylan Thomas put it.[83]

Al Young's words reinforce a number of my arguments here: Thomas's significance in 1950s America and the widespread comparison with

Charlie Parker in particular. More significantly, in a surprising and revisionist development of the primitivist terms in which Thomas was
appropriated by the Beats, Al Young testifies to the way in which Dylan
became a significant figure for African American artists themselves. The
African American responses to Thomas's work underline the fact that
'Dylan' became more than the sum of his parts in the United States. 'Dylan'
was, then, a culturally constructed figure of some significance as he got
drawn into broader, and often highly charged, debates on the relationship
between the cultures of black and white America, and between America
and Europe. While for Amiri Baraka, Thomas represented the oppressive
'worship of Europe', Al Young in his 'Poem to Dylan Thomas' speaks of
the Welshman's key role in encouraging a young black poet to voice 'all
I'd heard and seen and breathed / down there inside your dream, and mixed
it well / with wishes and bewitchments of my own'.[84]

V

When Dylan Thomas died in New York in November 1953 he was,
according to Igor Stravinsky, 'on the first leg of his journey to my home in
California, and we were both looking forward to getting better acquainted
personally and working on the idea of an opera'.[85] Thomas had met
Stravinsky in Boston the previous May, and following that meeting
discussed his ideas for a libretto with the organizer of his US tours, the
poet John Malcolm Brinnin:

> They would do a 'recreation of the world' – an opera about the only man and
> woman alive on earth. These creatures might be visitors from outer space
> who, by some cosmic mischance, find themselves on an earth recently devas-
> tated and silenced by global warfare; or they might be earthlings who
> somehow have survived an atomic miscalculation. In either case, they would
> re-experience the whole awakening life of aboriginal man. They would make
> a new cosmogony. Confronted with a tree pushing its way upward out of
> radio-active dust, they would have to name it, and learn its uses, and then
> proceed to find names and a definition for everything on earth. The landscape
> would be fantastic – everything shaped and colored by the dreams of primitive
> man – and even the rocks and trees would sing.[86]

It is by now a commonplace to describe modernism as a response to a
crisis of representation or a crisis of language; a crisis that took on a
revived immediacy following the atrocities of the Second World War.[87]
Thomas's libretto seems to enact a scene where language is re-constructed

anew, with a direct connection being re-established between word and referent, signifier and signified. The apocalypse gives rise, dialectically, to a utopia where language can be freed from corrupted social conventions and stifling historical associations. In 'From Love's First Fever' Thomas speaks of learning

> man's tongue, to twist the shapes of thoughts
> Into the stony idiom of the brain,
> To shade and knit anew the patch of words
> Left by the dead ...[88]

It is precisely his attempts at knitting language anew, at re-vivifying both poetic language and poetic forms, that marks the late-modernist impulse in Thomas's works.

Charlie Parker was also engaged in re-vivifying the vocabulary of jazz, and in doing so had turned to Stravinsky for inspiration. Parker's admiration for his classical contemporaries has been widely noted. Bill Coss observed in the 1950s that Parker 'seldom listened to jazz anywhere unless he happened to be on a job. His main interest was in classical music, mostly the moderns', and Ted Gioia has noted the 'strange and subtle ways' in which this interest manifested itself: he would often call his band up to the stage with a few lines of Hindemith's 'Kleine Klammermusik', he asked that Bartok be played at his daughter's funeral and towards the end of his life he approached Edgard Varèse asking for composition lessons.[89] In a Leonard Feather 'Blindfold Test' of 1948, Parker correctly identified Stravinsky's 'The Song of the Nightingale' and commented: 'Is that Stravinsky? That's music at its best. I like all of Stravinsky.'[90] Recalling his time in Parker's band, trumpeter Howard McGhee noted that Parker

> knew everything, and he hipped me to, like, Stravinsky and all those guys. I didn't know nothin' about Stravinsky. So Bird was the first one to tell me about it. So like, The Rite of Spring, he brought it over to the house and let me hear it. And I said, 'Yeah, this cat, he's kind of cool, you know; he knows what he's doing'.[91]

Alfred Appel, Jr. recalls an evening 'in the winter of 1951, at New York's premier modern jazz club Birdland':

> As Parker's quintet walked onto the bandstand, trumpeter Red Rodney recognized Stravinsky, front and almost centre. Rodney leaned over and told Parker, who did not look at Stravinsky. Parker immediately called the first number for his band, and, forgoing the customary greeting to the crowd, was off like a shot ... At the beginning of his second chorus he interpolated the opening of

Stravinsky's *Firebird Suite* as though it had always been there, a perfect fit, and then sailed on with the rest of the number. Stravinsky roared with delight, pounding his glass on the table, the upward arc of the glass sending its liquor and ice cubes onto the people behind him.[92]

It is a telling moment, for it was partly the assimilation of harmonic and rhythmic devices from contemporary classical music that led, in Martin Williams's words, to bebop's 'renewed musical language, with which the old practices could be replenished and continued'.[93]

The juxtaposition of tradition and renewal, of the modern and the primitive, characterizes Stravinsky's composition 'In Memoriam Dylan Thomas'. The piece was completed a year after Thomas's death, is scored for four trombones, string quartet and tenor, and is written in the serial style which Stravinsky began to experiment with in later life. The opening and closing instrumental passages were described as 'dirge-canons' and they frame the central portion in which the tenor sings Thomas's poem 'Do Not Go Gentle into That Good Night' accompanied by just the strings. The trombone is perhaps the most basic of brass instruments due to its reliance on varying the length of the tubing rather than on valves to achieve different pitches, and may thus be seen to represent the primitivist dimension in the works of both Thomas and Stravinsky. The string quartet on the other hand, associated in particular with Haydn and Beethoven, represents the Western classical tradition. It seems that Dylan, the writer of taut lyrics of formal and psychological complexity, is represented in the strings, while the brooding, disturbing, subversive, primitivist, Celtic, druidic Dylan is expressed by the trombones. Given Charlie Parker's open admiration for Stravinsky, this musical juxtaposition of the primitive and the modern offers a fitting conclusion to this chapter. For, in its juxtaposition of the 'civilized' and the 'primitive', Stravinsky's 'In Memoriam Dylan Thomas' may be considered a meditation on the paradoxical ways in which Thomas was perceived in the United States, and the identities that he had to adopt, adapt and perform in the American context.

Class and Identity: Aneurin Bevan and Paul Robeson

Aneurin Bevan was preoccupied with communication in August 1958. In *Tribune*, the weekly paper of the democratic Left, he discussed the relationship between China and the United States in the following terms:

> Communication is the very essence of civilised ways of living. It is a most monstrous offence against this principle that the most populous nation on earth should be cut off from communication with so many nations merely because the vision of the leaders of the United States falls so lamentably short of the material power they command.[1]

He had expressed similar thoughts a week earlier at the *Gymanfa Ganu* (congregational singing festival) of the National Eisteddfod in Ebbw Vale. 'The whole lesson of Eisteddfodau is communication,' he stated, 'and unless the people can freely communicate with each other there is no chance for civilisation.'[2] Sitting in the audience with his wife Bessie was the African American singer and activist Paul Robeson who, following Bevan's introduction, would rise to sing 'John Brown's Body', 'Water Boy' and 'We are Climbing Jacob's Ladder'.[3] In 1950 Robeson's passport had been taken from him and he was confined to the United States as the madness of Senator Joe McCarthy's campaign against alleged Communists dominated the political and cultural life of his country. Robeson's passport had just been returned when he visited Ebbw Vale in 1958, and Bevan proceeded to criticize the US government for denying Robeson his right to travel and expressed his hope that the ban would never be reinstated. To obstruct communication between individuals and countries was a threat to world peace, stated Bevan, and while he had heard of the United States's ambitions to 'encircle the moon', 'they might start off at first by encircling China'.[4]

If Bevan had one eye on the world, his thoughts on communication also engaged with the Welsh context. In order to allow Bevan to introduce Paul Robeson, the *Gymanfa Ganu* was moved from the last Sunday of the eisteddfod to the first. The eisteddfod had not been officially opened, and there was therefore no need to adhere to the *rheol Gymraeg* (the Welsh-language only rule), that was introduced in 1950 and would be in operation for the rest of the week.

> I must have my say about the Eisteddfod this evening for I shall be inarticulate during the rest of the week ... I want to say how much we in Ebbw Vale welcome the Eisteddfod and the visit of the people of Wales, together with our friends from overseas, to Ebbw Vale. You will find the true qualities of the Welsh people here in Monmouthshire, even though you may not always hear their sentiments expressed in the language of heaven.[5]

Having struggled during his career to overcome a stammer, and to give voice to the aspirations of his people, Bevan would have noted the strange irony of the fact that, for the remainder of the week, he would be rendered inarticulate in his own constituency.[6]

According to the *Merthyr Express*, there were in fact over 9,000 people packed into the pavilion on 3 August 1958 to listen to Bevan and Robeson and to participate in the *gymanfa*. Paul Robeson understood the nature of the event and, although he was linked to the Communist Party, expressed his pleasure at being able to contribute to a religious service.

> You may not know it but I was brought up in traditions very similar to yours. My father was a Wesleyan minister, my brother is one, and almost every Sunday I have taken part in similar hymn-singings to those you are enjoying tonight. I bring you greetings from my own people, who will appreciate, I know, the kind of welcome I have received here.[7]

Robeson had already been the recipient of Welsh hospitality. In 1928 he impulsively joined a group of marching Welsh miners singing in London's West End. The next ten years saw him donating money to, and visiting, Talygarn Miners' Rest Home, appearing in many concerts across Wales including an appearance at the Caernarfon Pavilion the night after an explosion had claimed 266 lives at the Gresford Pit near Wrexham, and, most famously, a visit to Mountain Ash in 1938 for the 'Welsh National

Memorial Meeting to the Men of the International Brigade from Wales who gave their lives in defence of Democracy in Spain'.[8] The 1930s also saw Robeson establishing connections with the multi-ethnic community in Cardiff's Butetown, which was also home to the political activist and pan-Africanist native of Philadelphia, Aaron Mosell, an uncle by marriage to Robeson.[9] The year 1939 saw Robeson playing the role of David Goliath, an African American seaman who settles in a mining village, in one of the few movies that he did not later disown, *Proud Valley*. Hounded during the McCarthy era for his Communist sympathies, Robeson had his passport confiscated from 1950 to 1958. The persistent invitations made throughout the 1950s for Robeson to appear at the Miners' Eisteddfod in Porthcawl led to the 'Transatlantic Exchange' of 1957 which allowed the eisteddfod audience to hear Robeson's voice via a telephonic link from New York. Following the return of his passport in 1958, he visited the National Eisteddfod at Ebbw Vale, where he was introduced by Bevan, and presented with a Welsh hymn book by the leading Welsh modernist poet, T. H. Parry-Williams. In the October of that year he finally appeared in person at the Miners' Eisteddfod in Porthcawl. His last significant contact with Wales occurred in 1960 when he appeared with the Cwmbach Male Choir at a Movement for Colonial Freedom concert in the Royal Festival Hall, London.[10]

Several commentators have used the relationship between Robeson and Wales to support their readings of Welsh history. For some, like Hywel Francis and Dai Smith, Robeson's connections with the Welsh working class underline the progressive socialist internationalism of the labour movement, and reflect the diverse and tolerant communities of the coalfield. Dai Smith, echoing Aneurin Bevan's emphasis on communication, states that

> South Wales, at its provocative best, contradicted the curtailers of human interaction anywhere and everywhere it could. The ideal was, perhaps, often merely, though movingly, emblematic as when south Wales miners arranged a transatlantic radio link so that Paul Robeson, deprived of his civil liberties and his passport in the USA, could sing at their Eisteddfod; or when Nye Bevan ... welcomed Robeson to the National Eisteddfod in Ebbw Vale in 1958.[11]

It is revealing to compare this reading with T. J. Davies's description of the *Gymanfa Ganu* in his Welsh-language biography of Paul Robeson. T. J. Davies draws on Robeson's 1935 comment that 'Negroes the world over have an inferiority complex because they imitate whatever culture they are in contact with instead of harking back to their own tradition', to argue that the African American singer touched:

gwythien ddofn ynom. Ninnau fel y Negroaid wedi cefnu, i fesur, ar ein diwyl-liant brodorol a mabwysiadu un Seisnig; eto, ym mêr ein hesgyrn yn gwybod bod ynddo rin a gwerth, a phan ddeuai Paul Robeson i'n mysg, yn lladmerydd huawdl i ddiwylliant dirmygedig, caem ynddo un a roddai lais i gri a foddwyd yn ein hisymwybyddiaeth ... Bid siwr, y mae elfen o dristwch yn y sefyllfa, y miloedd ym mhabell yr Eisteddfod yng Nglyn Ebwy yn ei gymeradwyo am eu bod yn cael boddhad mawr yng nghanu gŵr a gyflwynai ei ddiwylliant ei hun heb ymddiheuro; eto, yr un rhai, er yn gweld yr hyn a wnâi Paul Robeson ac yn falch o'i genhadaeth, yn methu cymryd y cam gwleidyddol i roi i'w cenedl hwy yr urddas y credent y dylai'r Negro ei gael.

[a deep vein within us. Like the Negroes, we have turned our backs, to a degree, on our indigenous culture and adopted an English culture; yet, in the marrow of our bones we are aware of its worth and value, and when Paul Robeson came to us, an eloquent spokesman for a derided culture, we found a voice for a cry that had been submerged in our subconsciousness ... There is certainly an element of sadness in the scene; the thousands in the Eisteddfod pavilion in Ebbw Vale applauding and enjoying the singing of a man who presented his own culture without apology; yet, those same thousands, despite seeing what Paul Robeson was doing and welcoming his message, were unable to take the political step that would give their nation the status that they believed should be granted to the Negro.][12]

I will return to some of the controversial assumptions informing this passage, but wish to emphasize here the fundamental difference between T. J. Davies's reading in Welsh, and Dai Smith's account in English. 'Robeson' features as a crossroads at which the cultural narratives of '*y Gymru Gymraeg*' (Welsh-speaking Wales) and 'South Wales' meet; those very narratives that the critic Raymond Williams referred to as the 'two truths' that influence and inform our ways of describing the Welsh experience:

The first draws on the continuity of Welsh language and literature: from the sixth century, it is said, and thus perhaps the oldest surviving poetic tradition in Europe. The second draws on the turbulent experience of South Wales, over the last two centuries, and its powerful political and communal formations.[13]

Indeed the meeting between Robeson and Bevan allows us to explore some of the intellectual strains within progressive thought in Wales in the twentieth century, and to address some of the key tensions within Welsh intellectual and political history today.

II

For many Welsh linguistic nationalists Aneurin Bevan is associated with the rejection of the 'indigenous culture' evoked by T. J. Davies in his description of the Welsh audience's response to Robeson above. In his popular history *Aros Mae* (1971), for instance, Plaid Cymru president Gwynfor Evans used the example of Bevan's family to illustrate the anglicization of Monmouthshire. Before noting that Bevan's father, David, was a member of the *Cymmrodorion*, a faithful chapel goer and a Welsh-language poet of some renown, Gwynfor Evans suggests that the 'situation in Monmouthshire' could be illuminated with reference to the:

> amgylchiadau cartref crwtyn bach a ddechreuodd fynd y pryd hyn i ysgol Sirhywi gyda'i chwiorydd, Myfanwy a Blodwen; byddai Arianwen a Iorwerth yn ymuno ag ef yno eto ... Ymhen ychydig flynyddoedd byddai'r Sistem wedi difa iaith a diwylliant cenhedlaeth tad Aneurin Bevan yn llwyr yn y fro honno.
>
> [domestic circumstances of a little boy who started going to Sirhowy school during this period with his sisters, Myfanwy and Blodwen; Arianwen and Iorwerth would join him there later ... Within a few years in that area the System would have completely destroyed the language and culture of the generation to which Aneurin Bevan's father belonged.][14]

In Gwynfor Evans's nationalist history Aneurin Bevan is not so much the founder of the National Health Service, nor is he the hero of Welsh socialists. Rather, he is a representative of how Labour proved to be an anglicizing force in Welsh culture, contributing to society's abandonment of the Welsh language and its culture. Bevan's subtle attack on the eisteddfod 'Welsh rule' at the *Gymanfa Ganu* of 1958 could be used to reinforce this interpretation. Furthermore, few Welsh nationalists would disagree with Angharad Tomos that Bevan more than anyone else prevented the idea of self-government, and legitimized opposition in Labour's ranks to any measure of constitutional status for Wales.[15]

This is not entirely true, for Bevan's support was key to ensuring that the establishment of a Secretary of State for Wales appeared as a policy in the Labour Party's manifesto for the general elections of 1959. The Tories won that election, but the policy stayed in place, leading to the establishment of Jim Griffiths in that post when Labour came back to power in 1964. Bevan's support for the policy of a Secretary of State surprised, and continues to surprise, many. Bevan had previously been consistent in his opposition to any political embodiment of Welsh identity. At the first day dedicated to 'Welsh Questions' in Parliament in 1944 Bevan admitted that he didn't know the difference between 'a Welsh sheep, and Westmoreland sheep and a Scottish sheep'.[16] He had objected to the idea of creating a Secretary of State for Wales in 1946 on linguistic grounds, fearing that the incumbent would have to speak Welsh. Unconsciously evoking the language of the 1847 'Blue Books', he stated that 'Our nationalist friends are making an enclave and the vast majority of Welshmen would be denied participation in the government of their own country'.[17] He believed that the people of Monmouthshire would be oppressed by Welsh speakers from Cardiganshire, and regretted that Welsh culture tended to be connected to the language.

Before rejecting such ideas, it is worth remembering that south Wales was represented as a cultureless space – the ground lost to Wales – by many linguistic nationalists. T. J. Davies's description of the Ebbw Vale audience having 'abandoned' their 'indigenous culture' is a case in point. 'Yma bu unwaith Gymru' ('Here once was Wales') was Saunders Lewis's dismissive verdict as he viewed industrial Merthyr in his apocalyptic poem 'Y Dilyw 1939' (The Deluge 1939). In a letter to Kate Roberts of 10 February 1927, Lewis expressed his exasperation at the audience of 'anwariaid syml' ('simple barbarians') who had turned out to listen to him in Blaen Dulais (Seven Sisters) and claimed that he would kill himself if forced to spend a day in their company.[18] More recently, when Christine James won the crown at the 2005 Eisteddfod, Archdruid Selwyn Griffith claimed that her time as a student in Aberystwyth had made Christine 'yn Gymraes' (Welsh woman). But given that she comes from Porth, in the Rhondda, what was she before that?[19] Plaid Cymru's Assembly Member for Caernarfon, Alun Ffred Jones, offered this analysis of English-speaking Wales in 1999:

[I] genhedlaeth sydd wedi ymwrthod â'r syniad o genedl at beth allan nhw droi? Does dim o'r nodweddion amlwg – yn gerddorol, yn grefyddol nac yn ddiwylliannol – sydd gan y Gwyddel Saesneg i droi atynt am gysur.

[What can a generation who have rejected the idea of nationhood turn to? They have none of the obvious characteristics – either musically, religiously or culturally – that the Anglo-Irish can turn to for comfort.][20]

Bevan was speaking against such views when he highlighted the essential Welshness of Ebbw Vale in his speech at the 1958 *gymanfa*, and there is no doubt that the contributions of Hywel Teifi Edwards from one direction, and Dai Smith from another, have been crucial in the ongoing process of describing and mapping the distinctive cultures of the south Wales valleys.[21] Dai Smith's fundamental point in his *Aneurin Bevan and the World of South Wales* (1993) is that 'imagining Aneurin Bevan's culture is an essential pre-condition to comprehending his politics'.[22] The challenge faced by the cultural historian is to describe the defining characteristics of that culture. Writing against English historians of the Labour Party, who tend to see Bevan's 'Welsh' background as a constraint frustrating his abilities to extend the relevance of his politics beyond 'narrow' working-class interests, Smith states:

> The whole direction of Bevan's life, and especially because of the experiences he underwent within the variegated culture of south Wales, was away from the bathos of nostalgia and the pathos of sentiment ... If it is the values of the south Wales of his youth that marked Bevan then those values were increasingly offensive not defensive.[23]

And one aspect of the 'offensive' nature of that new culture was its desire to reject the culture of the past. While this was something to regret for Gwynfor Evans, it is something to celebrate for Dai Smith:

> Aneurin attended two chapels as a boy; he left both after too close a disquisition of Darwinian evolutionism for the taste of the ministers. He was never baptized. He spoke no Welsh. And in all this he was typifying individually the self-confident progressive world of south Wales.[24]

'Progressive' may not be the most appropriate adjective for this social process. It seems in the quotation above that Smith's 'South Wales' is defined by what it is not, more than by what it is.

In this respect, it is interesting to note that when it became a matter of defining Welsh culture Aneurin Bevan tended to turn to 'traditional' practices and to notions of cultural continuity. While he warned against linking Welshness with the Welsh language, his grounds for arguing strongly for 'the re-unification of Monmouthshire and Wales' in Ebbw Vale in 1958 was that the 'characteristics of Monmouthshire were essentially Welsh', her 'legends were Welsh'.[25] A decade earlier, he made the following case in a *Tribune* editorial on 'The Claim of Wales':

> People from other parts of the country are surprised when they visit Wales to find how many Welsh people still speak Welsh, and how strong and even passionate is the love of the Welsh for their country, their culture and their unique institutions. In all this there is nothing to deplore. On the contrary, it is very much to the good that distinctive cultures, values, and institutions should flourish so as to counteract the appalling tendency of the times towards standardisation, regimentation and universal greyness ... In so far as Wales is different from England, it is the difference, and not the similarity, which requires special recognition and a special constitutional medium of expression. Wales is different, not in the fact that she possesses coal and steel, docks and harbours, factories and an intricate web of economic activities. These are

part of the common life of the United Kingdom. She is different in that she has a language of her own, and an art and a culture, and an educational system and an excitement for things of the mind and spirit, which are wholly different from England and English ways. It is in the commonality of this difference that Wales has a claim for special recognition and where she should seek new forms of national life.[26]

Bevan was clearly making a distinction between the political and the cultural spheres. Wales for Bevan was essentially a cultural entity. That cultural distinctiveness was not the basis for an independent nation state, nor did it imply that the cultural nation needed its own form of political expression. The reference above to a 'special Constitutional medium of expression' is ambiguous, especially as he specifically argues against the establishment of a Secretary of State in the same piece. For Bevan, the problems of coal, steel and agriculture should clearly be addressed at the British level. Britain is clearly the sphere of economics and politics. Wales is the sphere of culture.

It is noticeable, however, that Bevan does not use the terms 'province', or 'region' or 'principality' in describing Wales. Bevan's Wales is a 'nation', and it is worth noting that he was not opposed in principle to nationalism and, in some contexts, could see the benefits of dressing the socialist struggle in national costume. In his speech to the 'Chinese People's Consultative Conference' in 1954, for example, he noted:

the struggles which you have waged are at the same time a struggle for national independence against imperialism. This has the effect of super-charging the social struggle with the emotion derived from national self-consciousness and the yearning for liberation. You are therefore possessed of an emotional dynamic which is not present with us.[27]

Bevan was not opposed in principle to struggles for national independence. But, to the frustration of Welsh nationalists, he did not see his native Wales in those terms. The nationalist poet Harri Webb responded colourfully to Bevan's speech in China in the pages of *The Welsh Republican*:

Mr Bevan comes from the Tops of the Valleys. It is hard to believe that even in China he can have forgotten the difference between the exploitation of the English worker and the wholesale rape and ruin of that region where the epic desolation of Dowlais, the generation of despair that engulfed Blaina and Brynmawr, seal the utter damnation before God and man of the gentlemen of England.[28]

Bevan would never forget the suffering of the valleys. But he believed that the way to ensure the suffering would never return was for socialists to control the levers of the British economy.

If the concept of the 'nation' played a part in Aneurin Bevan's political world view, his politics was fundamentally grounded in the working-class struggle against economic inequality. His political vision evolved from a Marxist tradition of thought – 'Insofar as I can be said to have had a political training at all, it has been in Marxism' – and the tendency is to view that tradition as being opposed to cultural difference due to its emphasis on the class struggle as the only legitimate vehicle for the creation of a classless society in which differences of status and opportunity are eradicated.[29] This opposition to cultural difference can be traced back to the work of Marx himself. While being critical of British imperialism, Marx believed that the barbarism of the villagers of Hindustan was reflected in the fact that they worshipped nature. For Marx, the British Empire was a necessary historical force in civilizing and developing a society which would otherwise be worshipping Hamhuan the monkey and Sabala the cow.[30] Such cultural intolerance is generally absent from Bevan's writings, and unlike some of his constituency's future representatives, he respected the concept of Wales as a cultural entity manifested in its linguistic difference, its stories and legends. He also supported Indian independence and was a friend of the country's first prime minister, Jawaharlal Nehru.[31] But fundamentally, Bevan's politics were rooted in class. For him, cultural distinctiveness should never be a constraint on the struggle of the working class and the poor for economic and social equality. The desire to preserve distinctive cultures – as embodied primarily in the language movement in Wales – should never hinder a people's ability to communicate with each other and with others. His vision was one of common advancement and social betterment for the British people. This is a truth recognized and expressed eloquently by the novelist Gwyn Thomas:

> [Bevan] was a very interesting character. He was very much a man after my own heart. He was full of contempt, really, for the society that had begotten him. All he wanted was to get rid of that society. You could always feel that whenever Bevan set his eyes on these awful grey scabrous streets, [he believed] that they should never have been made. And yet, you see, one of the great things in Wales is that if you say this, you are accused immediately of spitting upon Aneurin Bevan's name: 'Aneurin Bevan would have crucified you if he heard you speaking about the lovely terraces of Ebbw Vale like this'.[32]

In noting the lack of nostalgia in Bevan's politics and in drawing attention to the fact that Bevan wanted to 'get rid of that society' which had 'begotten him', Thomas is, characteristically, drawing attention to a misunderstood, but absolutely central, dimension of Bevan's thought. Bevan's position was similar to that recently articulated by the American critic Walter Benn Michaels: 'When it comes to questions of economic inequality we should stop finding ways to ignore it. We should concentrate not on respecting ... cultural difference but on reducing the reality of economic difference.'[33]

III

Paul Robeson, like Aneurin Bevan, was a socialist. But he came to his socialism from a different direction, and represents a different tradition within socialist thought. When he described the 'hymn-singings' of his youth deriving from 'traditions very similar to yours' at the Ebbw Vale *gymanfa*, and proceeded to offer greetings from 'my people', he was drawing attention to his background in the African American Church, and to the distinctiveness of the African American people. As the African American critic Sterling Stuckey suggests, Robeson belonged to a tradition of black nationalist thought with its roots in the nineteenth century. 'Among Robeson's most lasting contributions', argues Stuckey,

> may be one we have, ironically, for a long time known the least about: after years of study and reflection, he succeeded in bringing together most of the salient strands of black nationalism while extending its meaning in a variety of ways ... In his thought, there is such a close link between cultural and political nationalisms that the two are virtually indistinguishable. In fact, he came to perceive art as an instrument of revolutionary change. Any dichotomy between the cultural and the political was, in the end, meaningless in his thought.[34]

Whereas Robeson has been celebrated for his universalist and internationalist socialist beliefs by Welsh labour historians, African American critics often foreground the black nationalist tradition that informed Robeson's thought. His careful American biographer Martin Duberman argues that it was this background that led Robeson to admire 'the ethnic insistence of the Welsh'.[35] Robeson, like many Welsh nationalists, adhered at times to the romantic notion that language lay at the root of national cultures. According to his close friend, the journalist Marie Seton, this sense of linguistic identity derived largely from his family background in the western areas of North and South Carolina where the Gullah language is spoken – a Creole language based on English but containing many words borrowed from African languages. In her biography *Paul Robeson* (1958),

Seton refers to this linguistic background while discussing the relationship between Robeson and Wales.

> [The Welsh] took him into their homes, fed him and wrapped him around tight and close in the intimacy of warmth and humour, and in the aspirations of a people in whom a national spirit had never died. The Welsh spoke Welsh to show they were themselves, just as Robeson's relatives in the Carolinas spoke the Gullah dialect because they, too, wanted to be themselves. Paul felt he was home.[36]

It seems that for Seton, language forms the basis of identity, and there's evidence that Robeson also thought of the relationship between language and identity in these terms. He was an excellent linguist and in 1951 recalled learning languages in order to sing the folk songs of 'the African, the Welsh, the Scotch Hebridean, the Russian, Spanish, Chinese, the Yiddish, Hebrew and others'.[37] There's actually no evidence that he ever did learn Welsh. 'Dafydd y Garreg Wen' is listed as 'David of the White Rock' in his concert programmes and presumably sung in English, and the final line 'Ar Hyd y Nos' is the only Welsh heard in his performances of the Welsh tune 'All Through the Night'. 'The Welsh language', stated Robeson at the Ebbw Vale Eisteddfod in 1958, 'is a language not to be trifled with and unless I could be perfect at it I would not attempt to sing in Welsh'.[38] However, Robeson was certainly interested in the Welsh language. He owned a Welsh-language grammar, and when asked to suggest an appropriate gift to mark his visit to the 1958 eisteddfod, he requested a Welsh hymnbook.[39]

The nationalist strain in Robeson's thought is something that is often ignored in Wales, and the tendency to see nationalism and socialism as opposed political forces in the Welsh nation's history leads to a misunderstanding of Robeson's life and thought. For Robeson's concert performances, from the mid-1930s onwards, offered a creative expression for the fusion of ethnic particularism and socialist universalism that informed his responses to other people and places.[40] His interest in the Soviet Union derived from an earlier interest in minorities. He first visited the USSR as a result of his interest in Africa, and went with the intention of studying 'the Soviet national minority policy as it operates among the people of Central Asia'.[41] During the 1950s, when he was not entitled to travel, he referred back to his first visits to the Soviet Union in the following terms:

> I saw for myself when I visited the Soviet Union how the Yakuts and the Uzbeks and all the other formerly oppressed nations were leaping ahead from tribalism to modern industrial economy, from illiteracy to the heights of

knowledge. Their ancient cultures blossoming in new and greater splendour. Their young men and women mastering the sciences and arts.[42]

Robeson's increasing adherence to Marxism from the mid-1930s onwards did not lead to a rejection of nationalism, but rather to an attempted combination of the Marxist notion that individual experiences are determined by social class, with a nationalist view that identity is rooted in language or race. This was reflected in his concert programmes where, from the early 1930s onwards Robeson expanded his repertoire beyond the spirituals to embrace the folk songs of other peoples. The programme of his 25 March concert in Wrexham testifies to his inclusion of the Russian 'O Ivan, You Ivan', the English 'O, No, John! No!' and the Welsh 'David of the White Rock' in his repertoire, and Martin Duberman notes that Robeson included performances of Russian songs arranged by Gretchaninov, the Scottish 'Turn Yet to Me' and the Mexican 'Encantadora Maria' in his British concerts of that year.[43] Robeson argued that he could interpret folk songs from around the world because of the fact that he 'came from a working-class people'.[44] This fusion of 'folk' and 'class' results in a view of class identity that is not the product of historical forces, of social position nor of active engagement in common cultural practices, but is rather a factor determined by race. Robeson argued that he failed

> to see how a Negro can really feel the sentiments of an Italian or a German, or a Frenchman, for instance ... I believe that one should confine oneself to the art for which one is qualified. One can only be qualified by understanding, and this is born in one, not bred.[45]

Nature ('born in one') it seems is more significant than nurture ('bred') in the making of a cultural sensibility, a view that Robeson reiterated unequivocally in 1934: 'I would rather sing Russian folk-songs than German grand-opera – not because it is necessarily better music, but because it is more instinctive and less reasoned music. It is in my blood.'[46] The key constituents of character and culture seem to be pre-determined 'in my blood'.

In an interview of 1958, recorded a few months before his visit to the eisteddfod, Robeson suggested that his particular fusion of class and ethnic identity emerged as a result of his experiences in Wales:

> And I went down into the mines with the workers, and they explained to me, that 'Paul, you may be successful here in England, but your people suffer like ours. We are poor people, and you belong to us. You don't belong to the bigwigs here in this country.' And so today I feel as much at home in the Welsh valley as I would in my own Negro section in any city in the United States. I

just did a broadcast by transatlantic cable to the Welsh valley, a few weeks
ago, and here was the first understanding that the struggle of the Negro people,
or of any people, cannot be by itself – that is, the human struggle. So I was
attracted by and met many members of the Labour Party, and my politics
embraced also the common struggle of all oppressed people, including especially the working masses – specifically the laboring people of all the world.
That defines my philosophy. It's a joining one. We are a working people, a
laboring people – the Negro people.[47]

This passage is striking due to the apparent tension between the declara-
tion of ethnic particularity – 'the Negro people' – and an internationalist,
universalist commitment to 'the human struggle'. It is not clear, however,
that Robeson would see this as a tension at all. He was deeply inspired by
early Bolshevik policy and by Stalin's *The National and Colonial
Question*. In spite of later attempts to curb internal, minority nationalist
impulses in the Soviet Union, the earlier policies inspired by Lenin and
Stalin laid the groundwork for a flourishing of national culture that was not
stopped by the repeal of cultural support. It was, according to Kate
Baldwin, the 'transnational formations of a Leninist tradition' that Robeson
strove to foster in his performances of national folk songs.[48]

What occurs from the 1930s onwards, then, is that Robeson attempted
to fuse his early commitment to African American cultural distinctiveness
with his increasing awareness of the importance of class consciousness.
This fusion of 'race' and 'class' allowed the son of a slave who had become
bourgeois through the success of his concert performances to identify with
working people, due to his membership of an oppressed race. That is, even
if you are middle class yourself, you can claim to be working class because
you come from 'a working-class people'. It was this fusion of class and
identity that, in Sterling Stuckey's words, allowed Robeson to bring
'together most of the salient strands of black nationalism while extending
its meaning in a variety of ways'.[49]

IV

I have sought to emphasize that Aneurin Bevan and Paul Robeson belong
to two different traditions within socialist thought. As I've noted, there is a
cultural awareness of national difference within Bevan's thought, and the
concept of class is important for Robeson. But Bevan's main emphasis is
on fighting economic inequality by means of a class-based politics.
Robeson's primary emphasis is on combating racism by securing rights by

means of an identity-based politics. Class is of most importance for Bevan. Identity is of most importance for Robeson.

In thinking about these figures in these terms we may generalize by stating that the intellectual tradition to which Robeson belongs has dominated literary and cultural analysis in the last twenty years, though it is Bevan's tradition that has been dominant in Welsh historiography. From the late 1960s onwards an influential generation of Welsh labour historians emphasized class as the key determinant of cultural and political formation, and were openly sceptical of studies focusing on national identity and ethnic consciousness.[50] Recent historical writing within this tradition is informed by a desire to unchain concepts of 'Welshness' from any cultural bases.[51] These arguments can be contrasted with those emerging in the fields of literary and political studies where the impact of postcolonial theory, feminist theory and so on has led to the Left's traditional emphasis on the redistribution of power and capital being replaced by the growing demand for recognition of minority rights and respect for differences based on race, gender, sexuality and language.[52] This shift from the redistribution of capital to a respect for identities has been described by Nancy Fraser as a shift 'from redistribution to recognition'.[53]

This shift can be traced in the political and cultural criticism of another son of south-east Wales, the critic Raymond Williams. Williams's career-making volume *Culture and Society* appeared, conveniently enough for my argument's purposes, in 1958.[54] The study was conceived as an analysis of the changing relationship between culture and society since the beginning of the Industrial Revolution, and is informed throughout by the author's awareness of the working-class's struggle to create a common democratic culture available to everyone by means of an equitable and just education system. Unlike a seat in the House of Lords, one cannot inherit this 'common culture', for it must be created and reinforced by society itself. Williams had hoped to see the creation of a society 'whose values are at once commonly created and criticised, and where the discussions and exclusions of class may be replaced by the reality of common and equal membership'.[55] His emphasis was on social class within a British context, and Williams admitted in 1979 that he wasn't particularly conscious of his Welsh background when writing *Culture and Society*.[56] Britain was his focus, and he argued in favour of a common culture based on the co-operative social values of the working class, which could be contrasted with the individualistic values of the upper classes in society. From the 1970s onwards, however, Williams became increasingly aware of the cultural and linguistic diversity of Britain, and became more self-consciously aware of his Welshness.[57] In a 1971 review of Ned Thomas's *The Welsh Extremist*, Williams placed the campaigns of the Welsh Language Society within the context of Black Power, feminism and campaigns for civil rights in Northern Ireland.[58] He argued in 1983 that the challenge for the Left would be to unite the feminist, environmental, minority nationalist and peace movements.[59] The question that arises is to what extent are these movements compatible with one another? To what extent is a politics based on working-class consciousness compatible with a struggle for gay rights, or the rights of minority-language speakers? Are these movements compatible with one other, or are they incompatible movements drawing upon competing solidarities?[60]

The trend today is to think of 'class' as an 'identity', compatible with other identities based on ethnicity, gender and language. 'Gender, class and race' are terms that appear in the titles of hundreds of academic books and articles. But, at least according to one influential formulation, class is not an identity. It is, rather, a way of describing an individual's position within the economic structure of capitalism.[61] In adopting this perspective, Walter Benn Michaels has argued that the political logic of a movement based on class is fundamentally different to the logic of a political movement based on identity. He notes that the whole point of a class-based politics is to eliminate economic and social divides, leading eventually to the elimination of the very class that gave rise to the movement in the first place. The whole point of a politics based on identity is to encourage society to respect difference, to foster cultural distinctions and to establish rights for the minority or group in question based on its particular needs.[62]

Today, where an emphasis on respecting cultural distinctiveness has replaced an emphasis on redistributing wealth, we tend to think of fairness in terms of social rights: the rights of citizens to avoid discrimination based on language or race or gender. This is to some extent an American influence on our political discourse, and has resulted in a great deal of innovative work and important social developments. But this emphasis on identity has resulted in the marginalization of class as a means of understanding social structures. The political logic of a movement based on 'class' is very different to that of a movement based on the struggle for identity. Walter Benn Michaels argues that a class-based politics does not generally ask us to respect the poor, to tolerate their cultural difference, to recognize their difference or to celebrate their culture. Class politics does not ask us to regret the fact that the poor are going to lose their marks of uniqueness through their integration into the higher classes of society. We do not tend to wish that the children of the poor remain poor themselves.

While people deserve the same respect regardless of background, I doubt whether we believe poverty deserves the same respect as wealth in the way that the speakers of Welsh deserve the same respect as speakers of English, or that an African American deserves the same respect as an Irish-American. A politics of identity is based on the belief that I am not inferior or subordinate because I am a Welshman, or a Jew or an African American. But inferiority and subordination are the basis of poverty, and the awareness that a whole social class is being exploited by others and therefore kept inferior and subordinated forms the basis of class politics. The poor are subordinate within an economic structure. The goal of class politics is not to eliminate the perception that the poor are inferior, but to eliminate poverty itself.[63] This is surely what Gwyn Thomas means when he speaks of Bevan desiring the eradication of the society that had begotten him. It is the poverty that was the economic source of that society's suffering that Bevan wished to eradicate.

This, I suggest, is what explains Aneurin Bevan's attitudes towards nationalism and towards Wales. The common nationalist dismissals of Bevan are oversimplified: he did not suffer from an inferiority complex regarding his Welshness, nor was he an 'Uncle Tom' when it came to the Welsh language and its culture. While certainly happy to work within a British political context, he did not evoke notions of Englishness nor wallow in a patriotic 'one nation' Britishness. Bevan was a politician from the Marxist tradition, his political views infused by the values of the working-class community in which he was bred. At the root of his politics was a desire to eliminate differences, to eliminate inequality, to eliminate the barriers to open communication and to the development of a truly democratic society. His attitudes towards nationalism and towards minority languages derived from this world view, and were consistent with his wider perspectives.

If his emphasis on the elimination of inequality explains Bevan's attitude towards nationalism, it also sheds light on the reason why many minority nationalists adopted conservative positions and located themselves on the political Right. For the Welsh linguistic nationalist Saunders Lewis, as for the Irish cultural nationalist W. B. Yeats before him, the desire to protect and maintain cultural traditions went hand in hand with a desire to maintain and protect the social structures that sustained those cultures. From the viewpoint of Saunders Lewis's medievalism, it was desirable that hierarchical social structures should be preserved. As Richard Wyn Jones has noted, Lewis defined nationalism in 'contradistinction to socialism, and in opposition to it'.[64] According to

Saunders Lewis, 'The National Party of Wales has a political philosophy which is based on the historical traditions of Wales and is wholly at odds with the philosophies of English Socialism, and of the Socialism of Marx'.[65] More recently, this is broadly the position adopted by Simon Brooks in his engaging collection of essays *Yr Hawl i Oroesi* (2009, The Right to Survive), where he argues that Welsh socialist governments are inevitably weak and ineffectual in relation to the Welsh language.[66] 'In a healthy country,' argues Brooks, 'Conservatism would be supportive of the language – because it is in favour of keeping things, and because it believes that some values (such as the language or soul of a nation) are timeless ... Unlike Socialism with its prejudice against all such abstractions.'[67] From this viewpoint, the essence of socialism is to eliminate differences, whereas conservatism aims to 'preserve for the generations to come the purity that used to be'.[68] Aneurin Bevan would have agreed. But he would have argued the opposite position, believing that the elimination of economic injustices was far more important than trying to defend an abstract 'purity' existing only in the minds of conservative nationalists.

Speaking broadly, the purpose of a movement based on a minority identity is to maintain and respect difference. The purpose of a movement based on the interests of the working class is to eradicate difference. Does it therefore follow that cultural nationalists should abandon the Left? Does it follow that the Left should reject all forms of minority nationalism? For Paul Robeson, as I have previously noted, there was no necessary hostility between minority nationalism and socialism. Robeson believed that the African American struggle for civil rights would have a very limited impact if it did not progress simultaneously with a struggle for economic equality. If racial discrimination has to be maintained by law, economic discrimination needs no legal support, for it can be sustained by the market. Indeed, capitalism encourages us to discriminate on the basis of wealth. Benn Michaels draws attention to an episode of the American cartoon *The Simpsons* in which the mother, Marge, goes to 'the rich people's mall' where the advertisement reads 'our prices discriminate because we can't'.[69] If a campaign against racism leads to a situation where the state can no longer discriminate on the basis of race, then so long as the majority of African Americans remain poor the market can discriminate instead. It is therefore clear that there are times when it is imperative that the struggle for economic equality coincides with the struggle for minority rights. The problem in Paul Robeson's political thought is that ethnic identity and class consciousness become fused. These are two categories, as Benn

Michaels convincingly argues, that follow divergent political logics. The result of the merger between the economic category of class and the cultural category of identity is that 'class' becomes an 'identity'.

We can turn to the novels of the Rhondda Communist, Lewis Jones, *Cwmardy* and *We Live*, to see the dangerous implications of this merger of 'class' and 'identity'. Jones's novels document the making of the Welsh working class, and tend to be treated as semi-realistic reflections of Welsh industrial history and a celebration of the working-class struggle.[70] But under the surface of these novels' fairly conventional realism lies a dark and troubling political subconscious. In *Cwmardy* and *We Live*, the workers have no choice but to stay true to the aspirations of their class, and those who deviate from the union line are likely to be punished. Will Smallbear is forced to join the Federation, and the response to his question 'do the federashon mean that workman have got to fight against workman?' is 'Yes, when a few stubborn workmen go against what is good for the majority'.[71] There is no room for individualism in this world, and in fact no room for anyone who fails to espouse the Federation's ideals. The shopkeeper Evans Cardi is a middle-class character whose son, Ron, turns his back on his family, renounces his Christian faith and joins the Communist Party. In a stomach-churning scene Evans Cardi responds by taking a razor to his wife's neck before proceeding to hang himself.[72] If poverty is largely responsible for his suicide, there is also the suggestion that the *petite bourgeoisie*'s time is running out. And indeed there is little future for any character who leaves the confines of the working-class community. Towards the beginning of *Cwmardy*, Jane, the sister of the main character Len, embarks on a relationship with Evan, the son of the mine's overman. She becomes pregnant, but there is no future for this product of two classes for mother and child die during childbirth. This incident sparks Len's sense of injustice and fires his desire to become a Communist leader who ultimately loses his life fighting Franco's fascist soldiers in Spain. Jane's death is made particularly harrowing by the closeness of her relationship with Len, which borders on incest.[73] Len snuggles up to his sister's body in early scenes, and following her death he suffers a surrealist nightmare in which 'Len's heart thrilled. He laughed happily and pressed the face of his sister to his lips. The short stiff hair on it hurt him. He looked again and found he had been kissing Evan the Overman's son.'[74] In a discussion of nationalism in literature the critic Marc Shell draws attention to the ubiquity of incest as a theme. The fear of contamination and of mixing blood lines which can be seen to lie within the nationalist unconsciousness manifests itself in narratives of incest within novels which purport to depict the 'national family'.[75] Keeping things 'in the family' is a way of keeping the blood line pure. It seems to me that Shell's analysis can be adapted for narratives of class. Lewis Jones's *Cwmardy* is not haunted by a fear of national contamination, but of the contamination and weakening of a class identity. The concept of class has become an identity, functioning similarly to a racially based national identity; it must be protected and kept pure. Class consciousness is transformed into class identity. To read *Cwmardy* and *We Live* today is to realize that Lewis Jones may inadvertently have exposed the factors within the Communist ideology, that he espoused, which led to the atrocities of Stalin and Pol Pot. The ideal of a classless world can be transformed easily into an ideal of a world that requires the destruction of other classes. The goal ceases to be the assimilation of all into a classless utopia, but the elimination of those of other classes. If a racial nationalism can lead at its most extreme to ethnic cleansing, then the fusion of class and identity, pushed to an extreme, can result in class cleansing. I would not wish to argue that Communism inevitably leads to such atrocities, any more than I would argue that nationalism inevitably leads to ethnic cleansing. But the historical record suggests that there's good reason to be wary of Robeson's desired fusion of class and identity.

V

So where does that leave us? While the emphasis on cultural difference may at times function as a diversion from the problem of economic inequality, it is surely an error to wish struggles for cultural distinctiveness, preservation and development away. It is not unreasonable to speak of working-class communities developing their own cultures, and wishing to see the values of their communities continuing to inform the practices of a future, more equitable, society.[76] The struggle for economic equality should not be aimed at allowing all peoples to assimilate into a rapaciously individualistic, culturally homogeneous and environmentally devastating capitalist system. Martin Bauml Duberman – Paul Robeson's biographer and a gay-rights activist – argues that the 'high-flown' rhetoric of the anti-culturalists, calling for the transcendence of identitarian allegiances in the name of 'universal human beings with universal rights', rings hollow. 'It is difficult', he notes

> to march into the sunset as a 'civic community' with a 'common culture' when the legitimacy of our differentness as minorities has not yet been more than

superficially acknowledged – let alone safeguarded. You cannot link arms under a universalist banner when you can't find your own name on it. A minority identity may be contingent or incomplete, but that does not make it fabricated or needless. And cultural unity cannot be purchased at the cost of cultural erasure.[77]

The Brazilian thinker Roberto Unger responds to this tension between universalism and particularism by suggesting that the contemporary Left should 'not only respond to the universal aspiration of the ordinary working man and woman for more opportunity by which to raise him and herself up', but should also 'turn democratic polities, market economies and free civil societies into machines for developing distinct and novel forms of life'.[78] That is, the general aspirations for social equality, and for distinctive identities, should underpin any progressive movement on the Left today. In this respect Bevan and Robeson continue to speak to our moment. Bevan was right to separate his national identity from the politics of class. But he was wrong to then devalue the struggles for the continued existence of Welsh distinctiveness as manifested in the spheres of language and culture. Robeson was right to place his people's culture and their civil rights at the heart of his socialist vision, but his fusion of 'class' with 'identity'has become increasingly untenable in recent decades with the exacerbation of class divisions within African American society.[79] I hope to have suggested that class and identity do not follow the same political logic and it is therefore crucial, at a conceptual level, that they are kept apart. But (*contra* W.B. Yeats and Saunders Lewis) cultural diversity and economic equality are not intrinsically incompatible. The challenge for the Left is to fight two distinct battles simultaneously: Bevan's battle for economic justice, and Robeson's struggle for the rights of minorities.

To Know the Divisions:
The Identity of Raymond Williams

I

> [Raymond] Williams was ... discomfited by the identity politics he associated
> with – and these are his words – 'many minority liberals and socialists, and
> especially those who by the nature of their work or formation are themselves
> nationally and internationally mobile'. In other words: not settled, not truly
> English, not truly part of the nation. He was uncomfortable with identity poli-
> tics ...[1]

In this passage from *Tradition and the Black Atlantic* (2010), the African
American critic Henry Louis Gates, Jr. reinforces an established view of
Raymond Williams. Since his untimely death in January 1988, a broad
critical consensus has emerged that Williams was a critic who espoused an
essentialist view of culture and whose writings were severely limited by
his neglect of the thematics of identity, race and empire. John Higgins
argues that Williams was 'constitutively blind to the politics of race and
gender, and the dynamics of imperialism'. Rajagopalan Radhakrishnan
describes Williams as 'incapable of dealing with the subtle nuances of the
politics of location'. Benita Parry is puzzled by the admiration that Aijaz
Ahmad expresses for Williams in light of the latter's English 'provincialism' and what Edward Said described as his 'stubborn Anglocentrism'.
Laura Chrisman is typical of many in lamenting the 'insularly English'
focus of Williams's work, and Cornel West laments Williams's failure to
see the 'affiliation between Imperialism and English culture'. More damn-
ingly, in an American collection of *Black British Cultural Studies*, the

editors describe Williams as sharing an 'ideological posture' with 'postin-dustrial English conservative racism and nationalism'.[2]

In offering a characteristically spirited account of the history of cultural studies, Henry Louis Gates, Jr. has added his influential voice to this consensus. He notes that 'writing in 1983' Williams advanced a

> seemingly organicist conception of culture based on ethno-territorial conti-nuity: 'The real history of the peoples of these islands ... goes back ... to the remarkable society of the Neolithic shepherds and farmers, and back beyond them to the hunting peoples who did not simply disappear but are also amongst our ancestors'.
>
> But if this is the 'real history', it follows that some of us – those not numbered among the possessive collectivity 'our ancestors' – must not be Britain's 'real people'. The passage reprises the Anglo-Saxonist myths of lineage that serve to buttress an exclusionary and imperialist ideology of 'Englishness'. (Remember, this is a country where in the 1950s Winston Churchill could suggest to Harold Macmillan that if the Conservative Party wanted to win elections, it should adopt the slogan 'Keep England White').[3]

In its own terms, and buttressed by selective quotation, the analysis seems persuasive enough. However, Williams's sentences read slightly differ-ently when placed in their original context:

> What is most intolerable and unreal in existing projections of 'England' or 'Britain' is their historical and cultural ignorance. 'The Yookay', of course, is neither historical nor cultural; it is a jargon term of commercial and military planning. I remember a leader of the Labour Party, opposing British entry to the European Community, asserting that it would be the end of 'a thousand years of history'. Why a thousand, I wondered. The only meaningful date by that reckoning would be somewhere around 1066, when a Norman-French replaced a Norse-Saxon monarchy. What then of the English? That would be some fifteen hundred years. The British? Some two thousand five hundred. But the real history of the peoples of these islands goes back very much further than that: at least six thousand years to the remarkable societies of the Neolithic shepherds and farmers, and back beyond them to the hunting peoples who did not simply disappear but are also among our ancestors. Thus the leader of a nominally popular party could not in practice think about the realities of his own people. He could not think about their history except in the alienated forms of a centralised nation-state. And that he deployed these petty projections as a self-evident argument against attempts at a wider European identity would be incomprehensible, in all its actual and approved former-European reorganisations, if the cultural and historical realities had not been so systematically repressed by a functional and domineering selective 'patri-otism'. All the varied peoples who have lived on this island are in a substantial physical sense still here. What is from time to time projected as an 'island

race' is in reality a long process of successive conquests and repressions but also of successive supersessions and relative integrations.[4]

Even if we might wish to take issue with Williams's use of the possessive collectivity 'our ancestors', it is surely wholly misleading to see this passage as reprising 'Anglo-Saxon myths of lineage'. Williams could not be more explicit in his desire to reject the 'existing projections' of 'Englishness'. To the contrary, the whole point of the argument regarding the 'real' history of the British Isles, the endless sequence of conquests, repressions and relative integrations, is to undermine, deconstruct and to reject the myths on which the contemporary evocations of Englishness and Britishness are based. Williams warns us of the ways in which a fundamentally plural present and past has been replaced by a 'domineering and selective patriotism'. He is not reinforcing dominant and exclusionary definitions of Englishness, but attacking them. It is surprising that a subtle close reader such as Gates should offer such a wholly misleading reconstruction of Williams's analysis. What explains this misreading, and what is at stake in this widespread misrepresentation of Williams and his work?

II

A partial answer to these questions lies in the fact that all of the critics mentioned above, without exception, make reference either explicitly or in a footnote to Paul Gilroy's critique of Williams's *Towards 2000* (1983). Gates offers a spirited reconstruction of Gilroy's critique and argues that it 'is worth quoting at length because as a minority critique of the provincialism of the English left, it has become a standard point of reference in subsequent debates'.[5] In his seminal account of the 'cultural politics of race and nation' in Britain, *'There Ain't No Black in the Union Jack'* (1987), Gilroy argues that Williams draws 'precisely the same picture of the relationship between "race", national identity and citizenship as [Enoch] Powell'.[6] Powell's infamous 'Rivers of Blood' speech of 1968 was, to quote *The Times*, 'the first time that a serious British politician has appealed to racial hatred in this direct way in our postwar history'.[7] Gilroy believes Williams's understanding of 'race' and 'nation' are 'redolent of other aspects of modern Conservative racism and nationalism', and finds evidence for his harsh and influential critique in the following passage from a chapter in *Towards 2000* entitled 'The Culture of Nations':

[I]t is a serious misunderstanding … to suppose that the problems of social identity are resolved by formal (merely legal) definitions. For unevenly and at

times precariously, but always through long experience substantially, an
effective awareness of social identity depends on actual and sustained social
relationships. To reduce social identity to formal legal definitions, at the level
of the state, is to collude in the alienated superficialities of 'the nation' which
are the limited functional terms of the modern ruling class.[8]

Due to the seriousness and severity of the critique it is worth quoting
Gilroy's discussion of this passage at some length. Gilroy refers back to
the previous passage in *Towards 2000* to note that Williams presents his
remarks as a response

> to anti-racists who would answer the denial that blacks can be British by
> saying 'They are as British as you are'. [Williams] dismisses this reply as 'the
> standard liberal' variety. His alternative conception stresses that social iden-
> tity is a product of 'long experience'. But this prompts the question – how
> long is long enough to become a genuine Brit? His insistence that the origins
> of racial conflict lie in the hostility between strangers in the city makes little
> sense given the effects of the 1971 Immigration Act in halting primary black
> settlement. More disturbingly, these arguments effectively deny that blacks
> can share a significant 'social identity' with their white neighbours who, in
> contrast to more recent arrivals, inhabit what Williams calls 'rooted settle-
> ments' articulated by 'lived and formed identities' ... His use of the term
> 'social identity' is both significant and misleading. It minimizes the specifici-
> ties of nationalism and ideologies of national identity and diverts attention
> from analysis of the political processes by which national and social identities
> have been aligned ... How these social identities relate to the conspicuous
> differences of language and culture is unclear except where Williams points
> out that the forms of identity fostered by the 'artificial order' of the nation
> state are incomplete and empty when compared to 'full social identities in
> their real diversity'. This does not, of course, make them any the less vicious.
> Where racism demands repatriation and pivots on the exclusion of certain
> groups from the imagined community of the nation, the contradictions around
> citizenship that Williams dismisses as 'alienated superficialities' remain
> important constituents of the political field. They provide an important point
> of entry into the nation's sense of itself ... Quite apart from Williams's
> apparent endorsement of the presuppositions of the new racism, the strategic
> silences in his work contribute directly to its strength and resilience.[9]

Gilroy's critique of Williams's rather simplistic contrast between the
'alienated superficialities' of political orders and the 'full social identities'
of cultural communities is both trenchant and insightful, and there is no
doubt that Williams tended to underestimate the impact of racism on the
constitution of social identities. It is wholly misleading, however, to argue
that Williams denies the indispensability of citizenship rights for

immigrants, a charge that has also been reiterated by Stuart Hall.[10] Indeed, Williams notes explicitly in the chapter that 'a merely legal definition of what it is to be "British" ... is necessary and important, correctly asserting the need for equality and protection within the laws'.[11] Williams's point is that such appeals to abstract legal rights, and to facile and patronizing ideas of 'assimilation' by politicians of both the Right and the Left, are unequal to the social strains of Britain's changing ethnic composition in the present, and betray an ignorance of Britain's ethnic diversity in the past. 'To reduce social identity to formal legal definitions, at the level of the state', notes Williams, 'is to collude with the alienated superficialities of "the nation" which are the limited functional terms of the modern ruling class'.[12] This argument is in fact in keeping with Gilroy's own analysis, a few pages later, of a Conservative Party election poster of 1983 which set an image of a black male above the caption 'Labour says he's black. Tories say he's British'. Gilroy argues that the term 'British' is being used here to suggest that 'the category of citizen and the formal belonging which it bestows on its black holders are essentially colourless, or at least colour-blind ... Blacks are being invited to forsake all that marks them out as culturally distinct before real Britishness can be guaranteed'.[13] This argument is similar, in content and structure, to Williams's own critique of the ways in which a dominant national identity can be used to obscure economic disparities and legitimate cultural and historical differences. In this respect, perhaps surprisingly, Williams's cultural materialist emphasis on the significance of human experience and the constitutive effects of 'actual and sustained social relationships' can be seen to share a number of features with Paul Gilroy's analyses of black history and cultural consciousness. Surely, one of the fundamental arguments of Gilroy's *The Black Atlantic* is that the experience and legacy of slavery determines the form and content of black artistic expression in the twentieth century.[14] Henry Louis Gates, Jr. notes the continuity between the thought of Williams and Gilroy, and states that the latter does embrace a notion of cultural continuity, especially when arguing that immigrants and 'their British born children have preserved organic links with it, in their kitchens and temples – in their communities'. Is this, asks Gates, 'Williams's rhetoric of lineage, organicity, and community in blackface?' 'Perhaps', he continues, 'but all blackface is not equal'.[15]

If we take Gates's problematic evocation of minstrel traditions as a metaphor for the adoption of identity as a site from which to speak in the world of theory, then the example of Raymond Williams suggests that little cultural capital accrues from being Welsh. In discussing Gilroy's harsh critique of Williams, Neil Lazarus wonders 'how Gilroy can insist that the historical experience of slavery remains materially constitutive of contemporary black Atlantic sociality while denying to Williams the right to make a similar claim about the determination of contemporary Welsh sociality'.[16] But Gilroy does not in fact deny the continuities of Welsh sociality, for he never registers the fact that Williams was Welsh at all. Williams is forced to wear an English mask in all the critiques listed above. He is an Englishman, furthermore, who is unaware of his insularity and provincialism and who reprises Anglo-Saxon myths of lineage. Williams was of course aware of those myths, but was more a victim of their effects, than a blind supporter of their continued use. He often recalled a contemporary at Cambridge attempting to put the Welsh working-class grammar schoolboy in his place by telling him that 'my family came over with the Normans'. Williams responded, 'And how are you liking it here?'[17] The joke of course relies on a sense of organicist continuity, of the connection between ancient Britons and the modern-day Welsh, and Williams admits himself that he was 'playing the game' of ancestral privilege in his response. Williams's own contingent sense of identity, based on his formation on the Welsh side of the Wales–England border, is expressed many times in his writings. One example might suffice.

> One of the central advantages of being born and bred among the presumed Welsh is the profusion of official identities. Wales and Monmouthshire, as it was for me at school, with special force since we lived in the appendage. England-and-Wales: that administrative, legal and even weather-forecasting area. Wales for rugby but All-England for cricket. Welsh Wales and English Wales. Wales and Cymru. To anyone looking for an official status it was a nightmare. To anyone trying to think about communities and societies a blessing: a native gift.[18]

Passages such as this are currently ignored because in describing Williams as an 'insular' and 'provincial' Englishman his critics are reinforcing a well-established narrative in which the early figures of the British New Left (especially Williams, but E. P. Thompson is also critiqued in these terms) were blind to questions of empire, imperialism and identity. According to this story it was not until the empire 'wrote back' in the 1980s that a new generation emerged who would give these issues a central role. Gates sees Gilroy's critique of Raymond Williams, especially the comparison with Enoch Powell, as a 'twisting' of the knife, which inaugurated 'a changing of the guard'.[19] The results of this apparently violent coup were modest, in that 'Williams's valorization of community and generational links was never jettisoned; it was merely pluralized'.[20]

III

There is certainly some truth to this history of British cultural studies. In his early career-making works *Culture and Society* (1958) and *The Long Revolution* (1961), Williams's emphasis was on a process of lived experience, a process of growing democratization and cultural participation that was the making of an emergent 'common culture'.[21] This notion of a 'common culture' embodies one of the deepest desires informing Williams's cultural thought in the 1950s: the desire to make connections in the name of a cultural 'wholeness' and 'general interest'. Capitalism is to be resisted as a system for it breeds divisions, of classes, of peoples, of nations. This dimension of his thought is particularly clear in the chapter on the 'The Growth of Standard English' in *The Long Revolution*, which ends with the observation that 'there will doubtless always be people and groups who are anxious to show that they are not as other men, but the deep process of the growth of the great international language will not be much affected by them, though they may for a time be blurred'.[22] It is this emphasis on a common human experience that informs the particular prestige that Williams gives to realism in the novel. Realism, for Williams, is conceived as a process, an aim in writing that calls for new forms and approaches as our world, and understanding of that world, changes. Rejecting those voices in the late 1950s who argued that 'the realistic novel … went out with the hansom cab', Williams argued, in a Brechtian mode, that realism was an 'intention' that did not require an adherence to an already established form.[23] 'Realism' does not refer to imitations of nineteenth-century conventions, for Williams insisted that new social realities would require new realisms. His conclusion was that 'a new realism is necessary' to capture the shape, and contribute to the emergence of, a common culture.

His first novel *Border Country* (1960) – written concurrently with *Culture and Society* and *The Long Revolution* and part of 'a body of work which I set myself to do ten years ago' – can be read as the fictional embodiment of Williams's theory of realism.[24] The novel is also significant, however, because it begins to register the problems inherent in the concept of a common British culture, and in this respect it anticipates future developments in Williams's thinking. This is particularly the case in relation to the novel's engagement with dialect and linguistic difference. Indeed, the question of discourse, of the process by which ways of seeing are reflected, embodied and constructed in ways of speaking, is a central, reiterated, theme in the novel. Characters are consistently identified by their speech. Harry, from 'this side of the river' has 'the quick Welsh accent', while his wife Ellen speaks 'with the slow, rich, Herefordshire tongue'.[25] Dr Evans's voice is a 'Welsh voice' but 'different from the Glynmawr accent: smoother with narrower vowels, and with the intonation of the mining valleys'.[26] Language is also significant in that it can be a barrier to, as much a mode of, understanding. Jack Price, for instance, teases his grandson with 'dialect words that he had known as a boy but that had gone out of use', and, more seriously, when the policeman comes to tell Ellen that her husband has died, she listens to the breaking news 'as if the men were speaking a language she did not understand'.[27]

This exploration of communication is most clearly pursued in relation to the submerged presence of the Welsh language in the text. For the 'Baptist anniversary' at the chapel, Will (the autobiographically based central character) is taught 'a little Welsh poem of two verses' by his father Harry, which the boy recites 'clearly' while standing 'nervously under the arch of the pulpit'.[28] Will is given a book entitled 'The Holy Child' for his efforts which he throws into the river, much to the embarrassment of his parents. In another scene Harry, who rarely expresses his emotions overtly, can't seem to control his anger when he hears the 'little minister' Joshua Watkins 'rehearsing his prayers and sermon. It went on for more than an hour, in Welsh, although the eventual delivery would be in English. The practice, it seemed, was to get the first flow right.'[29] Harry's anger is primarily a response to Watkins's unwillingness to help with spreading ashes on the frozen lane, followed by the minister's impertinence in asking Harry to empty his lavatory bucket. But it is surely significant that the issue of language difference appears at those moments of heightened emotional pressure in the novel, where character motivations become difficult to fathom, and where the realist narrator's claim to 'know' the characters' thoughts and inner beings breaks down. In terms of the influential post-structuralist critique of realism mounted by Colin MacCabe and others, it would seem that the Welsh language represents a discourse that the narrative meta-language (or omniscient third-person voice) 'cannot transform into an object', resulting in the 'loss of control of the novel' at those very moments where Will and Harry lose control of their own contained emotions.[30]

The role of Welsh in the novel reaches its climax in the section on the eisteddfod.[31] Here, the boundaries between languages, between generations, and between Will and the culture which surrounds him, become dissolved in the performances of the choirs which are followed by the communal singing of the Welsh national anthem:

It was time now for the choirs, and Will knew, looking up, that it was no use at all even trying to stay separate ... The drop of the raised hand, and then not the explosion of sound that you half expected, but a low, distant sound, a sound like the sea yet insistently human; a long, deep, caressing whisper, pointed suddenly and sharply broken off, then repeated at a different level, still both harsh and liquid; broken off again, cleanly; then irresistibly the entry and rising of an extraordinary power, and everyone singing; the faces straining and the voices rising around them, holding moving, in the hushed silence that held all the potency of these sounds, until you listening were the singing and the border had been crossed. When all the choirs had sung, everyone stood and sang the anthem. It was now no longer simply hearing, but a direct effect on the body: on the skin, on the hair, on the hands.[32]

Will's desire to 'stand apart' is clear, but when the choirs begin to sing, that position of detachment becomes untenable. We're told that a 'border had been crossed' as listener becomes singer in an act of empathy that again seems to lie 'outside the control' of the narrator's meta-language. Indeed, the eisteddfod in *Border Country* can stand metonymically for Welsh culture itself: it is a transformative space in which 'I. Morgan, Watch Repairer', becomes 'Illtyd Morgan y Darren', in which a border is crossed as the power of the art produced by a community has a 'direct effect on the body'.[33]

If Wales, as Williams was to note later, tends to be viewed as 'unusually singular' from an English perspective, he reverses the gaze in *Border Country*, where it is on the Welsh side of the border that identities become unstable, that variousness and openness replace an English reserve and insularity.[34] On the novel's very first page Matthew (known as 'Will' during his childhood in the border country, but by his official registered name 'Matthew' now that he is a historian in London) notes the 'contained indifference' of the English capital, where 'you don't speak to people', and goes on to generalize that 'in fact you don't speak to people anywhere in England; there is plenty of time for that sort of thing on the appointed occasions'.[35] England is seen later to be

a great house with every room partitioned by lath and plaster ... If you went out of your own cupboard, to see a man in another cupboard, still you must wait for the cupboard door to be opened, with proper ceremony, and by a proper attendant.[36]

Wales, on the other hand, is a place of openness. The 'ease' of speech 'that had almost been lost' that Matthew encounters in the 'West Indian conductress' in the novel's opening scene is mirrored upon his return to Glynmawr when the tense and formal exchanges between Matthew Price and his father's friend Morgan Rosser give way to the native rhythms of the border as Price notes that 'it was easy at last, and enough had been re-established'.[37] This ease of speech is mirrored in an openness observed at several points in the novel. In Glynmawr, the men 'walk slowly, showing all three layers. Mack open, jacket open, cardigan open, waistcoat open, collar-band open – nothing, you see, to hide.'[38] The binary terms of this distinction between English reserve and Welsh openness is too simplistic and is not sustained throughout the novel. Welsh Nonconformist puritanism is compared to English social liberalism in the scene, discussed in chapter 2, where the men leave 'dry' Wales for a Sunday pint in England, for example. But the fictional contrast between Welsh 'ease' and English reserve can be seen to inform Williams's later engagements with his native country where he argued that 'the most valuable emphasis in Welsh culture is that everybody should speak and have the right to speak'.[39]

While Christopher Prendergast is certainly right to note that Williams is similar to Georg Lukács in 'preferring to the art of dispersal and fragmentation promoted by the sanctioned versions of modernism an art that connects, especially … forms that join, as mutually necessary for intelligibility, individual experience and social formation', matters are slightly different in relation to his evaluation of Welsh literature.[40] For, while championing the writings of the 1930s realists (Gwyn Jones and Lewis Jones in particular), Williams was primarily attracted to two non-representational narratives where the controlling voice of the omniscient realist narrator gives way to a chorus of competing voices, and where the view of the world is coloured by wild hyperbole and black comedy: Dylan Thomas's 'play for voices' *Under Milk Wood* (1953) and Gwyn Thomas's *All Things Betray Thee* (1949). Both works can be seen to illustrate Williams's notion that 'Welsh writers cannot accept the English pressure towards a fiction of private lives'.[41] In Williams's revealing readings, Dylan Thomas follows Joyce in discovering a 'living convention' that juxtaposes the 'language of dream' with the 'public language of chorus and rhetoric', while Gwyn Thomas creates a 'composition of voices' that will express a historical experience not confined to the 'flattened representations or the applied ideological phrases'.[42] This celebration of dialogue and plurality in the writings of Gwyn Thomas and Dylan Thomas reinforces Williams's emphasis that Wales 'has been a plurality of cultures' resulting in a situation in which 'any formulation becomes a challenge'.[43]

This presentation of the internal variedness and plurality of a Wales viewed from a dominating external perspective as singular and static is one of the key characteristics of Border Country. In this respect, Williams can be seen to be offering a fictional enactment of an argument developed in *The Long Revolution*. If Matthew's career in London has led him to view the Wales of his youth as a static, idealized, periphery in the novel's opening scenes, then his perspective is shared by many English novelists in their representations of other places. Williams revealingly selects E. M. Forster's *A Passage to India* (1924) as a 'good example' of a novel that romanticizes the 'actual society to the needs of certain of the characters':

> This is quite common in this form: a society, a general way of living, is apparently there, but is in fact often a highly personalized landscape, to clarify or frame an individual portrait rather than a country within which the individuals are actually contained.[44]

As Matthew Price crosses the border into Wales to be at the bedside of his dying father, he considers the map of 'pig-headed Wales', and proceeds to observe the 'usual photographs' at 'the sides of the map': 'On the far side was the abbey, that he had always known: the ruined abbey at Trawsfynydd that had not changed in his lifetime. On the near side was the front at Tenby.'[45] Matthew is reminded of these images the following day when, upon waking in his childhood bed in Glynmawr, he picks up a county history describing the village church as 'distinguished by its relics', its 'Norman porch' and 'Saxon tomb' located in a landscape where the 'bloodiest of border castles' and the 'Stone of Treachery' are to be found. 'Yesterday the pictures in the train, and now this', muses Matthew, 'the pieces of past and present that are safe to handle. Here, in this living country.'[46] Against the living history of which, as both a historian and a native of this place, he is all too aware, Matthew turns to those ways of seeing that offer to fix that ever-changing experience thus making it 'safe to handle'. He describes the historical work that he is doing on 'population movements into the Welsh mining valleys in the middle decades of the nineteenth century' in scientific terms. 'The techniques I have learned have the solidity and precision of ice-cubes, while a given temperature is maintained. But it is a temperature I can't really maintain; the door of the box keeps flying open.'[47] If the empirical work of the historian is approximate to scientific observation, the human experiences on which that work is based force Matthew to consider other, less easily measured, considerations: '[I]t wasn't a piece of research, but an emotional pattern', he notes.[48] *Border Country* continually juxtaposes different ways of seeing and knowing as, upon his return to Wales, Matthew feels a growing sense of uncertainty about his work as a historian, the trajectory of his life and ultimately his own sense of identity.

Thus, as a returning exile, Matthew seems to find some solace in the fixed images of the train carriage and the descriptive accounts of popular history. These are ways of seeing that turn the fluidity of experience back into ice cubes. At the novel's outset Matthew's past does seem 'another country', best imagined in static, unchanging ways closely related to his own childhood memories, as is suggested by his observation that the images in the train were 'more than thirty years old: nearly his own age'.[49] As the narrative proceeds Matthew begins to question the assumptions that he brings to bear on this landscape, questioning the values that inform his conception of reality:

> In Gwenton he had met nobody he knew, and the simple shopping had been difficult, after London: the conventions were different. He had felt empty and tired, but the familiar shape of the valley and the mountains held and replaced him. It was one thing to carry its image in his mind, as he did, everywhere, never a day passing but he closed his eyes and saw it again, his only landscape. But it was different to stand and look at the reality. It was not less beautiful; every detail of the land came up with its old excitement. But it was not still, as the image had been. It was no longer a landscape or a view, but a valley that people were using. He realized, as he watched, what had happened in going away. The valley as landscape had been taken, but its work forgotten. The visitor sees beauty; the inhabitant a place where he works and has his friends. Far away, closing his eyes, he had been seeing this valley, but as a visitor sees it, as the guide-book sees it: this valley, in which he had lived more than half his life.[50]

As he learns again to become an inhabitant within a living space as opposed to a visitor who sees only the image, Matthew comes to realize the extent to which he moulds the landscape and environment of the border country according to his own changing perspectives.

This analysis echoes Matthew's realization, quoted above, that 'the visitor sees beauty; the inhabitant a place where he works and has his friends'.[51] Forster's India is a subjective projection rather than an actual society. We may begin to see here the influence of Williams's formative work on the emergence of postcolonial criticism. In *Orientalism* (1978), Edward Said traced the tension between the tendencies to visualize and narrativize within descriptions of the colonial 'Other'. 'Against the static system of "synchronic essentialism" I have called vision', noted Said,

> there is a constant pressure. The source of pressure is narrative, in that if any Oriental detail can be shown to move, or to develop, diachrony is introduced into the system. What seemed stable – and the Orient is synonymous with stability and unchanging eternality – now appears unstable.[52]

There is evidence, especially in the later writings, that Williams was fully aware of the ways in which the 'marginalized' or 'oppressed' can become fashionable symbols of resistance, most strikingly in the novel *Loyalties*, where Emma, a middle-class radical, is seen in the 1980s to replace her picture of the 'green heads of miners' with 'an embroidered African landscape'.[53] Against such primitivist pitfalls Williams emphasizes historical change and human mobility. Matthew's development in *Border Country* sees him rejecting the tendency to see Wales in static, visualized terms, as he becomes increasingly, and troublingly, aware of the inherent instability of his native country. The novel's contrapuntal movement back and forth between Matthew's experiences in the present and the longer historical sections centring on Harry Price and the General Strike of 1926 aims to allow for an emphasis on personal perception but always within a deep social contextualization that foregrounds social and historical change. In the movements back and forth between Wales and England, which is characteristic of all the novels in the 'Welsh Trilogy', Williams is arguing that all places and peoples have lives and internal tensions of their own; nowhere exists merely as a static, unchanging and idealized background for something or someone else.

IV

What Henry Louis Gates, Jr. misses in drawing attention to the potential discriminatory implications of 'common culture' as a concept is that Williams was already exploring the tensions and limitations of his thought in relation to his own Welsh formation. This exploration took the form of fiction in the 1950s and 1960s. When challenged by his *New Left Review* interlocutors in 1979 about the lack of any reference to 'nationalism or imperialism' in *Culture and Society*, Williams responded as follows:

> There are in fact two places in the book which do refer to the imperial experience, although in a way they confirm your general emphasis – the discussion of Carlyle's criticism of emigration as a social solution, and the analysis of the magical function of departures to the empire in the fiction of the period. But otherwise there is nothing about it … I think one of the reasons for this is that the particular experience which ought to have enabled me to think much more closely and critically about it was for various reasons at that time very much in abeyance : the Welsh experience. The way I used the term community actually rested on my memories of Wales as I've said. But the Welsh experience was also precisely one of subjection to English expansion and assimilation

historically. That is what ought to have most alerted me to the dangers of a persuasive type of definition of community, which is as once dominant and exclusive.[54]

It is this passage that Edward Said had in mind when he recalled that Williams related the absence of 'Empire' in *Culture and Society* to the 'unavailability at the time of [his] Welsh experience' that wasn't 'as important ... then as it later became'.[55] This would seem to suggest that any discussion of Williams's engagement with the question of colonialism should take place in the light of his meditations on his Welsh experience. Unfortunately, the Welsh dimension of Williams's thought is never referred to by Said in the influential reading of *The Country and the City* (1973) that appeared in *Culture and Imperialism* (1993).[56] In that analysis Said registers the fact that Williams 'does address the export of England to the colonies' but argues that he does so 'in a less focused way and less expansively than the practice actually warrants'.[57] He proceeds to criticize Williams for having limited his discussion of imperialism to the mid-nineteenth century and after. This is a criticism that could be justifiably made of the entry on 'Imperialism' in *Keywords* (1976), but is less applicable to *The Country and the City* where in his chapter on 'The New Metropolis' Williams brings the question of colonialism into the centre of his analysis:

> In 1700 fifteen per cent of British commerce was with the colonies. In 1775 it was as much as a third. In an intricate process of economic interaction, supported by wars between the trading nations for control of the areas of supply, an organized colonial system and the development of an industrial economy changed the nature of British society.[58]

Following this discussion of how the consolidation of the plantation economies was dependent on the slave trade, Williams comments that 'The unprecedented events of the nineteenth century, in which Britain became a predominantly industrial and urban society, with its agriculture declining to marginal status, are inexplicable and would have been impossible without this colonial development.'[59] The tendency to universalize a particular formation (of which Williams is himself guilty in *The Long Revolution*) is criticized throughout *The Country and the City*, most powerfully and memorably in Williams's rejection of the Marxist tendency to demean and ridicule the 'idiocy of rural life':

> In the *Communist Manifesto* Marx and Engels argued that 'the bourgeoisie has subjected the country to the rule of the towns ... has created enormous cities ... has made barbarian and semi-barbarian countries dependent on the

civilized ones': the familiar history of capitalism and imperialism. They argued that these relations of centralisation and dependence had created the conditions for revolution, and in one sense they were right.

But there was an ambiguity at the core of the argument. They denounced what was being done in the tearing progress of capitalism and imperialism; they insisted that men must struggle to supersede it, and they showed us some ways. But implicit in the denunciation was another set of value-judgements: the bourgeoisie has 'rescued a considerable part of the population from the idiocy of rural life'; the subjected nations were 'barbarian and semi-barbarian', the dominating powers 'civilised'. It was then on this kind of confidence in the singular values of modernisation and civilisation that a major distortion in the history of communism was erected ... This difficulty worked itself through in a surprising way, in our own century. Revolutions came not in the 'developed' but in the 'undeveloped' countries ... Thus the 'rural idiots' and the 'barbarians and semi-barbarians' have been, for the last forty years, the main revolutionary force in the world.[60]

As a result of this new perspective *The Country and the City* marks the moment in Williams's work when, as Dai Smith has noted, 'the wider, encompassing, anglocentric references are often brought up against Irish, Scottish and, more unknown to his readers, Welsh sources of enquiry'.[61] It should be noted further, however, that these Celtic references were themselves supplemented by discussions of Indian and African writers whose names were in more limited circulation in 1973 than they are today: Achebe, Nwankwo, Ngugi and Narayan. *The Country and City* expanded the boundaries of literary study as it was practised in 1973, and can hardly be regarded as the work of a man who, according to Gauri Viswanathan, 'consistently and exclusively' studied 'the formation of metropolitan culture from within its own boundaries'.[62]

It should now be clear that unlike Enoch Powell and the various ideologues of the New Right in Britain, Raymond Williams never compared an unproblematic, rooted, 'Britishness' with the newer, less rooted, less 'authentic', identities of immigrants. At no point in *Towards 2000*, nor in any of his other writings, does Williams deny, in Gilroy's words, 'that blacks can share a significant social identity with their white neighbours', nor does he ever suggest, as Gilroy alleges, that the 'origins of racial conflict lie in the hostility between strangers in the city'.[63] Williams preceded the passages quoted by Gilroy in *There Ain't No Black in the Union Jack* by noting that

What is from time to time projected as an 'island race' is in reality a long process of successive conquests and repressions but also of successive supersessions and relative integrations ... [I]t should be obvious that this long and unfinished process cannot reasonably be repressed by versions of a national history and a patriotic heritage which deliberately exclude its complexities and in doing so reject its many surviving and diverse identities.[64]

Cultural diversity thus pre-dates twentieth-century immigration. Williams reinforces this insight towards the end of the chapter where he typically relates the preceding discussion to Welsh history and his own Welsh experience:

> It happens that I grew up in an old frontier area, the Welsh border country, where for centuries there was bitter fighting and raiding and repression and discrimination, and where, within twenty miles of where I was born, there were in those turbulent centuries as many as four different everyday spoken languages. It is with this history in mind that I believe in the practical formation of social identity – it is now very marked there – and know that necessarily it has to be lived. Not far away there are the Welsh mining valleys, into which in the nineteenth century there was massive and diverse immigration, but in which, after two generations, there were some of the most remarkably solid and mutually loyal communities of which we have record. These are the real grounds of hope.[65]

Far from denying that immigrants can share a significant social identity with the settled population, Williams actually turns to the diversity of the south Walian experience as 'the real grounds of hope'. By the late 1970s Williams was defining himself as a 'Welsh-European', and even when a young boy 'British' was a term that 'was not used much, except by people one distrusted'.[66] It would also be a mistake to see Williams rejecting an oppressive Britain in favour of an equally essentialist, if minoritarian, Wales. For if Williams never defined himself, nor considered himself, 'British', his writings on Wales are also characterized by the rejection and problematization of the idea of an unitary identity. In his 1971 *Guardian* review of Ned Thomas's 'little red book' of the Welsh-language movement, *The Welsh Extremist*, Williams adopted a strategy that he would repeat many times in his later writings on Wales: he locates himself in the border country of his youth – a place 'so special and in other ways so marginal' – and looks westwards towards the two societies that have formed the bases for the dominant, and bitterly divergent, images of Wales in the twentieth century: the 'powerful political culture of industrial South Wales' on the one hand, and 'the more enclosed, mainly rural, more Welsh-speaking west and north' on the other.[67] Revealingly, in both cases, Williams's knowledge of these Welsh communities derives more from research than experience: he recalls 'focusing first' on the history of south

Wales, before turning his attention to the Welsh-speaking west and north that 'in the beginning ... was much more remote'.[68] This position of outsiderness is put to good effect in the review article 'Community' of 1985. Here, Williams compares novelist and critic Emyr Humphreys's celebration and analysis of the 'continuity of Welsh language and litera- ture ... from the sixth century' with historian Dai Smith's critique of notions of national continuity in his emphasis on 'the turbulent experience of industrial South Wales' since the late nineteenth century.[69] Attempting to see beyond the bitterness of Welsh cultural and political debates, Williams seeks to effect a unity of the various ideas of Wales that he had encountered in his life and work. He notes his particular awareness 'of the common elements of authenticity in each apparently alternative case', and, despite the divisions, argues that 'the more profound community is its area of discourse'.[70] Williams suggests that this argument develops from 'seeing the matter in my own living conditions from both inside and outside', an ambivalent location that lies at the heart of his fictional and theoretical engagements with Wales and Welshness and his engagements with questions of nationalism and national identity.[71] Williams emphasizes in several essays that he was 'born on the border, and ... talked about the "English" who were not us, and the "Welsh" who were not us'.[72] This border experience forms the basis for a pluralistic conception of nation- hood that is wholly at odds with the racially essentialist view of the nation espoused by Enoch Powell and his followers.

V

Despite the simplistic clichés which now circulate Williams and his work, he was not – to use Gates's words – 'discomfited by identity politics'. He was, rather, a prophetic interpreter of the historic and contemporary tensions within the idea of 'Britain'. In Williams's second novel, *Second Generation* (1964), the experience of the British working class in the 1960s is increasingly related to the legacies of empire. This thematic thread reaches its climax at a party where the central character Peter Owen engages in the following conversation with two representatives from the West African Federation.

> 'I have been having an argument with the Minister', Okoi said. 'I have been saying our nationalism is now too evident, and that we are not doing enough in the struggle with poverty.'
> 'The distinction is false', Akande said. 'But this is still the class struggle, only now between nations ... Nationalism' he said precisely 'is in this sense

like class. To have it, and to feel it, is the only way to end it. If you fail to claim it, or give it up too soon, you will merely be cheated, by other classes and other nations.'

'I agree', Peter said. 'This is what I've been learning.'

'Then I wish you luck, Mr Owen'.

'I wish you luck, Mr Akande. Both of you', he added, smiling across at Okoi.

'It will be more than luck, it will be struggle, Peter', Okoi said.[73]

What Peter 'has been learning' is arguably reflective of Williams's engagement with the relationships between class, nationhood and identity. Two reiterated positions, which emerge in his discussions of the national question, are implicit in this dialogue. First, that while class and nation are distinct social categories they may both offer possible resources for communal identity and political action. A politics based on 'class' or 'nation' will be partly played out on a terrain defined by one's antagonists, but these forms of identity cannot be circumvented; they must be embraced and worked through towards alternative forms of being and belonging. Secondly, while the British Left has traditionally been opposed to nationalism in all its forms (whilst being blind to its own national biases), Akande's words suggest that it is in fact necessary to discriminate between nationalism's emancipatory and oppressive forms. In his writings from the early 1970s onwards Raymond Williams would increasingly apply these issues – discussed here by a second-generation member of Oxford's Welsh diasporic community and two representatives of newly independent African nations – to his own Welsh experience, and to his analyses of Britain's cultures.

But it is probably worth concluding by noting in the bluntest terms that I am not advocating that we think of Williams as the prophet of a devolved Welsh socialist utopia rooted in an appreciation of cultural difference. While Patrick Parrinder described Williams 'withdrawing into the redoubt of his Welshness', and James A. Davies's referred to Williams's 'alternative Wales' as 'a Celtic commune under threat but indomitable', Williams was in fact rarely a nostalgic romanticizer.[74] He is a figure who continues to trouble the unthinking assumptions of the contemporary 'Left' in both its Welsh, 'Yookayan' and 'Anglo-American' guises. While many have celebrated the shift from 'ethnic' (based on language, religion, culture) to 'civic' (based on political institutions) identities, national identity can never be purely civic for Williams. For him, all nationalisms are cultural nationalisms whether they recognize it or not, for no political articulation can precede cultural formation. What we are asked to face by Williams's emphasis on the cultural constitution of contemporary identities is how far is it possible to travel away from an insistence on distinctiveness and authenticity, with their inherent dangers of nativism, racism and xenophobia, before a culture is stripped of any specificity? This is a question of particular importance in Wales where, from the late nineteenth century onwards, a nationalist desire to transcend cultural differences in order to forge a viable sense of a single national identity, has co-existed with an awareness of the cultural diversity of a modern Wales that emerged with the Industrial Revolution, and a struggle to maintain a minority Celtic language still spoken by over 20 per cent of the population. This is also a question of central importance to the European Left as it tries to make sense of the supranational and regional ties being forged within the context of Europeanization and placed under increasing strain during a period of economic depression. In the post-devolution 'Yookay', where Britishness is being re-defined under internal and external pressures, Williams's should be heard as a prophetic voice. Beyond Wales that voice is currently silenced by the reiterated charge of insularity and provincialism. Possible lines of communication and bases for solidarity may yet emerge, however, from the realization that while there ain't no black in the Union Jack, Wales ain't there either.

'American Freaks': Welsh Poets and the United States

I

In his fragmentary travelogue, *To Babel and Back* (2005), Robert Minhinnick recalls sitting in a park in Jack Kerouac's home town of Lowell, Massachusetts, musing on the irony that the words of America's leading mythologizer of the open road are now to be found statically 'reproduced on marble slabs'.[1] Having noted that what 'might live on the page has no vitality on a menhir', Minhinnick takes a book from his bag 'and settles to a chapter'. Like thousands of tourists to America, from the early 1990s onwards, the book he reads is Bill Bryson's *The Lost Continent*, which becomes a catalyst for further thought:

> Bill Bryson is a reductionist. *The Lost Continent* took middle America and dumbed it down, more deeply down, more subterraneanly down than it had ever been dumbed down before … Not that America doesn't ask for it. The US has destroyed its history and environment. It delights in the disneyfication of its own psyche. But the US teems with mysteries. Despite the wagon-trains, Hollywood and rock 'n' roll, it remains unexplored. Jack Kerouac attempted the task, but *On the Road* is a muddied stream of consciousness, and subsequent works too full of half-baked zenology. But no matter the failure of *On the Road*. Crucially, it admitted the ritualistic possibilities of the US. It paid homage. It praised. It did not reduce but suggested that here was a world where the imagination might blossom. Ironically, it was Kerouac, the homebird, the substance abuser, the self-styled Breton princeling, who was one of the first pop culture invaders of mainstream art. Kerouac's ilk created the climate in which Bill Bryson flourishes. But any study of *On the Road* and *The*

Lost Continent will make clear what has been sacrificed in the democratisation of art since the 1950s.[2]

Two widely held views of the United States are embedded within this passage. First there is the America of Hollywood, of rock and roll, of Disneyland, of a rampant capitalism which generates a seemingly lamentable 'democratisation of art'. Secondly there's America as a land that 'teems with mysteries', 'ritualistic possibilities' and where the 'imagination might blossom'. Bryson is the postmodern, mass-produced, chronicler of the first view, whose 'Fartville and Coma are not satisfying satirical constructs because they are fogged by the author's air of knowingness'.[3] Kerouac is the 'tormented' and 'damned' chronicler of the second America, whose works are characterized by an 'unknowingness' which allows the 'secrets of America' to retain their mystery in a land that is 'vast with possibility'.

In stating that 'Kerouac and his ilk created the climate in which Bill Bryson flourishes', Minhinnick suggests that his two Americas are historically connected. Bryson was brought up in the America being critiqued by the Beats, which I discussed in chapter 3. Emerging in a period of American military dominance, consumer craving and political conservatism, the Beats' 'inva[sion] of mainstream art' in the mid-1950s marked a moment in which a new generation of American writers bared the dark side of national affluence. Like many counter-cultural artistic movements, the Beats sought to construct in their writings an alternative set of values to those of a dominant money-driven society. Minhinnick, in describing Kerouac as 'a proclaimer ... an intimate proclaimer', reflects the fact that the Beats turned increasingly away from the printed page in an excited interest in their own bardic tradition, stemming from Emerson and Whitman, and paving the way for the American performance poetry of the following decades. And as I suggested in chapter 3, Dylan Thomas, whose four visits to America took place in the early 1950s, was amongst the key catalysts for this shift.[4]

Jack Kerouac's admiration for Thomas was informed by an awareness of his Breton, and thus Celtic, ancestry. While this has already been discussed earlier in this volume (see pp. 52–3), Kerouac's references to Matthew Arnold's 1866 lectures *On the Study of Celtic Literature* in his letters are of relevance to my argument here, for in revealing one of the main sources for his sense of his own Breton identity, he was also tracing one significant source of Minhinnick's concern at the increasing 'democratisation of art'. For, as I noted earlier, in his essay 'Democracy' (1861) Arnold asked 'what influence may help us to prevent the English people from becoming, with the growth of democracy, "Americanised"'?[5] Arnold's words suggest that by the 1860s 'Americanization' was already being used as a concise way of referring to the sweeping changes occurring as a result of the social movement towards democracy, as manifested in the decline of the aristocracy's influence on the political and cultural life of the nation. This process left the middle class to determine the future tone of the national life, a prospect that could not be welcomed, for Arnold believed that the middle class in England was characterized by its narrow, uncultured and 'philistine' conception of what that life should be. In Arnold's lectures the counter-force to Saxon philistinism lay in a Celtic resistance to industrialization manifested in that race's sensitivity, femininity and attraction to 'natural magic'.[6] This view was in keeping with Arnold's English Unionism, predicated as it was on the belief that these valuable Celtic attributes of 'femininity' and 'natural magic' would reach their full maturity when combined with masculine Saxon rationality, in the making of the hybrid, superior, Englishman. However, as R. F. Foster notes, Arnold's essays ultimately 'reinforced an interpretation of Celticism that strengthened irreconcilable ideas of separatism'.[7] W. B. Yeats, like many members of the Irish Renaissance, evoked Arnold's lectures in support of his view that 'the flood-gates of materialism are only half-open among us as yet in Ireland; perhaps the new age may close them before the tide is quite upon us'.[8] Such ideas were to have a lasting impact in Wales. As the twentieth century proceeded, and America emerged as the leading capitalist super power, a wide range of writers and thinkers, from a variety of political and cultural persuasions, tended increasingly to equate America with a rampant individualist capitalism, while imaginative, poetic and communitarian Wales was seen to offer a valuable counter-force.

   The percolation of Arnoldian Celticism, via the Irish Revival, into the literature of twentieth-century Wales is particularly apparent in the writing of R. S. Thomas.[9] Where Arnold began his Celtic lectures by turning from the 'steamboats' and 'Saxon swarms' of Liverpool to 'the eternal and mild light' of Wales 'where the past still lives, where every place has its tradition, every name its poetry', R. S. Thomas, travelling by train from Cardiff to Shrewsbury, turns from the 'plains of England' to the west where 'the hills rose dark and threatening as though full of armed men waiting for a chance to attack. There was in the west a land of romance and danger, a secret land.'[10] The romance is in keeping with Arnold's Celticism, but the armed fighters suggest a nationalist re-working of Arnoldian Unionism similar to that engineered in the writings of W. B. Yeats. If Yeats often alluded to 'the dream of my early manhood, that a modern nation can return to Unity of Culture' thus bypassing the 'modern, utilitarian, commercial civilization which has been organized by a few great nations', R. S. Thomas, when he 'was young and under the influence of the Anglo-Welsh revival', dreamt of creating 'an alternative culture' based on the Welsh 'possession of qualities and values which were steadily eroded by a material culture'.[11] While Yeats and Thomas primarily lamented the encroachment of 'English' industrial civilization on Ireland and Wales respectively, both writers also used 'America' as a signifier of the forces which they opposed.

Yeats visited an America suffering from the 'degradation of industry' in 1903, and his solution for the ills bred by the 'democratisation of arts' (to use Minhinnick's term a century later) lay in the fostering of an aristocratic class: 'As your aristocracy grows the passion for beautiful things will grow. In the growth of that aristocracy lies your hope.'[12] R. S. Thomas attacked a contemporary Wales 'fuddled with democracy' and lamented the loss of 'a Welsh-speaking nobility that succoured music and poetry'.[13] In his poem 'Afallon' from *No Truce with the Furies* (1995), his imagined Avalon is a place where a Welsh-speaking David has 'floor[ed]' the Goliath of 'a world / oscillating between dollar / and yen'.[14] Some years earlier, in his review of Dee Brown's *Bury My Heart at Wounded Knee*, Thomas evoked the indigenous peoples of America as part of his primitivist resistance to industrialization:

> Here was yet another of the primitive peoples of the world who had followed a particular way of life since time immemorial; a way of life which was beautiful and in keeping with nature itself. It was confronted by the mechanised way of life, a money-gathering life based on the machine and the gun, and like every other culture, it collapsed before this soul-less Leviathan.[15]

This romanticization of the American Indian's 'beautiful' life leads Thomas back to his youthful 'dream of a different society':

> When I was younger, I used to dream of a different society in Wales. The population was comparatively small; there was a distinctive language; there was space. Most of the country had not yet been built on; most of the inhabitants worked on the land – except for the industrial monster in the south. Language is important; it partly reflects the personality of a people and it partly moulds it. Would it not be possible, by means of Welsh, to avoid the over-industrialisation that had taken place in England, the bottomless pit into which so many western countries were rushing? The years went by. The industrialisation increased. The Welsh countryside was covered in forests; the cottages and smallholdings were taken by Englishmen. The dream receded.

Today, having read this book; having realised that the Indians, with their comparatively simple ideas, were right; having begun to realise the extent of the crisis which faces England and its imitators because of over-industrialisation, its over-population, the greed of its businessmen, the wish to turn these islands into a shop in which others can buy, I see that the dream was not so unfounded after all.[16]

The encounter with Dee Brown's sympathetic history of American Indians leads R. S. Thomas to reiterate the central values at the heart of his remarkably consistent, if simplistic, social philosophy. The adherence to an identity rooted in language, the idealization of a pre-industrial past, the dismissal of 'the south' as an 'industrial monster', are all characteristics of Welsh cultural nationalism in the early twentieth century, but draw on a long tradition of responses to industrialization. For many contemporary critics, such views mark Thomas out as an 'essentialist', the promoter of a racial definition of nationhood, and the romanticizer of a Wales that never existed. The emergence of a new generation of Welsh poets is frequently deemed to be a reaction to Thomas's outmoded cultural nationalism. Thomas cultivated an image as someone existing outside the mainstream, publishing a collection of his most nationalistic poems in the volume *Welsh Airs* in 1987 as a counter-blast to what he saw as the waning of the nationalist spirit in the work of Wales's English-language poets. M. Wynn Thomas notes that Robert Minhinnick spoke for many in defining the new poetry against the 'sixties generation, which had given itself such tiresomely Welsh airs'.[17] Wynn Thomas identifies and describes the way in which Minhinnick's generation rejected their predecessors' 'misty-eyed reference to remote Welsh history, their cliché trove of romantic images. Their gung-ho nationalism and their psychological hang-ups about their monolingualism.'[18]

Yet, to encounter Minhinnick lamenting the increased 'democratisation of the arts' in *To Babel and Back*, and to see him identifying that democratization with the worst features of American culture, is to realize that the gulf between generations can be overemphasized. Indeed, in celebrating R. S. Thomas's eightieth birthday, Minhinnick expressed his admiration for the poet while simultaneously distancing himself from his views. The significance of Thomas, for Minhinnick, is that he 'speaks publicly of matters that not long ago were treated with ceremonial secrecy' and has thus 'mapped and named the cultural divide between various groupings of the Welsh people'. Thomas's example also helps Minhinnick to define the groupings in contemporary Welsh poetry:

It is a sobering, indeed lacerating, experience to listen in person whilst the poet lectures, for example, the non-Welsh-speaking Welsh on their linguistic treachery and gutlessness. Yet it is difficult to convey this to the many English-born or bred writers who now live and publish in Wales, because, for them, it is a less culturally – and environmentally – compromised country than England or America.

   Raymond Garlick, Jon Dressel, J. P. Ward, Jeremy Hooker, Joseph Clancy ... whether they have learned Welsh or not, would applaud many of the poet's cultural stipulations. And all honour to them for doing so. But they would not understand, as say, Mike Jenkins or Nigel Jenkins or Steve Griffiths would understand, the nuances and the personal implications of the lecture. I doubt if they would reel, as I have done, out of a public room after listening to the poet, feeling that I was a cancer in my own society.[19]

This seems to me a suggestive division of (male) Welsh poets which depends less on age and generation and more on cultural positioning. The first group are those who have come to Wales and identified sympathetically with a version of Welsh culture that, broadly, isn't far removed from that espoused by R. S. Thomas. The second group feel moved by Thomas's words and example, but are distanced from them as he is in effect mounting an attack on the legitimacy of their Welshness. There is also a third group, not mentioned by Minhinnick, who would respond differently again to Thomas's lecture, for they would have no sympathy with his opinions, and would view Thomas's brand of ethno-linguistic nationalism as being the real cancer in Welsh society.

   The poets that I will be discussing in this chapter can broadly be positioned within these three camps: Jon Dressel belongs to the first, Nigel Jenkins to the second and Duncan Bush to the third. All three have held their identities as Welshmen and poets up to the, at times affirming, but often distorting and troubling, mirror of America. And, as I hope will become clear in the following discussion, what they see in the reflection is often coloured by the intellectual tradition that I have attempted to map out broadly above.

II

It is not surprising that America should be of central importance in the writings of the St Louis-born poet of Welsh descent, Jon Dressel. Writing retrospectively in 1994, he could see that a 'romantic infatuation' had informed his earlier views of Wales, 'partly rooted in a revulsion to the Vietnam War in the late 1960s and early 1970s'.[20] The keynotes of that romanticism are struck in a letter of Dressel's addressed to *The*

Anglo-Welsh Review in 1977. He was responding to critic John Pikoulis's opinion that Raymond Garlick's poem 'Fourth of May' was 'utterly disgraceful' in its comparison of Wales with Nazi-occupied Holland. Dressel, who viewed Pikoulis's response as belonging not to 'literary criticism, but to ... outraged authority', could see the merits of Garlick's worrying comparison:

> Is there not a sense in which the threat of cultural annihilation is as terrifying as the physical threats of conquest and brutal occupation? Might not the impending destruction of a national identity be as awful to contemplate as the destruction, let alone the mistreatment, of individual human beings? The Nazis, after all, were militarily defeated (with not a few Welsh lives given in the process); their occupation of Holland did end, but the economic and psychological occupation of Wales has gone on for centuries, and goes on now. The crisis of the Welsh spirit, the threat of Welsh cultural annihilation, is real, present, continuous.[21]

This alleged 'Welsh spirit' manifests itself, for Dressel, in the 'affirmation of alternative values, call them agrarian if you will' against the overwhelming force of 'what R. S. Thomas has called the "hyper-industrialised Anglo-American anti-culture"'.[22] Dressel concludes his dramatic letter by hoping that Wales may yet prove to be one of those 'places on earth fortunate enough in terms of geography, history, persistence of cultural tradition to avoid total engulfment by consumer industrialism'.[23]

It would seem, then, that Minhinnick is right to include Jon Dressel amongst those sympathetic outsiders who 'would applaud many of [R. S. Thomas's] cultural stipulations'. In fact, when compared to Thomas, the distinction between a rural ideal and an urban reality is arguably more consistently central to Dressel's work. 'Prytherch is dead' is the opening sentence in his early poem 'Dai, Live', where a Carmarthen drunkard, who 'grunts a little rugby' and 'digs around the village, roads / sewers', replaces R. S. Thomas's peasant as a symbol of unfathomable otherness.[24] A Prytherch-like synthesis of simplicity and sublimity is also foisted on 'The Shop Girl', who 'was born / to the council house', works in Littlewoods, hangs around bus shelters and

> Having
> no larger needs or illusions, I will
> be happy enough, and die, if I am lucky,
> at my ease with Sunday telly at the age
> of eighty-two. What is the dream
> of Wales to me? Even the poet who
> toys with me on this page understands

> that in my kept inertial dullness I am
> utterly invincible, and make his hand go slack.[25]

The actual urban Welsh whom Dressel encounters fail to live up to his national ideal; they are akin to the living dead in which the 'Welsh spirit' has been extinguished. He reflects a structure of feeling that is prevalent in Welsh literature in both languages, but takes on a heightened charge for an American Welshman who wishes to take pride in his ethnic roots. Tony Conran argues perceptively that the issue of devolution in the 1970s

> was central to Anglo-Welsh perspectives as it never really was to Welsh-speaking Wales. This is not a matter of who supported what; only that a Welsh Assembly automatically would have revolutionized the status of Anglo-Welsh writers while it would have left Welsh ones very much as it found them.[26]

Perhaps for a Welsh American, the 'No' vote of 1979 was particularly cataclysmic, for at a time in the late 1970s when a whole generation of Americans were rejecting the 'melting pot' and attempting to reclaim their various 'ethnic' roots, the few who embraced a conscious Welsh American identity saw the nation with whom they wished to identify denying its own separate existence. Dressel recognizes that his 'immediate sympathy' with the goals of Welsh nationalism in the 1960s was based on his 'very American' belief that 'Wales was of course a nation, and had a right to govern itself'.[27] The nationalist expectations that Dressel harboured throughout the 1960s and 1970s 'crashed, of course, in 1979', and he would later admit that 'whatever disillusion I had with America has been fully balanced by disillusion with Wales'.[28] The sense of total despair is captured in his 'A Diary for St. David's Week, 1979'. A Welsh version by T. James Jones was famously awarded the Crown at the Eisteddfod of 1979, only to be disqualified as a collaboration.[29] What became known as the 'Ianws' poems represented 'the limit of my ability to psychically identify with Wales'.[30] What followed was a thematic return to America in Dressel's poetry:

> Turning to the question of my American identity was no doubt, at first, a defensive reaction; the Welsh majority, having been, as it were, dragooned to the front, had broken and run, and so I beat a psychic retreat to the American lines. The question, however, soon became one of just what and where were the American lines, and whether indeed I could wholly retreat to them.[31]

If disillusion with American society drove Dressel to embrace Wales in the 1970s, disillusion with Wales led to 'the matter of my American identity' and the realization of 'how Southern my formative American experience had been'.[32]

The product of that realization is the long sequence *The Road to Shiloh*. Formally the poem is characteristic of Dressel's work as the majority of stanzas are three lines long, occasionally curt and abrupt, at other times long and meditative, but always attempting to capture the cadences of the human voice. Dressel is himself the owner of a Welsh bar in St Louis, and one assumes an autobiographical dimension to the character of the bar's 'boss', the poem's main protagonist, who is also an amateur historian. The sequence follows the 'boss' as he explores the past of one Captain Delbert Stubbs, a Unionist soldier shot at Shiloh; it is a technique that allows the poet to take us from war memorial, to registrar's office, to Stubbs's home town of Prairie Country, to the battlefields of the Civil War. Around this central narrative a plethora of minor characters appear, speaking their own range of voices: they include the ghosts of General Grant and Albert Sidney Johnston (the Unionist and Confederate commandeers at Shiloh respectively); a bartender who views his boss as an 'old white liberal' who is 'patronizing' to African Americans; Woodrow and Juke, two contemporary African American characters, the first a drop out who comes around the bar selling pictures, the second a porter living in East St Louis; and the ghost of the African American author, philosopher and sociologist, W. E. B. Du Bois, who engages the 'boss' in an imaginary discussion on the meaning and legacy of the Civil War. The sequence's multi-voiced structure makes it profoundly dialogic, not only in the literal sense that many of the poem's sections are dialogues between the saloon owner and one of the many characters, but also in the Bakhtinian sense that language is itself a site of conflict and contest in which 'historical and social distinctions … power relations and hierarchies' are registered.[33] Mikhail Bakhtin's remark that 'it is precisely the diversity of speech, and not the unity of a normative shared language, that is the ground of style' is particularly applicable to *The Road to Shiloh*, and Dressel's major achievement is to constantly dialogize one voice against another and in doing so to challenge the notion of an unitary account of the Civil War.[34]

If this diversity of voices is a strength at the level of form, it is also simultaneously the sequence's major weakness at the level of content. For, surely, some accounts of the Civil War are more ethically, morally, and historically, valid than others. In his remarkable study of how the Civil War was remembered and mythologized, David Blight identifies 'three overall visions of the Civil War' in American memory:

> [O]ne, the reconciliationist vision, which took root in the process of dealing
> with the dead from so many battlefields, prisons and hospitals …; two, the
> white supremacist vision, which took many forms early, including terror and

violence, locked arms with reconciliationists of many kinds, and by the turn of the century delivered the country a segregated memory of the Civil War on Southern terms; and three, the emancipationist vision, embodied in African Americans' complex remembrance of their own freedom, in the politics of radical Reconstruction, and in conceptions of the war as the reinvention of the republic and the liberation of blacks to citizenship and Constitutional equality.[35]

This process of isolating three divergent narrative strains within a varied and complex field proves particularly useful in reading Dressel's sequence, for all three narratives jostle for authority in *The Road to Shiloh*.

The reconciliationist vision is voiced intermittently throughout the poem. The ghost of General Grant sees a nation united in tragedy:

After Shiloh, Cable wrote, the South
Never smiled. Nor, in truth, said Grant, did we –[36]

The poem's narrator, similarly, sees a nation 'bound' in the blood of battle:

– ... the covenant was there,
and it was a covenant of men and women,
bound together by the bloody American ground.[37]

And Dressel himself, in introducing the sequence, emphasizes the 'rightness' of the reconciliationist vision: 'I understand that, for all my sympathies with the Southern predicament, all my distaste for Yankee moral posturing, it was right, and hugely so, that the North prevailed in the Civil War.'[38] Dressel develops this train of thought in relation to the other 'reconciliation' attempted in the poem, that between his identities as 'American Southerner' and 'Welshman':

And indeed on this point the analogy [between the American South and Wales] must falter, for I do not think it was right, in any comparable sense, that England conquered Wales. In both cases superior power, with which it is fruitless to take historic issue, triumphed, but the matter of black slavery makes a profound difference in the American equation. White Southern dignity, in transcending defeat, has had to do so under the burden of a kind of original sin.[39]

Perhaps this particular comparison should be laid to rest having acknowledged this point, but after addressing the differences, Dressel goes on to emphasize the similarities.

But if the Civil War was ultimately about slavery, it was also about the need to defend your land against invasion, and about the opposition of essentially agrarian values to those of an industrial and mercantile society in which the profit motive was increasingly superseding all considerations of human fair dealing ... Here the parallels with Wales run truly close, for there is a sense (call it mythic if you will, but remember as you do so the myth of 'progress') in which the struggle of both the South and of Wales has been one of trying to preserve traditional, small-scale human values against mechanistic forces driven essentially by capitalistic greed.[40]

This structure of argument suggests that Dressel has not rejected his 'romantic infatuation' with Wales, but extends the rural vs. urban distinction manifest in his 1977 letter to *The Anglo-Welsh Review* to encompass the American South itself. We are back in the land where a mythic ruralism stands opposed to a mechanistic society, and it is here that Dressel's thought is in danger of reinforcing what David Blight describes as the 'white supremacist' reading of the Civil War.

In seeking to establish an intellectual and poetic space for what he problematically describes as 'white Southern dignity', Dressel turns to a form of anti-industrialism which he associates with Wales, but is in fact a characteristic of reactionary thought in the American South.[41] His anti-industrialism is close to that of the Southern Agrarians, for example, who vented their dislike of industrialism, urbanization, immigration and the American Left in their manifesto *I'll Take My Stand* of 1930. For the agrarians, Northern 'industry', rather than abolitionism or federalism, had been the South's main adversary in the Civil War.[42] More recently Southern anti-industrialism has been linked to an essentially 'Celtic' agrarianism in the writings of latter-day Confederates. In his *Cracker Culture: Celtic Ways in the Old South*, the military historian and Confederate sympathizer, Grady McWhiney, argues that 'Southerners lost the war because they were too Celtic and their opponents were too English'.[43] 'Viewed through this prism', notes Tony Horowitz,

> The War of Northern Aggression had little to do with slavery. Rather, it was a culture war in which Yankees imposed their imperialist and capitalistic will on the agrarian South, just as the English had done to the Irish and Scots – and as America did to the Indians and Mexicans in the name of Manifest Destiny.[44]

The 'Celtic' myth of the south helps to reinforce a racial, and often racist, myth of Southern identity in which the true South is 'Celtic' and therefore 'other Souths (notably African American) ... become illegitimate and inferior'.[45]

If there are worrying parallels between Dressel's construction of Southern history and that of neo-Confederates, it has to be emphasized that Dressel is no white supremacist. He stresses that the African American experience is 'inextricably interwoven' into the history of the South, and the power and impact of *The Road to Shiloh* derives partly from the way in which the poet's desire to create a poetic space for 'white Southern dignity' comes up against African American voices and concerns in the text.[46] We encounter Woodrow, an African American street artist selling paintings of jazz musicians copied from books and stamps, early on. 'Seven years, in Illinois / I learned to draw in prison, man', explains Woodrow, and by placing Woodrow back in a 'correctional' facility at the end of the poem, Dressel is clearly reflecting the ongoing racial legacy of slavery and the Civil War.[47] The other African American voice is Juke who helps the saloon owner to stack his beer. Juke is one of eight brothers, and has 'twelve sisters, too', 'Same momma and daddy, all of us' still 'down in Tennessee'.[48] Juke is the voice of homespun truths in the poem, a kind of chorus, who represents a better future. The sequence's penultimate poem ends with 'Juke / and the others waiting on the stoop' to enjoy the 'cold beer, hot food, good talk' of Memorial Monday, 1991:

> Things would get better,
> Had to get better, but it would be hard,
> Another hundred years. There was too much
> History yet to be paid for, too much ghetto,
> Too much jail, too many Woodrows doomed to do
> grim time.[49]

Neither of the African American characters is as educated as the narrator, who is given the last word here – and expresses a characteristic liberal, gradualist, viewpoint. In one of the poem's most striking scenes the narrator finds himself in dialogue with the ghost of the philosopher and activist W.E. B. Du Bois (1868–1963) who is familiar with the 'long term view' that 'allows you the old white luxury, evasion'.[50] Du Bois offers an internal critique of the poem from an African American point of view, seeing 'Juke and Woodrow' as 'possible avenues of expiation' for the narrator (and by extrapolation, the poet):

> You find Juke
> and Woodrow remarkable not because one
> is competent and the other is talented
> but because they are reasonably so
> in spite of the handicap of being black.[51]

Du Bois's discussion with the narrator moves to an engagement with the nature of white racism. Having dedicated decades of his long life to the struggle for human rights Du Bois eventually abandoned America to spend his final years in Nkrumah's newly independent Ghana. It is the

disillusioned Du Bois of his final years in the 1960s who speaks in
Dressel's poem of an ultimate white 'recoil from blackness'.[52] While the
African American philosopher is a striking presence in *The Road to Shiloh*,
by making Du Bois speak in the despondent tones of his later years, his
earlier, well-documented, views on the Civil War are omitted. In 1928 Du
Bois wrote:

> It is the punishment of the South that its Robert Lees and Jefferson Davises
> will always be tall, handsome and well-born. That their courage will be phys-
> ical and not moral. That their leadership will be weak compliance with public
> opinion and never costly and unswerving revolt for justice and right. It is
> ridiculous to seek to excuse Robert Lee as the most formidable agency this
> nation ever raised to make 4 million human beings goods instead of men.
> Either he knew what slavery meant when he helped maim and murder thou-
> sands in its defence, or he did not. If he did not he was a fool. If he did, Robert
> Lee was a traitor and a rebel – not indeed to his country, but to humanity and
> humanity's God.[53]

The closest Dressel gets to reflecting this kind of sentiment in his poetry
occurs as the narrator meditates before the inscription on a monument to
Confederate soldiers:

> The hands of a loving and grateful people:
> a final, eloquently humble, phrase,
> or so it might seem, but was it an eloquence
> of criminal disregard, impervious
> to Klan terror, to mob rule and lynching,
> and every other lesser, hardly speakable
> indignity inflicted on the black, down all
> the years? He did not want to think it, yet
> he had to, it was the price of his being
> moved, the *sine qua non* of his understanding
> that the words rang not untrue. That gratitude
> and love were real, and what was more, deserved,
> he could not doubt, despite the moral rightness
> of the South's defeat, a rightness that resisted
> all of Yankee cant, and guilt. Yet the right
> of it was hard, another right had been there,
> the right, and need, to defend your land.[54]

The development of this passage reflects the broader trajectory of the
sequence itself. The African American experience is registered, Klan
atrocities are registered, but they cannot extinguish the suffering and willingness of Confederate soldiers to defend their land. The problem is that
once African Americans are fully included in one's definition of 'the

South', then it can be questioned how many Southerners actually supported the Confederacy. Dressel's 'South' is thus ultimately a white South. African American voices are heard in the text, but they belong to its margins. Woodrow and Juke are in fact rather like 'Dai' and the 'Shop Girl': they are types, viewed from some distance, and one feels that the poet would prefer to put them aside so that they may cease to worry his constructions of 'the South' or of 'Wales'. This is precisely what he does ask us to do in the final poem in the sequence where the war is described as 'not Civil' but for 'Southern Independence':

> Leave
> the slaves for now. Each one must know that
> too, but here we look on something else ...
> Consider Dixie, Wales, though it is more through
> than you. Waterloo, Sebastopol, Mafeking,
> World War, crown your high streets, sanctify
> your squares. Where are the hard tall figures
> of the men whose fight was just their own, and yours?
> A stone for Llywelyn, a cairn for Glyn Dŵr,
> right where they are, are not enough.
> Lee and Jackson in the noon at Richmond
> ride against the blue where thousands move.
> Who can imagine the midday gray of Cardiff
> under such spectacular, less vain, assault?[55]

In order, ultimately, for the comparison between Wales and the South to be sustained the 'slave must be laid aside'. But to construct a South, or a history of the Civil War, that marginalizes the experience of slavery is ethically repugnant, and historically inaccurate if not 'utterly disgraceful'. In a brief discussion of the sequence M. Wynn Thomas repeats, apparently approvingly or at least without dissent, the poem's question as to why there are no statues of Glyndŵr and Llywelyn in Wales equivalent to the statues of Lee and Davis in Southern towns.[56] Given Dressel's historical fantasy that 'parallels between Robert E. Lee and Owain Glyndŵr' are 'remarkable indeed', perhaps our response to his question should be: 'is it not time those statues to Confederate leaders were torn down'?[57] There are, undoubtedly, similarities between the ruralist fantasies of the Southern Agrarians and those of Saunders Lewis and others, as there are similarities between the elements of defeat and perseverance in the nationalist thought of Wales and the American South, and in the experiences of rapid and uneven industrialization. But to draw parallels is quite different to suggesting that we should endorse the particular forms of ethnic

nationalism that inform a Southern identity, or that the South should function as a model for Wales to follow. If Wales is to 'consider Dixie', we
should also consider African American novelist Ishmael Reed's response
to those who believe that Confederate monuments 'represent a heritage':
'A heritage of whipping people'.[58] Dressel tells us that his 'road to Shiloh
... is a road that runs through Wales'.[59] Whatever the strengths of the
poetry, it is not a road to follow.

III

If Jon Dressel's journey took him through Wales to the American South,
Nigel Jenkins spent several summers guiding American students along the
roads of Wales. In a diary about the weeks leading up to the referendum on
Welsh devolution in 1997, Jenkins describes one of these bi-annual
'mystery tours':

> The place that moves them most is the drowned valley of Tryweryn, espe-
> cially if the water's low, exposing the road, the hump-back bridge and the
> outlines of fields and houses. The Americans are shocked that this entire
> community was wiped out – not in medieval times but as recent as the 1960s
> – so that Liverpool Corporation could build a profit-making reservoir. They
> find it difficult to believe that although the Welsh were united, for once, in
> their opposition to the plan (with the exception of George 'Viscounts Against
> Devolution' Thomas and one or two other quislings) they were powerless to
> stop it. 'Everyone in Wales should come and take a look at this sad place', said
> a student on one of our visits. Yes, indeed.[60]

While the students are sensitive enough to appreciate the significance of
this 'sad place', as members of the world's capitalist superpower they find
it hard to understand the impotence of a small, peripheral, nation. The
drowning of the Tryweryn Valley, a key event for Welsh nationalists,
represents the way in which a people's concerns are made secondary to a
'corporate', capitalist mentality for Jenkins. This is a consistent and reiterated theme in his work. For example, on the way back to Syracuse during
a reading tour of America, Jenkins, like R. S. Thomas before him, dramatizes the ways in which a people's culture is of secondary concern to
economic demands with reference to American Indians.

> On the way back to Syracuse we passed near the controversial new Mohawk
> gambling centre at Turning Stone. The biggest Indian casino in the States, it
> has divided the Mohawks locally and caused bitter dissent among Native
> Americans everywhere. The 'modernisers' maintain that running casinos may

be difficult to square with native traditions but, where unemployment is destroying the Native American soul, it's an activity that brings in big bucks and the possibility of survival. What's the use of such 'survival', argue their opponents, if the price that's paid for it is the abandonment of the tribe's fundamental customs and beliefs? A pathetic dilemma with disturbing echoes in the culture of one's own lottery-obsessed tribe.[61]

The comparative reference back to Wales is a repeated gesture in Jenkins's work. If American corporate capitalism colonizes at home, it does so abroad too. The poem 'Colonial' is based on the 'ten months I spent bumming around Europe and North Africa in the early 1970s', an experience seen later as the 'clincher' in a long process of reclaiming a 'Welshness' that Jenkins describes as having been denied him during his childhood.[62] What he encounters in Morocco is a generation of young pimps – 'Wan'/ maybe fuck Moroccan chick?' – selling off their women, language and their culture in assimilating to an American norm.

> They old, no good. Me
> No Moroccan, me
> English, me American freak.[63]

The poem's final two lines are reminiscent of Harri Webb's poems 'Israel' or 'For Fanon', but rather than following Webb in overtly spelling out the terms of the comparison, Jenkins merely asserts

> Yes, sometimes, David bach,
> Sometimes Morocco springs to mind.[64]

The 'bach' of the penultimate line, as M. Wynn Thomas has noted, functions as a synecdoche for the whole of the Welsh language, and stands in contrast to the 'Anglo-American idiolect' spoken by the Moroccans.[65] It is of course common for Western tourists to lament the increasing homogenization of the world's cultures, while contributing to that very process by their presence, and here differences of geography, economy and culture are momentarily transcended as the colonial mentality of the Welsh is made equivalent to that of the Moroccans. There is no space here to explore the problematic implications of the comparison (there's by now a considerable secondary literature on the merits or demerits of seeing Wales in colonial terms), but it is indicative of the world view that informs Jenkins's poetry in the 1970s and 1980s.[66] Both the Welsh and the Moroccans are seen to be the victims of a rapacious American consumerist culture which is itself the subject of Jenkins's powerful sequence 'Circus'.

'Circus', like 'Colonial', is based on personal experience, in this case a period Jenkins spent in the 1970s as a 'roustabout and butcher' selling

popcorn 'nuts n cotton candy' in a travelling circus.[67] The job allows him
to see capitalism at its most exploitative as he's urged to 'dry the fuckers
out' with popcorn and nuts and then 'hit em' with the drinks 'and watch
those sweet-assed dollars fly'.[68] The 'Circus' of Jenkins's poem is both a
lived reality, and a metaphor for America itself, and the influence it has on
world culture. It comes and leaves by night leaving nothing 'but a hill of
garbage'.[69] The circus animals approximate a parade of the world's
peoples, showing different characteristics and thus calling on different
tactics in order to bring them in line. The seal 'is conveniently addicted to
fish', the elephant 'is yours if broken by violence at an early age', while
those who prove resistant need to be kept apart: 'Be aloof and wear a
gun.'[70] In case we miss the point, a trainer responds to an elephant who
'wouldn't bow, wouldn't rear' by shouting

> Ya stubborn fuckin cow of a
> gook fuckin' bitch …![71]

The Vietnam War is in the background throughout, with some of the circus
workers carrying 'treasured' wallets of 'snaps':

> Gook. Gook headless.
> Gook hanging by his heels.
> Gook without body. Gook suspect
> Dragged half to death by a truck.[72]

The 'America' of 'Circus' is a nation brutalized by war. Animals are brutalized as are women. A circus man recalls sending a favourite stripper 'a
gook ear' but hears nothing back 'the whole war long'. His sense of disap-
pointment is alleviated at a strip club as 'Labia major gets down, takes his
dollar in her cunt.'[73] This takes place in a 'clean town' where billboards
celebrating 'America the Proud' co-exist with signs claiming 'I made
Linda Lovelace gag!'[74] In the world of the circus, pornography, war,
nationalism and capitalism fuse into a crude, debasing, if heady, mix. The
America depicted in the sequence has no redeeming qualities. If the US is
represented in general terms as an all-consuming capitalist circus, the few
specific voices in the poem are all complicit with the debasing system:
circus workers direct their visceral prejudices at women, animals, the
elderly and the disabled, and the voice that comes from beyond the circus
world is that of a redneck who clothes his bigotry in piousness:

> No fags, no niggers,
> no mother-fuckin reds: we gotta
> way roun here a keeping things clean,
> y unnerstan me, boy?[75]

In the face of this relentless process of dehumanization the poet tries to remind himself that

> my name
> is Jenkins, my country Wales

but these badges of identity are wholly irrelevant in a life reduced to

> flogging nuts n
> cotton candy – these are the facts.[76]

If his boss recognizes that Jenkins's accent may prove useful in selling 'sno-cones', he's ordered to tell the punters 'you're English – who the fuck's heard of Wales?'[77] In the hierarchy of global powers America is the 'greatest land in all the free world', Englishness might have its uses, but Wales is rendered meaningless and invisible.[78] This is significant, for if we are to find the resources for alternative values to those of the capitalist behemoth in Jenkins's work it is to his conception of Wales and Welsh culture that we must turn.

To contrast the depiction of American culture in 'Circus' with Jenkins's views of the Welsh language, as expressed in his poetry and prose, is to realize the extent to which his world view is conditioned by the binary terms that I discussed in the introduction to this chapter. In 'Yr Iaith' the language is vested with a set of values deriving from a rural way of life that is defined in opposition to urban Swansea where 'there were killings to be made' – a phrase that relates both to the financial motivations for moving from the country to the city and the rejection of a prior Welsh-language culture that accompanied that movement.[79] Elsewhere Jenkins describes his knowledge of Welsh – 'grotesquely ungrammatical and mismutated' – as keeping 'the door at least ajar' to a language in which

> significant values and powerful emotions seem much less inclined to raise a snigger and do a quick bunk. Fortunate indeed is the *bardd* who has at his or her disposal a language apparently uncompromised by the jingoistic slogan-ising and huge public deceit to which English, in common with French, German, Russian and certain other 'big' languages, has been forced in recent times.[80]

While reinforcing the binary terms that can be traced back to Arnold's Victorian era, where the ancient Welsh language carries an alternative set of values to those of industrial civilization, Jenkins also explicitly rejects both R. S. Thomas's form of 'finger wagging admonition ... that without the language you are not Welsh at all', and Emyr Humphreys's view 'that the sole function of the English-language writer in Wales is to protect and succour the Welsh language'.[81] He prefers to align himself with Tony Conran who argues that the English-language writers of Wales should use the Welsh language 'as a weapon', as 'the jawbone of an ass against our Englishness', but in order for it to function in this way in Jenkins's writing the language is freighted with a cultural significance that is ultimately suffocating.[82] The truth is that from Victorian paeans to the role of little Wales in the British Empire, to speeches and sermons advocating recruitment during the First World War, Welsh has been as adept a vehicle for 'jingoistic sloganising' as any other language. Jenkins may wish to reject the excesses of R. S. Thomas and Emyr Humphreys but finds himself caught in the same binary terms which set a defiled English culture and language against an 'incorruptible' Welshness.

Yet, the italicized 'apparently' that Jenkins uses in discussing the 'incorruptibility' of the Welsh language suggests that he is aware that his view of the language is a product of his own romanticization. The rigorous binary terms in which R. S. Thomas develops his cultural criticism begin to be blurred in Jenkins's writings, a blurring that can be detected in his treatments of America. If the American students in this section's opening quotation are unable to identify with the experience of Welsh peripherality, they are sensitively responsive to the significance of Tryweryn, a sensitivity which Jenkins also detects in the distress that the Americans express 'at the churches up for sale and the chapels turned into curry houses and bingo clubs' in Wales, while 'we natives' are 'zonked on a newer trinity of Shopping, Telly and the Holy Lottery, and perhaps less inclined to sorrow at the sight of a corpsed Bethel'.[83] Jenkins's America is thus not consistently the cesspit of pornography and violence depicted in 'Circus'. American popular culture in the form of 'pop music, blues, country and jazz' reappear as sources of inspiration in his work, such as when Brad Mehldau's piano is evoked as a backdrop to the hallucinatory landscape of 'Hotel Gwales'.[84] Elsewhere, it is the addictive generosity and enthusiasm of the people that strike the poet while touring the US with the Welsh-language poets Iwan Llwyd and Menna Elfyn, and the 'complex, enviable variety' of the nation.[85] The 'Welsh-made town' of Remsen, New York State, is remembered fondly in 'A Round for Remsen' as 'brotherly' and 'quietly diasporate', words that evoke an America quite different to that of 'Circus'.[86]

In thinking of Jenkins's views of America as a whole, however, it is the brutality and exploitation of 'Circus' that abide. As I was preparing to write this chapter, the connections that Jenkins sets up thematically, formally and linguistically in that poem between economic and sexual exploitation, capitalism, war and pornography were reinforced in the photos from Abu Ghraib prison in Iraq. The hunched backs of Iraqi prisoners, one piled upon another, as they are forced to masturbate, the terrified faces of men being attacked by growling dogs, the prisoner lying naked on a bloodstained floor, are all images that resonate with the language and imagery of Jenkins's sequence. For many the images seemed to reflect a basic truth about American popular culture, with Susan Sontag, shortly before her death, being typical of many in arguing that the pictures 'seem part of a larger confluence of torture and pornography... And you wonder how much of the sexual tortures inflicted on the inmates of Abu Ghraib was inspired by the vast repertory of pornographic imagery available on the internet ... What is illustrated by these photographs is as much the culture of shamelessness as the reigning admiration for unapologetic brutality'.[87] Jenkins's 'Circus', despite being written in the 1970s, seems to reflect and reinforce these insights.

And yet, the fact that 'Circus' was written before the age of the internet may cause us to register the fact that defenders of human morality have been railing against American pop culture – from jazz, film and comic books to the 45rpm single and onwards – for the best part of a century. War breeds brutality. The decimation of American Indians in the nineteenth century, the Holocaust, the gang rapes that accompanied genocide in Rwanda, and so on, took place without the assistance of internet pornography or slasher films. At its weakest, 'Circus' merely replays an all too familiar form of anti-Americanism, where the Welsh 'we' tend to be the peripheral, the dispossessed, the struggling dissenters, mavericks and critics, while the American 'they' are the power of capital, the state, the condescending, the exploiters. There may be times of political conflict where these sharp binaries can usefully be brought to bear, but their overall effect is to 'oversimplify political choices and obscure the interlocking kinds of role and agency' that political and cultural processes involve.[88] At its best, 'Circus' blurs and problematizes these binaries, for at the heart of the poem, as M. Wynn Thomas has noted, lies a tension: if contemporary American popular culture is being critiqued at the level of content, Jenkins is in fact using the 'rawness and abrasiveness' of that culture to revivify Welsh poetry.[89] The use of invective is reminiscent of a Scorsese or a Mamet, the range of voices reflects the dialogism of pop or jazz, the voyeuristic sexuality draws on the visual grammar of pornography, the shift in registers from the demotic to the meditative reflects the switching of TV channels. A great deal of the linguistic vitality and force of the sequence derives from the very popular culture whose debasing, corruptive influence is being exposed at the level of content. Jenkins's recreation of the American vernacular in the poem itself underlines the limitations of binary models when discussing the relationship between Wales and America. The US attracts and repels in about equal measure in Jenkins's poetry. Despite the all-devouring capitalist circus, there is also the generosity of 'diasporate Remsen'. Wales, in both its main languages, is joined at the hip to both.

IV

In relation to the poets discussed so far, Duncan Bush occupies a very different place in the political and cultural landscape of contemporary Welsh poetry. Nevertheless, while often self-consciously seeking to complicate and problematize outworn generalizations, he tends to base his poems and essays on the familiar binary distinction between American individualism and Welsh communalism discussed in the introduction. He is quite different to Jenkins and Dressel, however, in that he values the individualism of America more than the alleged communalism of Wales. Rather than constructing an imagined Wales as a place from which to attack the excesses of the 'hyper industrialised Anglo-American anti-culture', Bush adopts a self-consciously (if conditional) 'American' form of individualism to attack what he sees as the excessively restrictive, conformist and debilitatingly communitarian culture of his native land.[90] Like Minhinnick and Dressel (and many others), Bush defines his position in relation to R. S. Thomas:

> The word ['community'] also gets cited in the context of 'spokesman for, conscience of, a community', etc. – phrases sometimes used of the bard-like role adopted by a poet like R. S. Thomas (abbreviated with coy familiarity to 'R.S.' by his devotees). This is of course an accreditation out of all proportion to the importance of the poet's work; and out of touch with reality in the sense of any actual community or constituency for his views on politics or language. The only people he speaks for are xenophobes and extremists. And his actual cultural position is, apparently, one of faintly misanthropic isolation. This might seem a natural, even admirable, position for the writer in our society – but the trouble is that this poet has listened to sycophants and other admirers, and is himself persuaded he's the mouthpiece for a nation. Once this happens, the transition from poet to demagogue is under way.[91]

Against this 'kind of cultural-borderline-antagonism or siege-mentality which many of us don't even recognise as existing', Bush consistently

posits an individualism which he detects in favourite writers such as André
Gide and Amy Clampitt, and which he traces in his revealing prose memoir
'Lash Larue and the River of Adventure' to a fascination with America
during his childhood in Cardiff.[92] Bush notes that 'Anti-British feeling' in
the late 1940s was a 'natural result of six years of war on a working-class
population exhausted from the experience'.[93] This Anti-Britishness did not
result in the embrace of Welshness, however, for questions of national or
tribal affiliation 'were of small account'.[94] 'Intellectual emancipation and
national sentiment' were seen, rather, to be issues of an 'imaginative
choice' or 'elective allegiance', embodied in an idea of America.[95] While
Bush can, retrospectively, see how his childhood view of America was
gleaned from comics and movies and was based on 'ignorance and several
thousand miles', the world's dominant power is seen by the child in 1950s
Cardiff as a 'technological and ludic wonderland', 'a country where
oranges grew on trees' and, crucially, a place that offers 'the famous possibility of becoming what – and who – you choose to be'.[96] While Bush
recognizes that the America of his childhood imagination is a myth based
on ignorance – 'in 1953, when they were finally executed, I'd never heard
of the Rosenbergs' – it is an enabling myth, and continues to offer a significant point of orientation for the poet's later writings where he is often still
'looking for America'.[97]

Thus, against the alleged Welsh obsession with 'community', America
stands for individualistic self-expression. Bush is fully aware that
'individualism creates its own problems in ethics', and (as we shall see),
like many American writers, he often seeks to explore the disjuncture
between national ideals and social realities.[98] But the individual, as
opposed to community, is consistently valued in his work and is reflected
in his own wish to stand outside the 'group'. 'I actually think that the
noblest role for a writer is that of the eternal renegade or maverick: that
annoying, irritating, frequently-resented presence – the complete antithesis
of the 'group mentality'.'[99] Bush consistently represents himself as
standing outside the group mentality that he associates with nationalistically
minded writers. He describes his work as seeking to 'fly by those ranged
nets of nostalgia and local colourism, not to mention other forms of Celtic
Moonshine', and directs his most critical remarks at a 'Welsh literary
culture' which 'is still in a state of provincialism and immaturity'.[100]
Dismissive comments about the Welsh language have of course always
been available on tap in many of our nation's pubs, but it is disappointing
to find a writer of Bush's sensitivity forcing his readers into a corner with
his finger-jabbing pronouncements on the alleged narrow-minded

provincialism of modern Wales. While he does not speak Welsh he nevertheless knows that the programmes on the Welsh-language channel S4C are 'bad television' for 'it's what you can expect from any form of cultural protectionism', and believes that to 'celebrate [the English language] without guilt' is to 'incense a number of people in Wales, but that's already reason enough to say it'.[101] There's little evidence that his celebration of English actually 'incensed' anyone. In fact, many of Wales's anglophone writers have celebrated their use of the English language, and several authors write 'without guilt' in both English and Welsh. It is of course common for writers to depict themselves as 'marginal' or 'maverick' figures within their respective national cultures, and Bush's self-dramatizing self-description of himself as a 'renegade' has atrophied into a set of predictable responses.[102] Bush emphasizes the fact that he resists the seductiveness and simple answers offered by 'narrow, pugnacious, forms of nationalism', but succumbs to an equally insidious kind of seduction, described by Stefan Collini in a different context as 'the glamour of dissent'.[103]

It is perhaps significant that Bush's views on contemporary Welsh culture are rarely reflected in his subtle and probing poetry. If his reiterated individualism has led to a regrettable unwillingness to understand the positions adopted by those who, by historical necessity, have had to articulate their cultural and political desires in communal terms, that individualism also informs those aspects of his work that are most distinctive and valuable. It leads to a desire to inhabit the minds and thoughts of the characters who speak in his poetry, leading to an absence of that personal or autobiographical voice that is consistently (either explicitly or implicitly) present in the works of Dressel and Jenkins. 'I prefer to hide in my poems rather than display myself', states Bush, 'there are so many more interesting topics than the ninth letter of the alphabet'.[104] These thoughts were expressed before the appearance of the overtly autobiographical collection *Midway*, but draw attention to a significant characteristic of Bush's writings. It may seem paradoxical for an individualist poet to seek to omit his own voice, but it reflects Bush's desire to register the particular individuality of the personae constructed in his poetry. This characteristic of his work can be traced to his American influences:

> American writing is itself often based on the demotic much more than British literary English is – this is the source of the strength and vitality of a lot of modern American poetry as well as prose. And for me the single most influential work in American literature is probably Huckleberry Finn, which liberated

the American voice – the ordinary, uneducated, demotic voice – definitively from English and European literary tradition. Also, narratively, the teller was himself henceforth responsible for all the implications of the tale – the novelist became invisible – which was also very important. This led to Faulkner's great multi-narrational novels, for example – or to a wiseacre character such as V. K. Ratliffe. It also led to those everyday, unconscious oral poets Studs Terkel taped. It was part of the great liberal tradition.[105]

This authorial invisibility, deriving from American influences, leads to a necessary questioning of stereotypes and generalizations in Bush's poetry. While the Americans we encounter in Jenkins's 'Circus' tend to be brutalized Vietnam veterans and racist rednecks, the 'hillbillies' Bush encounters in Arkansas, despite sharing similar names and driving similar vehicles, resist homogenization. They are individuals that challenge the lazy stereotypes:

> Even the professors down here
> Drive pickups to class,
> Have names like Mary Sue or Billy Bob.
> Clinton voters, they're no rednecks.[106]

The related respect for individuality and suppression of the autobiographical 'I' fuse powerfully in the sequence 'Are There Still Wolves in Pennsylvania?'. Like Dressel's *The Road to Shiloh* and Jenkins's 'Circus', 'Are There Still Wolves in Pennsylvania?' originated in a meditation on the legacies of the Vietnam War. Bush traces the gestation of his poem to his encounters with W. D. Ehrhart, John Del Vecchia and John Pratt – American writers who are also Vietnam veterans – at a conference in Swansea, followed a year later by a period teaching at Penn State University.[107] If the poem 'began in Wales' and draws on personal experience, the poetic 'I' is absent, as are any signs of Welshness, with the poet adopting the voices of a Vietnam veteran and his wife. Both characters speak in a similar American vernacular which continually seems to break through the four-line stanzas into which their thoughts are arranged. Wesley speaks first, fingering the scar on his left shoulder which is what remains of the 'frag-blast' which led to his 'planeride home'.[108] He is the centre of the poem, meditating on his own experiences, while his wife watches him, concerned about his behaviour while also trying to conceal her affair with another man. We follow Wesley on a hunting trip where his thoughts take him back to his pre-war life and his graduation, where he was 'weird and lost' enough to call himself 'G. I. Bill' while unsuccessfully chatting up a 'young Physics major'.[109] Moving back to the present

we witness him faking illness to leave work early in order to catch his wife
making love in a truck, and trace his thought process as fantasies of a
murderous revenge turn to despairing thoughts of suicide.

> The shotgun's on the back seat.
> When I loaded the shells
> I thought of
> him putting it in.
> One time. And then
> again … And I thought,
> now there's one for each
> of them or both
> at once, out here in the wood,
> taking it into my mouth.
> Then them in the trailer scared,
> listening for a second shot,
> and me palate, brains, the whole
> top of my head
> blown clear at last,
> clear right up
> through the trees,
> a roar I didn't even
> hear.[110]

Sexuality, power, love and violence are the key components of Wesley's
psychology, and the final two sections seek to reveal the ways in which his
essential humanity has been warped by life experiences. The penultimate
section centres on the military values that he was forced to adopt, and
which transformed his proudly owned 'Zippo', made in 'Bradford,
Pennsylvania', into a weapon:

> Like the seargent said:
> *Never leave*
> *A doorway that ain't burning …*
> We was all Local Boys –
> but not from any ville round there.
> My lighter was a Zippo made
> in Bradford Pennsylvania,
> came guaranteed against
> repair for life.
> It kept right through
> my eleven months
> the closing snap
> a good knife
> and used up more

> gas than a jeep.
> […]
> Mine had my initials
> drill-etched on it.
> (*I want to hear*
> *it crackle,*
> *the lieutenant said.*
> *The whole damn place.*)[111]

While the guaranteed lighter, made in Pennsylvania and etched with the soldier's initials, represents a link with home and his pre-war identity, there is no simple way to 'repair', or to guarantee recovery from, the damage wrought by Wesley's experiences in Vietnam. The final section dramatizes the effect of militaristic brutality on the individual solider in battle, and explains the source of the trauma that Wesley's thoughts and language have been circling around throughout the poem. Having shot at escaping Vietnamese villagers, Wesley discovers upon inspection that he's killed a 16-year-old girl. 'Hell of a shot' says a fellow soldier who has been 'brought up on / rifles in the woods', and who goes on to suggest:

> *Why don't you*
> *Fuck her?*
> *She's still warm …*[112]

Wesley recoils from this brutalized, misogynistic voice to a compensatory dreamscape where his bullet has missed its target, the body in the field is that of an old woman who is still alive and who reaches up towards him 'and says / *I'm yours*'. This dramatic confluence of maternal redemption, and disturbing sexuality, forces Wesley back from the dream to his contemporary traumatized reality where he states defensively,

> I don't need no Dr Freud or
> fucking V.A. shrink to
> work this out.[113]

Bush's 'Are There Wolves' is a notable late meditation on the legacies of the Vietnam War. It has a strong narrative development which has required this level of reconstruction to give a sense of the sequence's development. The distinctiveness of Bush's poem may be brought into focus by contrasting it with Jenkins's 'Circus'. For both poets, Vietnam casts its shadow over the social and personal dimensions of a post-war American culture in which the crass masculinism, misogyny and degradation of a soldier's life are the crucial viewfinders for focusing on the American national psyche. Both poets seek to expose the ways in which people are reduced to animals, for if America is a circus for Jenkins, it approximates a hunt for Bush. The key difference is one of perspective. The veterans running the 'Circus' are observed from a position of a critical, self-consciously, Welsh detachment in Nigel Jenkins's poem, as they share 'their treasured wallet of snaps' of 'Gook hanging by his heels./ Gook without body.'[114] Bush eschews detachment, seeks invisibility and enters the mind of the veteran himself. Wales, for Jenkins, is a victim of the crass American culture depicted in his poem, and the Welsh are another marginalized people powerless in the face of an all-consuming Anglo-Americanism. Whereas the meaning of what it means to be Welsh is itself a subject of Jenkins's 'Circus', Wales is wholly absent in Bush's sequence. In entering the minds of his American personae, and in making his own self invisible, Bush makes the reader of his poetry complicit with the thoughts being expressed. If Bush recalls feeling American in post-war Cardiff, the disturbing results of that identification are explored in the post-Vietnam landscape of 'Are There Still Wolves in Pennsylvania?'. The Welsh poet who wears the American mask is in some ways complicit in the acts being described. The poem exposes the fact that it is easier, due to historical connections and cultural influence, for a Welshman to narrate the experience of Vietnam from an American rather than Vietnamese perspective (and the choice of Pennsylvania, the state most associated with Welsh immigration, may be significant in this respect). There is no alternative ground – whether rooted in a minority language or in a sense of peripherality – on which the poet can stand. If Bush identifies with the America of the 'good war' against fascism, the America that seemed to reflect his own multi-ethnic, anti-nationalist, individualism in Cardiff, he is no romanticizer of American realities. 'Are There Still Wolves in Pennsylvania?' forces us, implicitly, to contemplate the dark underbelly of the 'American Wales' described with some affection in *Midway*. Bush's writings reveal the sobering truth that to identify with the America dream is also to take some responsibility for the nightmare.

V

'America' stands as an ambivalent symbol in contemporary Welsh poetry. The nation that offers the poet the freedom to cultivate an alternative self is also the nation that napalmed Vietnam. Kerouac's land of possibilities and of the open road co-exists with the bland consumerism of Bill Bryson. As I noted earlier, critics of what Minhinnick describes as the 'democratization of the arts' have always complained about 'Americanization', as the capitalist-consumerist giant continued to consume new markets. But 'Americanization' can also be seen to promote a healthy diminished deference towards London and Europe as the traditional centres of 'Culture'. The continual fascination with America in contemporary Welsh writing has occurred at a time of growing national and cultural self-assertion, which itself reflects a loss of deference to the long internalized values of Britishness. What is incarcerating from one perspective may be liberating from another.

The power and significance of the poetry discussed in this chapter deserves better than a bland conclusion which notes that in writing about America, Welsh writers are ultimately writing about themselves – although this is no doubt the case. The cultural stakes are somewhat higher than that, at a time when, in the wake of 9/11, the wars in Afghanistan and Iraq have ignited a wave of anti-Americanism through much of Europe. 'Dialogue', 'correspondence' and 'exchange', while useful terms in the rarefied world of comparative literary studies, seem insufficient in relation to the engagement with the United States in the works of Dressel, Jenkins and Bush. Can the specific commentaries of this chapter lead to any useful general points in conclusion? First, what I hope to have suggested here is that it is all too easy to critique the ugly aspects of modernity while ignoring the unpalatable aspects of pre-modernity, as it is, conversely, to attack the alleged 'provincialism' or 'backwardness' of minority cultures without registering the power of the forces threatening their very existence. We should expect more from our poets than the romanticization of marginalized peoples or 'lost causes' on the one hand, or the unquestioning reflection of majoritarian cultural prejudices on the other. Secondly, it would seem that for these Welsh anglophone poets, an engagement with American culture has been, simultaneously, linguistically liberating and thematically traumatic.

Singing Unchained: Language, Nation and Multiculturalism

I

The French Marxist philosopher Étienne Balibar usefully identifies 'two great competing routes' to the production of ethnic difference: language and race. While both routes may at times be articulated simultaneously – such as when an individual's 'foreign' accent or language marks him or her as belonging to a specific hereditary group or 'race' – for analytical purposes Balibar insists that the two routes must be separated, for their cultural and political effects are distinct. Balibar notes that while the language community seems the 'more abstract notion', in reality 'it is the more concrete since it connects individuals up with an origin which ... has as its content the common act of their own exchanges'.[1] The linguistic community thus 'possesses a strange plasticity: it immediately naturalizes new acquisitions'.[2] If the linguistic community is inherently open (since anyone can learn a language), the racial community is inherently closed (since no one can change their ancestors). This distinction is crucial for understanding Welsh culture, and for envisaging a multicultural future that is not homogeneously anglophone on the one hand, nor dangerously discriminatory on the other.

II

Balibar's analysis sheds light on one of the problems in contemporary English-language literature and criticism in Wales, for Welsh anglophone critics often equate linguistic and racial differences. This is partly a result of the fact that language difference rarely figures in the cultural debates of the Anglo-American academy, and if it features at all it is usually equated with 'race'. This pattern is replicated in Wales where, for example, it is the equation of 'language' with 'race' that allows Ian Gregson and Chris Wigginton to offer misleading accounts of Raymond Williams's distinction between 'two distinct models of cultural and national identification still operating in Wales'.[3] Raymond Williams begins the article being critiqued, a review essay of works by the novelist Emyr Humphreys and historian Dai Smith, as follows:

> Two truths are told, as alternative prologues to the action of modern Wales. The first draws on the continuity of Welsh language and literature: from the sixth century, it is said, and thus perhaps the oldest surviving poetic tradition in Europe. The second draws on the turbulent experience of industrial South Wales, over the last two centuries, and its powerful political and communal formations.[4]

Chris Wigginton discusses the passage in the following terms:

> According to Williams, the first version venerates origin and essence in its prescription of an authentic Welshness, and tends to operate in terms of closure and restriction, as it predicates identity as a natural given, rather than a cultural construct. The other version emerges from south Wales, and imagines identity less definitely, consequently accommodating a more fluid definition of nationality.[5]

The problem in this analysis is that Raymond Williams makes it clear that he sees both 'truths' as 'cultural constructs'. He expresses his awareness of 'the common elements of authenticity in each apparently alternative case', and, while drawing attention to limitations and blindnesses in each account, concludes that the Welsh response to the 'dissolution of community and identity' has been to attempt to 'remake communities and identities which will hold'.[6] Emyr Humphreys detects the resources for this remaking 'in a cultural tradition' while Dai Smith 'finds them in the communal struggles and loyalties of a Welsh industrial proletariat'.[7] Wigginton is thus incorrect in suggesting that we are dealing here with a 'naturally given' sense of identity pitted against a 'more fluid definition': both 'truths' are culturally contingent and open to revision and redefinition. The first truth is not rooted in 'race', but in 'language and literature'. Ian Gregson quotes Wigginton's analysis approvingly in his analysis of *The New Poetry in Wales*, and proceeds to conflate 'language' with 'race' throughout his study. He reads Robert Minhinnick's description of attempting to speak Welsh in Beddgelert in terms of a 'racial alter ego', for example, and reads Gwyneth Lewis's account of language difference in relation to Toni Morrison's account of racial difference.[8] This equation of language with race is not limited to literary criticism and has been a characteristic of British political discourse on the Welsh language for more than a century. Simon Brooks and Patrick McGuiness, for example, documented the ways in which those embracing a dominant, 'common sense', liberal individualism dismissed those fighting for the communal rights of Welsh speakers as 'racist nationalists'.[9]

But the conflation of language and race is not limited to those opposed to a perceived 'linguistic culturalism'. Even writers sympathetic to linguistic difference and cultural pluralism tend, at times, to represent the linguistic community as a closed community and Welsh-language culture as impenetrable and not open to others. Far from being a community that Balibar identifies as possessing 'a strange plasticity' and which 'naturalizes new acquisitions', the Welsh-language world is often presented as a closed culture, inaccessible to others. Language in these instances approximates 'race', and this unfortunate view of language in 'racial' terms is particularly apparent in Welsh writing in English. Some examples might suffice to illustrate this point. Consider, for example, R. S. Thomas's poem 'Welcome':

> You can come in.
> You can come a long way;
> We can't stop you.
> You can come up the roads
> Or by railway;
> You can land from the air.
> You can walk this country
> From end to end;
> But you won't be inside;
> You must stop at the bar,
> The old bar of speech.[10]

Language functions here as a 'bar' to entry, an impermeable borderline between external and internal realms. You're welcome to Wales, but you'll see nothing of Cymru. Language is the key to an inner sanctum that lies beyond the tourist's gaze, a barrier to the incomer's integration. Though the poem's narrator is unable to stem the tide of incomers, he can compensate for that by suggesting that there's a unique experience that lies beyond the visitor's comprehension, and beyond the poem's implied anglophone reader. A fully historicized account of the poem would locate it within the cultural debates of the 1960s, the drowning of Tryweryn, the rise of Cymdeithas yr Iaith and so on.[11] In this respect the poem may be read as a rhetorical defensive strategy, an act of 'strategic essentialism', challenging the monolingual complacency of the English tourist and evoking a sense of bravado in the face of potential cultural death.[12] The structure of feeling evinced here, where the language is a bar to entry, is reflected in a significant body of post-war Welsh poetry, however, and transcends the particular moment of Thomas's composition.

Gillian Clarke's 'The Water Diviner', for example, also presents Welsh-language culture as a separate domain, one in this instance that cannot be fully accessed by the poem's narrator.[13] Here, the forgotten Welsh language lies buried deep in the earth and it takes the skill of the water-diviner to bring it to the surface.

> His fingers tell water like prayer.
> He hears its voice in the silence
> through fifty feet of rock
> on an afternoon dumb with drought.
> ...
> we dip our hose
> deep into the dark, sucking its dryness,
> till suddenly the water answers,
> not the little sound we know,
> but a thorough bass too deep
> for the naked ear, shouts through the hose
> a word we could not say, or spell, or remember,
> something like 'dŵr ... dŵr'[14]

By leaving the last words untranslated, the poet creates a work that enacts its own meaning for the non-Welsh-speaking reader. The diviner seems literally to bring the feminized landscape to life, allowing it, via the hose, to give expression to its repressed Welshness. Language is connected to land which is linked metaphorically to the female body.

These connections are evoked in more complex ways in Christine Evans's poem 'Second Language' which shares water imagery with Clarke's poem, but is about the experience of teaching English to schoolchildren whose first language is Welsh.

> I watch their faces rise to meet me
> from the green depths of a culture
> older than I can fathom. They glide
> as if weighted by dreams or water
> through my lessons, taking notes ...
> Five girls and a boy riding a name out of myth
> whose language fills the mouth like fruit
> who have grown in the delicate light
> of an old walled garden that was once the world.[15]

The title is teasingly ambiguous as the poem's narrator encounters the reality of a linguistic culture other than her own, while introducing English to her Welsh-speaking students. Welsh-language culture is a walled, verdant, garden in this poem. It is an enclosed, pastoral space that, as the symbols pile up, exists beneath the surface, immersed under water but now threatened by another, more powerful, language and culture. In penetrating the virginal, Edenic, 'walled garden' of the Welsh-language culture, English functions as a source of emancipation and a threat. This ambiguity is embodied within the tense multiple negatives of the poem's closing lines:

> In their calm faces I can find no clues
> that they are still at ease in their own skins
> that dredging for this voice has drowned no other
> and my teaching has not made them strangers.[16]

It seems that the teaching of a second language has resulted in feelings of guilt, but as the troubled teacher looks for 'clues' as to the effects of her 'dredging' she can find none and is left to meditate self-reflexively on the positive and negative implications of her vocation. Is she violating a cultural space by imposing a dominating anglophone culture on her students, or is she emancipating her class by introducing another world view?

What I wish to emphasize here is that, despite their different trajectories and approaches, these poems represent Welsh-language culture as lying beyond the reach of the English-language text, beyond the comprehension of the poem's narrator in the case of 'The Water Diviner' and 'Second Language', and beyond the understanding of the non-Welsh speaker in each case. These poems by Thomas, Clarke and Evans pose a challenge to the widespread belief that literature is a mode of accessing other cultures, that reading and writing are, in Carlos Fuentes's words, 'activities aimed at introducing civilizations to each other'.[17] These poems challenge the assumption that educated anglophone readers should be entitled to understand and to know that which they are reading. The critic Dale Peterson argues that there can be 'no persuasive representation of a distinctive "native" mode of expressivity without creative experiments that replicate an unbridgeable gap – those linguistic lacunae and cognitive lapses that emanate from exchanges between literate outsiders and indigenous insiders'.[18] Peterson is asking us to register the fact that some texts will deliberately resist interpretation, and urges us to be aware of the techniques adopted by non-English-speaking, and other 'ethnically marked', writers to achieve this aim. Such deliberately alienating literary works will position the reader as an outsider and keep her there. They will seek to reveal the existence of an inner culture, an alternative cultural realm, but will try to preserve that culture's sense of difference and otherness.[19] Against the dominant culture's universalist desire to know and to colonize the other, R. S. Thomas, Gillian Clarke and Christine Evans seek to evoke, and to respect, the existence of an inaccessible, alternative, inner realm of experience. They ask us to notice the cultural signs that affirm a respectful distance as a condition of both aesthetic effect and of political justice.

This seems admirable. The anglophone writer is showing an awareness of, and a respect for, the Welsh language and its culture within his or her work. But, if the notion of an internal language or culture is enabling at an aesthetic level, such a conception of minority languages is potentially disastrous for those of us who wish a viable future for the Welsh language. Once the Welsh language is portrayed as a 'walled garden', or as a suppressed water source, or as a 'barrier' to entry, then it is difficult to conceive that the language and its culture might be developing entities. Indeed, Christine Evans's depiction of the 'green depths' of an Edenic culture seems to draw on an Arnoldian conception of the 'natural magic' and feminine purity of Celtic cultures discussed elsewhere in this book. This kind of imagery contributes to a structure of thought that leads to the equation of language and race. To conceptualize linguistic difference in this way ultimately denies the possible existence of a multicultural society expressing itself through the medium of Welsh. Language is perceived as a 'closed' system. Once a language dies it can move from being a mode of communication to becoming a symbolic marker of ethnicity. Symbolic language functions like race – it is a practice or characteristic of past generations which cannot be opened up to new members in the present. A living language, however, in Balibar's terms, 'immediately naturalizes new acquisitions'. This is not to say that racism doesn't exist in minority-language communities: it does, and must be resisted. But the fact remains that the implications for multicultural tolerance are very different for forms of identity rooted in language, and those rooted in race. A living linguistic community is inevitably an evolving entity that is open to anyone who learns to speak its language.

A tolerant Welshness thus requires the preservation of the Welsh language as a mode of communication. A genuine multiculturalism in the contemporary nations of the British Isles must register the reality of multilingualism. Anglophone multiculturalism is, for example, different from Welsh '*aml-ddiwyllianaeth*', a point made forcefully by Ned Thomas:

> What is often meant within English-language discourse in Britain is tolerance and even encouragement of a number of background cultures and languages within a society which has English as the foreground language – or to be plain, the dominant language. Many speakers of immigrant languages are happy to accept such a place for themselves, always providing that sufficient resources are made available to support their background culture and that it is respected. Welsh speakers on the other hand, like other European territorial minorities, claim a historic space in which their culture too can be a foreground culture, allowing people of different backgrounds to participate. This yields a more European view of Britain, like continental Europe, as a mosaic rather than a melting pot, and requires a rather different account of multiculturalism.[20]

The monolingual, anglophone, form of multiculturalism informing much cultural debate in Britain today is rooted in the belief that the English language is the only legitimate bearer of all civic-democratic nationality, and that those lying beyond its generously catholic embrace are little better than atavistic racists. But the Welsh-language world cannot be a closed world if it is to survive. Once Welsh-language culture is conceived of in racial terms, as a closed system, and as a constraint on communication between peoples, it becomes easy to wish that it should disappear.

III

To insist that the Welsh language can itself be the crucible for multicultural citizenship is crucial for its vitality and development, but the reach of Welsh-language culture is currently limited in a Wales where around 20 per cent of the population speak the Celtic language. Welsh-language culture is not then commensurate with Welsh culture, and strategies for fostering a diverse and open Welsh-language culture will have limited relevance to areas where it is rarely spoken. The creation of Welsh political institutions have foregrounded this fact, for whereas previous generations of language activists might have claimed that their struggle was for 'Wales' and for 'Welshness' against a hostile British state, they increasingly find today that their actions are targeted at Welsh-based institutions and representatives. One legitimate response to this situation is to develop different policies for the differing linguistic profiles of geographical areas.[21] Putting the problems of creating such geographical boundaries to one side, the danger of this approach at a cultural level is that the Welsh language is seen as wholly irrelevant to a large percentage of the Welsh population, and those communities for whom Welsh is an everyday language begin to view themselves in increasingly exceptionalist terms with their culture seen to be a 'retreat', a 'redoubt', and their language harbouring a 'spiritual inheritance'.[22] The possibility of a bilingual culture, created and owned in common by the citizens of Wales, breaks down in this scenario into Welsh-language communities forced, due to the pressures upon them, to conceive of themselves in increasingly defensive and essentialized terms on the one hand, and an assimilationist dominant anglophone culture, either indifferent or hostile to linguistic difference, on the other. This is, perhaps, the likeliest future. But there are alternatives.

To think of Welsh culture as thoroughly bilingual would still require the 'radical psycho-cultural restructuring of the country' that M. Wynn Thomas called for in 1999, but the years since political devolution have witnessed signs of significant cultural shifts in this direction.[23] In the last twenty years, some Welsh writers in English have proceeded to think beyond binary conceptualizations of language difference towards other, possibly emergent, structures of feeling. Geraint Evans has recently traced an increasing sense among Welsh writers of both main languages that 'it is not multilingualism that kills languages' but 'the abandonment of one monolingual culture for another', and argues that a 'growing linguistic self-confidence' among writers is manifested in the fact that the language of literary composition in Wales 'can be as plural as identity itself'.[24] Evans traces the source of this growing hybridity to R. S. Thomas, a deliberately counter-intuitive move given the stridency of Thomas's opinions and overt linguistic nationalism. While, in his public statements, R. S. Thomas claimed that Cymru and Wales were incompatible entities, the practice of his poetic and prose writings was to undermine the stark binary terms of his thought. Indeed part of the cultural prestige accorded to R. S. Thomas was a result of the fact that he offered a model for the 'new generation of Welsh writers who had been raised with bilingual education and Welsh broadcasting and for whom the codes of language use were no

longer defined in the old ways'.[25] Evans suggests that different parts of R.
S. Thomas's output in different languages 'increasingly made a coherent
whole, one of which was not fully understandable without the other'.[26] In
particular, from the early 1970s in prose works like 'Y Llwybrau Gynt' and
'Abercuawg', Thomas was writing for a bilingual audience whose
'knowledge of his bi-lingual work informs a reading of his English
poetry'.[27] The potential audience being interpellated, or imagined into
being as ideal readers, in Thomas's work was increasingly a bilingual
audience.[28] In writing a series of interconnected texts in two languages
Thomas creates a situation in which 'a knowledge of one becomes a
precondition for understanding the other, so that it is only, in some ways,
the readers of the Welsh texts whose readings of the English poems are
fully informed'.[29] Evans thus regards Thomas as the 'first truly national
literary figure in post-industrial Wales, whose work crosses the border
between Welsh and English'.[30]

If R. S. Thomas's central role within Welsh literary culture was partly a
result of the rise of a readership that increasingly defined itself in bilingual
terms, there are other notable examples of linguistic border crossing. Emyr
Humphreys, as M. Wynn Thomas has argued, had initiated a similar
strategy in his own work with his Welsh novel *Y Tri Llais* and in Welsh-
language interviews in which he offered significant commentaries on his
much more substantial English-language oeuvre.[31] The rise of a bilingual
audience, partly called into being by writers such as Humphreys and
Thomas, may explain the attention given in recent years to Margiad
Evans's novel of 1932 *Country Dance*. Re-published as one of the first five
texts of the Welsh Assembly Government funded Library of Wales series
in 2005, *Country Dance* can be read as a meditation on the effects of
linguistic difference, and the aesthetic possibilities of bilingualism. The
folk song which forms the novel's epigraph, in the original Welsh followed
by an English translation, tells the reader that:

'Ti gei glywed os gwrandewi / Sŵn y galon fach yn torri'
[Thou shalt hear if thou listen / The sound of the little heart breaking][32]

This line resonates with the reference to 'native ears attuned to hear' in the
novel's penultimate sentence, and also alerts us to the bilingualism of the
world that we are about to enter. In the nineteenth-century border landscape of *Country Dance*, characterized by a persistent ethnic struggle
between the Welsh and the English, the narrator Ann Goodman is familiar
with the dominant and multiple subdominant discourses of the novel's
ethnically divided and gendered society. This burden and gift of speaking

in tongues is represented most clearly in a celebrated scene depicting the death of Ann's mother.

> I take my father his tea in the bottom meadow, where he is loading hay with the rest: when I come back there is my mother on the floor beside her bed, gasping for breath.
> 'What is it? What have you' I cry, running to her.
> 'My heart!' she answers.
> I lift her up in my arms and lay her on the bed. Her face is grey like ashes and damp with sweat; every minute it seems to me that she must die under my hands.
> 'Mae arnaf eisiau gweld John,' she gasps. 'I want to see John'. She has fallen into her own tongue, that she has not spoken since she was married.
> There is no time lose: from the window I can see my father down in the meadow, working by the gate. I lean out with my fingers to my mouth and give the shepherd's whistle; he looks up.
> 'Father!'
> He throws down his fork. I wait but a moment to see him start on the way before going back to my mother, who is groaning. [...]
> [W]hen he comes to her bed and tries to speak to her, she does not seem to know he is there.
> 'What is she saying? What does she want?'
> 'She is asking for you, Father.'
> 'Myfanwy, Myfanwy, I am here. Speak to her, Ann! Can't you? Speak her own tongue!'
> 'Father is here,' I tells her.
> She grasps my wrists.
> 'Oh, be quick, Ann dear, be quick, I am dying'.
> 'He is here,' I cry over and over.
> At last I tells my father to say:
> 'Rwaf [sic] yma wrth eich ymyl'.
> He tries, word for word, after me, and she smiles as best she can ...
> There is nothing we can do to hinder her, but she is still alive when the doctor comes into the room. He looks at her once, and a minute after we see that she is dead. Without a word or another glance my father pulls the curtains and goes away downstairs.[33]

Marriage has literally meant the silencing of one dimension of the mother's identity in a striking equation of linguistic and gender suppression. The mother's last gesture is to smile 'as best she can' (whether ruefully or with pleasure is not clear) at the father's belated attempt at speaking her own language. I have discussed this passage in detail elsewhere, as has Kirsti Bohata, but what I wish to emphasize here is the daughter's role as a cultural mediator.[34] Ann Goodman can speak and understand the Welsh

that her mother 'has not spoken since she was married', and can thus translate her dying mother's words to her monolingual English father. It is this
that makes the scene particularly resonant today, for a generation of
contemporary female writers are in the process of carving out a bilingual
creative space within Welsh literature.

The aesthetic manifestation of bilingualism takes different forms in the
works of Menna Elfyn and Gwyneth Lewis, for the former writes in Welsh
but publishes volumes with parallel-facing English translations, while the
latter writes original poetry in both languages. Both writers mediate
between, and meditate upon, the linguistic boundaries that have constructed
Welshness in the twentieth century, while simultaneously voicing well-
founded anxieties about the possible implications of their creative practice.
While there are some notable precedents to the practice of publishing
bilingual editions of poetry (Euros Bowen's *Poems* (1974), Gwyn
Thomas's *Living a Life* (1982) and R. Gerallt Jones's edited anthology
Poetry of Wales 1930–1970), Menna Elfyn's lauded collections proved
controversial as she had been a prominent language activist who had spent
time in prison.[35] In dedicating the first of these, *Eucalyptus* (1995), 'to the
new Welsh speakers', Elfyn indicated a desire to reach outwards towards
the increasingly significant numbers of monoglot English speakers who, in
the last two decades of the twentieth century, had moved to the mid Wales
where she resided.[36] M. Wynn Thomas offers a shrewd analysis of the
politics informing Elfyn's cultural strategy:

> she has realized that by identifying herself, through translation, with a
> women's movement that has developed a powerful international and interna-
> tionalist discourse, she is able both to overcome prejudices about the supposed
> 'narrowness' and 'backwardness' of Welsh-language culture, and to render
> that culture potently current.[37]

Yet, that internationalism could only be assessed by a wider audience due
to the English translations, and several Welsh-language critics expressed
their misgivings at the fact that Elfyn's increasingly 'European' standing
would inevitably be determined by analyses of her works in translation.[38]

Her poems indicate that Elfyn is fully cognisant of this danger. 'Rice
Papers', for example, is a poem that derives directly from the poet's
'international standing' and her desire to explore new publics for her work.
Dedicated 'I'm cyfieithydd Trinh yn Hanoi', to 'Trinh, my interpreter in
Hanoi', the poem recalls a meal at an expensive restaurant that the poet
shared with her translator.

> Hi oedd fy ngwestai. Hi fy nhafod.
> Hi yn ganghellor, hefyd fy morwyn.
> 'Mae'n rhy ddrud i mi fynd i fwytai
> heblaw gyda foreigner yn talu.'

> She was my host, my voice
> my chancellor, my maid.
> 'Too expensive to eat in places like this
> except with a foreigner paying.[39]

Trinh has never been to such an establishment, and is there because of the funds available to the Welsh poet. The poem responds to Vietnam's contemporary poverty and its violent past, and closes with the poet noting that 'I dined on the sight of her feasting for me'. While the closing evokes Elfyn's pleasure in the fact that her presence enables her translator to enjoy a rare feast, the final line may also be read as a meditation on translation itself. The act of translating allows the English language to feed on the other languages which it mediates (Welsh and Vietnamese in this instance). The poem seems to be asking, self-reflexively, whether the English translation of a Welsh-language work allows a new audience to feed on the literature. Does English feed on Welsh on our behalf, thus allowing Welsh culture to be appreciated by new international audiences? Or does the feeding metaphor allude to a dominant language's ability to devour minority languages leaving a carcass in its wake? The implications of these questions are of course intensified by an awareness that English was the language of the American culture that waged war on Vietnam for more than a decade, causing the rice shortages to which Trinh refers. In 'Rice Papers', Elfyn is in the economically dominant position, able to enjoy the fruits of her generosity, able to assuage her Western guilt, but also uneasily reversing the relationship between 'visitor' and 'host'. She is reliant on the international poetry circuit for this temporary wealth, and knows that it has been gained through the translations of her writings. Lines of economic inequality cross uneasily with lines of linguistic and cultural inequality in a poem that can be read as an extended meditation on metaphors of poverty, power and translation.

If Elfyn characteristically places the translator's act of feasting on a minority language within a specific cultural and political context, the oscillation between the destructive and enriching opportunities offered by the movement between languages takes on a profoundly personal, and intensely psychological, form in the works of Gwyneth Lewis. As in Christine Evans's 'Second Language', the acquiring of languages is often linked to the process of sexual maturity in Lewis's writings. But unlike

Evans, Lewis's focus in the poem 'Mother Tongue' is not on the guilty teacher but on the seemingly autobiographically based school pupil slowly facing the complexities of a bilingual existence where each language has its own web of cultural, historical and familial connections. The narrator confesses to having 'started to translate in seventy-three / in the schoolyard'.

> For a bit of fun
> to begin with – the occasional 'fuck'
> for the bite of another language's smoke
> at the back of my throat ...[40]

The sequence *Keeping Mum*, from which this poem is taken, is structured as a psychoanalytic detective story, with the poet seeking to identify who killed the Welsh language (her mother tongue) only to discover that she is herself complicit in its death. In this respect the collection builds on the themes of her earlier sequence 'Welsh Espionage', which very firmly associates the Welsh language with her mother, and the subversive English influence with her father. In the disturbing fifth section of that sequence a barely articulated sexual attraction, bordering on incest, informs the re-construction of the poet's illicit access to the English language.

> Welsh was the mother tongue, English was his.
> He taught her the body by fetishist quiz,
> father and daughter in the bottom stair:
> 'Dy benelin yw *elbow*, dy wallt di yw *hair*,
>
> *chin* yw dy ên di, *head* yw dy ben'.
> She promptly forgot, made him do it again.
> Then he folded her *dwrn* and, calling it fist,
> held it to show her knuckles and wrist.
>
> 'Let's keep it from Mam, as a special surprise.
> Lips are *gwefusau*, *llygaid* are eyes'.[41]

Needless to say, the 'mother was livid' once informed of the flirtatious ritual, exclaiming 'We agreed, no English till four years old!'[42] The mother's shock is shared by the reader, as both are exposed to the sexual terms in which the infant child's acquiring of another language is represented. The child is left to wonder whether 'it was such a bad thing to be daddy's girl?', and is thus exposed from the earliest years to the ways in which familial and cultural tensions are embedded in linguistic difference within a bilingual milieu. The English language, whether experimented with behind the bike shed, or acquired beyond the seemingly oppressive gaze of the mother, is the source of creativity and subversion. But, whatever the early subversive attraction of English, Gwyneth Lewis is almost unique in her ability to create poetry of equal complexity and allusions in Welsh and English which reflects a commitment to the development of her mother tongue and an awareness of the individual and communal action required for its continuance. She notes that 'losing a whole culture is an existential nightmare for a Welsh-speaker, fraught with questions of one's own responsibility in preserving collective values without becoming a parrot from the past. To most English speakers, it can't seem any more important than the loss of Morris dancing.'[43] Much of her work in English, however, seems predicated on the notion that there is a non-Welsh-speaking audience 'concerned with wider linguistic ecology – after all, if endangered plants offer cures for cancer, what essential directions might be hidden in obscure Welsh proverbs about never ploughing at a run?'[44] The poem 'What's In a Name?' makes the connection between linguistic and natural ecology explicit:

> *Lleian wen* is not the same as 'smew'
> because it's another point of view,
>
> another bird. There's been a cull:
> *gwylan*'s gone and we're left with 'gull'
>
> and blunter senses till the day
> when 'swallows', like *gwennol*, might stay away.[45]

As in much of Gwyneth Lewis's work, an apparent lexical simplicity leads to a complex multitude of potential interpretations. The equation of the loss of a language with the loss of a species is clear enough, but this leads to an ambiguity in the final line. Are we dealing here with ecological catastrophe: that the 'blunter senses' of the monoglot English speaker 'will remain' until the human species disappears like the Welsh words in the poem? Or are we to read this line within the context of Welsh-language politics, where the assimilationist act of swallowing is what needs to 'stay away', allowing a cultural space for the Welsh language to reclaim lost ground? Given that *Keeping Mum* appeared in 2003 when the movement Cymuned was attempting to develop an anti-colonialist language to champion the rights of Welsh-speaking communities in north-west Wales, there may also be a non-determinist trajectory within 'What's In a Name' which gestures towards a conclusion other than linguistic obsolescence and ecological catastrophe. Language death may be averted if the holiday-makers and their second homes, occupied during the summer months when the swallows are in Wales, can be encouraged to 'stay away'. Such a reading may be too divisive, however, for progressive directions in Welsh politics have been forged, periodically, in recent years through collaborative initiatives between linguistic and ecological conservationists.[46] Lewis creates a poetic space for such a dialogue and rapprochement to take place, while also subtly indicating the potential cultural strains within any such political alliance.

In their conscious efforts at moving between languages both Menna Elfyn and Gwyneth Lewis are poets who, to adapt Chana Kronfeld's phrase, 'mark the unmarked'.[47] To write from a minority culture is to destabilize majoritarian norms, 'colorising the colourless, particularising the universal'.[48] But to write as women within the minority culture, to write of the minority culture itself from a position of gendered 'otherness', is also to challenge its value systems, preconceptions and cultural norms. Experience itself becomes gendered in the works of writers whose female perspective is in itself a challenge to the patriarchal norms informing a society that, in Welsh or English, treats the masculine as the 'unmarked' universal position. Elfyn and Lewis do not envisage the Welsh and English cultures of Wales as inevitable antagonists. Writing from self-consciously female perspectives, both writers can see the incarcerating and emancipatory elements within both language cultures. It is perhaps not surprising that in Lewis's poetry English is the language of the father, for patriarchy and the English language constitute the norms informing our 'common sense' view of the world. To write as a Welsh speaker, and as a culturally and politically conscious woman, is to subvert those norms. Yet the English language is itself a vehicle of emancipation from a monologic Welsh-language world for the young protagonist of Lewis's poems, just as it is the language that allowed Menna Elfyn to construct an international space for a female voice that had been infamously marginalized by leading male elders of the Welsh bardic tradition.[49] Drawing on their bilingual heritage and feminist consciousness, Lewis and Elfyn resist the romanticization of Welsh-language culture as much as the unacknowledged dominance of British anglophone norms. These poets are not only engaged in the deconstructive process of defamiliarizing the familiar, for they are also engaged in the process of imagining a bilingual cultural space characterized by tolerance and dialogue in the face of dominance and division. But behind these dreams of tolerance remains the nightmarish possibility that bilingualism is a way-station in the journey from Welsh monolingualism to English monolingualism; a temporary mastication in preparation for swallowing.

IV

This book began with Rhys Davies, and argued that the Rhondda writer's novels were informed by a racial view of the Welsh. This was a claim initially made by Pennar Davies in an article of 1947 entitled 'Anti-Nationalism among the Anglo-Welsh' written for Plaid Cymru's English-language newspaper *The Welsh Nationalist*.[50] Pennar Davies expressed his regret that so many Anglo-Welsh writers 'define essential Welshness as a species of racial character rather than as a developing national life which must be given fair play in the sphere of economics and politics'.[51] He refers in particular to Rhys Davies. As I noted in chapter 1, Rhys Davies argued that 'the Eisteddfod, the Nationalist Party, Welsh MPs and all Welsh writers' are 'fundamentally useless'. For Rhys Davies the pure Welshmen were those who lived in isolation.

> There are several Welsh people in Wales, on remote farms, in dreamy chapels, tending sheep on hill-tops. But they have never heard of Wales. If you ask them 'Welsh you are?' they will look at you in a puzzled way. These are the only Welsh; they will always exist if left alone.[52]

Pennar Davies saw a great danger in thinking of Welshness in this way, for in abandoning the idea of a political nation – made of institutions in which people can participate – Rhys Davies was embracing a racial, essential conception of identity to which no one from outside the group could contribute. Pennar Davies argues that the Anglo-Welsh writers' anti-nationalism resulted in a view of the nation as a static and racial entity, rather than as a living thing to which a plurality of people could contribute.

This is an interesting stance, because the tendency among those who are vehemently opposed to nationalism is to suggest that all nationalisms hide a racial or atavistic essence. That is, even when attempts are made to put some civic lipstick on the ethnic gorilla, all nationalisms ultimately share a desire to keep the race pure and to keep others out.[53] But Pennar Davies turns this thinking on its head by suggesting that racial attitudes are the basis for anti-nationalist positions. Pennar Davies suggests that authors such as Rhys Davies and John Cowper Powys ('one of the most interesting of the Welsh racialists') replace a view of the nation as a civic, democratic, territorial space in which all citizens are allowed their voice, with an essentially racial view in which Welshness is based on ancestry.[54]

The form of Britishness embraced by Rhys Davies racializes the Welsh, and might be traced back to Matthew Arnold, or further to Shakespeare's *Henry V*. In each case a seemingly plural, liberal, Britain relies on racialized subgroups to function as the ingredients in its melting pot. If we adopt Werner Sollors's influential distinction between notions of identity based on 'consent and descent', we see that Britain in its liberal guises is conceived in consensual terms, while the Celtic peoples and other minorities are envisaged in terms of descent.[55] In a revisionist account of nineteenth-century British culture, the historian Peter Mandler suggests that a 'civilisational' rather than 'racial' perspective characterized the thought of the period.[56] The problem is that he concentrates wholly on how the English conceived of England and Englishness. Arnold's writings (discussed in chapter 1) indicate that a 'civilizationist' view of England can happily co-exist with, indeed may actually be predicated upon, a racial view of the Celts. This structure of thought is not limited to the British Isles for, as Slavoj Žižek has indicated, it is one of the ways racism functions subtly in contemporary discussions of multiculturalism:

> I am often accused in a very strange way – which I really cannot understand – of being a Slovene anti-Serb nationalist. When I converse with members of the so-called Serb democratic opposition, they say they are in favour of a cosmopolitan democratic Serbia whose defining quality is citizenship and not national belonging. OK, I accept this. But this is where the problems begin, because if you speak with them a little bit longer, you discover a certain political vision that tries to disguise cultural particularity as democratic universalism. For example, if you ask them about Slovene autonomy, they will argue that Slovenia is a small self-enclosed nation and that they, by contrast, are in favour of an anti-nationalist democratic society which is not self-enclosed. But in reality what they are practising is a kind of two-level nationalism in which they go on to affirm that the Serbs are the only nation in Yugoslavia that is so structured that it can sustain this open principle of democratic citizenship … So we have this double logic. On the one hand they criticize the Milosevic regime from a democratic standpoint – claiming that the Serbs are fundamentally democratic and that Milosevic perverted them – but, on the other, they deny this democratic potential to other ethnic groups of ex-Yugoslavia (you Slovenes want to be a state but in reality you are a primitive Alpine tribe) … And this is often how racism functions today – at this disguised reflexive level. So we should be careful when people emphasize their democratic credentials: do these same people allow the Other to have the same credentials?[57]

The problem that Slavoj Žižek identifies in the relation between Serbs and Slovenes is mirrored, if in a less charged manner, in the relationship between England and Wales. British nationalists employ the same 'double logic', espousing the progressive potential of their own national identity, while denying it to the minority nations who may wish to decide the forms of governance suitable to their own still-forming interests and identities. On the Left, 'Britain' has been separated from its connections with empire and racial superiority, and is espoused as the multicultural face of Englishness. The debate regarding 'cultural nationalism' in Britain today is a debate about the frames, or crucibles, within which a multicultural society is allowed and able to develop. The true British democrat, following Žižek's astute analysis, is one who is prepared to argue that Scotland and Wales have the same democratic and multicultural potential as England within the geographical space that we call Great Britain. To develop the political autonomy of Wales and Scotland is not to reject British multiculturalism, but is to deepen multicultural citizenship. It is surely time to move beyond the 'double logic' by which 'my nation is progressive and cosmopolitan' while 'your nation is separatist and divisive'.

If a case needs to be made for Welsh multiculturalism, this process of allowing the same rights to the Other pertain within the devolved nations themselves. Persuading the dominant anglophone society that minorities can be multicultural has been an abiding concern of Welsh-language activists, for example. As I noted earlier, quoting Ned Thomas, the danger for those of us who live in minority-language communities and value linguistic plurality and difference is that our languages are perceived to belong to a specific racial group, and are therefore closed to outsiders. Even those supportive of linguistic difference will tend to conceive of the speakers of the Celtic languages as belonging to an ethnic minority within their respective countries, with English functioning as the civic language of the nation, as the universal language in which a multicultural society communicates. Pennar Davies could see the danger of such thinking for minorities, and was in a position to do so as a writer who began life as an English-language poet, deeply indebted to Dylan Thomas, learning Welsh later in life and developing his most distinctive voice in his second language.[58]

Perhaps, somewhat counter-intuitively, as political nationhood develops, the chains binding race-language-place are eroding. This process is unlikely to lead us to a transnational utopia. But, as in the prophetic poetry of Gwyneth Lewis and Menna Elfyn, it may force a more creative engagement with the relationship between state and language, politics and culture. As Raymond Williams noted, 'the familiar intellectual jump to this or that universality' is an insufficient response to the process of globalization.[59] No political formation can develop without a cultural underpinning and, as I've argued elsewhere, both allegedly 'ethnic' and allegedly 'civic' nationalisms inevitably have a cultural as well as political component.[60] Of course, the way culture is interpreted varies from nation to nation. Some nations define their culture in racial terms, some linguistic, some religious, others do not. These variations are crucial to understanding why some nationalisms are peaceful, liberal and democratic, while others are xenophobic, authoritarian and expansionist. These are the real grounds of difference, rather than the spurious 'civic' vs. 'ethnic' binary division. Indeed multicultural 'civic' nationalism, as Žižek suggests, is often just a mask used by dominant nationalisms to hide the inevitable ethnic dimension of their make-up. So as Wales moves towards a more mature form of political nationhood, we should not jettison our cultural past for a post-national future. We should, rather, aim to pluralize our definitions of Welshness and *Cymreictod*. Raymond Williams, as I noted in the introduction, encouraged us to foster 'ideas, and ways of thinking, with the seeds of life in them', while undermining and breaking those chains 'perhaps deep in our minds' that connect us to ideas harbouring the 'seeds of a general death'.[61] It is hoped that this book, in tracing internally developed and externally imposed conceptions of Welsh identity, has been a modest contribution to that process.

Notes

Notes to the Introduction

1 See Douglas Tallack, *Twentieth-Century America: The Intellectual and Cultural Context* (London: Longman, 1991), p. 4.

2 Alfred Zimmern, *My Impressions of Wales* (1921), quoted in Dai Smith, *Aneurin Bevan and the World of South Wales* (Cardiff: University of Wales Press, 1993), p. i.

3 Dai Smith, *Wales! Wales?* (London: George Allen and Unwin, 1984), pp. 152–3.

4 Cornel West, *Keeping Faith: Philosophy and Race in America* (London: Routledge, 1993), p. 11.

5 See Alan M. Wald, *The New York Intellectuals: The Rise and Decline of the Anti-Stalinist Left from the 1930s to the 1980s* (Chapel Hill: University of North Carolina Press, 1987).

6 Alfred Kazin, 'The Posthumous Life of Dylan Thomas', *Atlantic Monthly*, 200 (October 1957), 164–8. Collected in Georg Gaston (ed.), *Critical Essays on Dylan Thomas* (Boston: G. K. Hall and Co., 1989), pp. 35–42. Kazin had personal reasons for writing, for Thomas had been involved in an intense love affair with his sister Pearl. See Jeff Towns (ed.), *A Pearl of Great Price: The Love Letters of Dylan Thomas to Pearl Kazin* (Cardigan: Parthian, 2014).

7 Kazin, 'The Posthumous Life', 39. On Alfred Kazin see Alan M. Wald, 'Alfred Kazin in Retrospect', in idem, *Writing from the Left: New Essays on Radical Culture and Politics* (London: Verso, 1994), pp. 28–39. Alfred Kazin, *On Native Grounds: An Interpretation of Modern American Prose Literature* (New York: Harcourt, Brace and World inc., 1942).

8 Irving Howe quoted by Smith, *Aneurin Bevan*, p. 139; Smith, *Wales! Wales?*, pp. 10–11. Smith also notes that 'I have found that critics like Leslie Fiedler and Irving Howe ... have often spoken more directly to my experience of south Wales, by being sharply acute about literature in America, than have either the boosters or the denigrators at home'. *Aneurin Bevan*, p. 344.

⁹   See Dai Smith's account of Aneurin Bevan's upbringing, quoted in chapter 4.

¹⁰ Thomas J. Ferraro, *Ethnic Passages: Literary Immigrants in Twentieth-Century America* (Chicago: University of Chicago Press, 1993), p. 3.

¹¹ Henry Louis Gates, Jr., *The Signifying Monkey: A Theory of African-American Literary Criticism* (Oxford: Oxford University Press, 1988).

¹² See, for example, Jerry Hunter's recent application of theories deriving from Native American and Celtic studies to the analysis of Welsh missionary activity among the Tsalagi (Cherokee) in *Llwybrau Cenhedloedd: Cyd-Destunoli'r Genhadaeth Gymreig i'r Tsalagi* (Caerdydd: University of Wales Press, 2012).

¹³ Smith, *Aneurin Bevan*, p. 275.

¹⁴ Smith, *Wales! Wales?*, pp. 154–60; Raymond Williams, *Marxism and Literature* (Oxford: Oxford University Press, 1977), pp. 121–7; D. Hywel Davies, 'South Wales history which almost excludes the Welsh', *New Welsh Review*, 26 (autumn 1994), 8–13.

¹⁵ Werner Sollors, *Beyond Ethnicity: Consent and Descent in American Culture* (New York: Oxford University Press, 1986) was particularly influential. Ferraro traces the shifts in American ethnic literary studies in *Ethnic Passages*, pp. 1–17. Others describe this shift as being from 'class' to 'identity', although class itself tends be discussed today as an identity. See chapter 4 in this volume for an account of this shift.

¹⁶ M. Wynn Thomas, *Internal Difference: Literature in 20ᵗʰ-Century Wales* (Cardiff: University of Wales Press, 1992) and idem, *Corresponding Cultures: The Two Literatures of Wales* (Cardiff: University of Wales Press, 1999); Jane Aaron, *Pur fel y Dur: Y Gymraes yn Llên Menywod y Bedwaredd Ganrif ar Bymtheg* (Caerdydd: University of Wales Press, 1998).

¹⁷ Will Kymlicka, 'Liberal Nationalism and Cosmopolitan Justice', in Seyla Benhabib, *Another Cosmopolitanism*, ed. Robert Post (Oxford: Oxford University Press, 2006), p. 129.

¹⁸ Ibid.

¹⁹ Chris Williams, 'Problematizing Wales: An Exploration in Historiography and Postcoloniality', in Jane Aaron and Chris Williams (eds), *Postcolonial Wales* (Cardiff: University of Wales Press, 2005), pp. 7, 10.

²⁰ Richard Wyn Jones, 'The Colonial Legacy in Welsh Politics', in ibid., pp. 23–4.

²¹ Williams, 'Problematizing Wales', p. 7; Christopher Clapham, *Third World Politics: An Introduction* (Madison: University of Wisconsin Press, 1992), p. 21f.

²² Williams, 'Problematizing Wales', p. 16; Jones, 'The Colonial Legacy in Welsh Politics', p. 36.

²³ Williams, 'Problematizing Wales', p. 16.

²⁴ Ibid.

²⁵ Terry Eagleton, *Crazy John and the Bishop and Other Essays on Irish Culture* (Cork: Cork University Press, 1998), p. 316.

²⁶ Williams, 'Problematizing Wales', p. 16.

²⁷ Idem, *Democratic Rhondda: Politics and Society, 1855–1951* (Cardiff: University of Wales Press, 1996), p. 212.

²⁸ Glenn Jordan, '"We Never Really Noticed You Were Coloured": Postcolonialist Reflections on Immigrants and Minorities in Wales', in Aaron and Williams (eds), *Postcolonial Wales*, pp. 70–1.

29   Charlotte Williams, *Sugar and Slate* (Aberystwyth: Planet, 2002).
30   Jones, 'The Colonial Legacy in Welsh Politics', pp. 35, 33.
31   Williams, 'Problematizing Wales', p. 9.
32   Ibid., pp. 9–10.
33   Raymond Williams, 'The Importance of Community' (1977), in idem, *Who Speaks for Wales? Nation, Culture, Identity*, ed. Daniel Williams (Cardiff: Cardiff University Press, 2003), p. 183.
34   Williams, 'Problematizing Wales', p. 4; emphasis added.
35   Raymond Williams, 'The Culture of Nations' (1983), in idem, *Who Speaks for Wales*, p. 200.
36   Williams, 'Problematizing Wales', p. 16.
37   Slavoj Žižek, 'Notes towards a politics of Bartleby: the ignorance of chicken', *Comparative American Studies*, 4, 4 (December 2006), 377.
38   Tom Nairn (in conversation with Richard Wyn Jones), 'Ukanian Discussions and Homo Britannicus', in Gerry Hassan and Rosie Ilett (eds), *Radical Scotland: Arguments for Self-Determination* (Edinburgh: Luath Press Limited, 2011), p. 280.
39   Ibid.
40   Raymond Williams, *Culture and Society* (1958; London: Hogarth, 1990), p. 338.

Notes to Chapter 1

1   George Ewart Evans, 'The Valleys', *Wales*, 3 (autumn 1937), 128.
2   John Carey, *The Intellectuals and the Masses* (London: Faber, 1992); Anthony Julius, *T.S. Eliot, Anti-Semitism and Literary Form* (Cambridge: Cambridge University Press, 1995).
3   Rhys Davies, 'Arfon', in idem, *Collected Stories Volume 1*, ed. Meic Stephens (Llandysul: Gomer, 1996), p. 17.
4   Idem, *Print of a Hare's Foot* (London: Heinemann, 1969), pp. 198, 184, 197.
5   See my discussion in Daniel G. Williams, *Black Skin, Blue Books: African Americans and Wales 1845–1945* (Cardiff: University of Wales Press, 2012), pp. 121–2.
6   Werner Sollors, *Beyond Ethnicity: Consent and Descent in American Culture* (New York: Oxford University Press, 1986).
7   Davies, *Print*, p. 140.
8   Idem, *My Wales* (London: Jarrolds, 1937), pp. 12–13.
9   Ibid., p. 13.
10   Ibid., p. 15. See Tony Brown, '"The Memory of Lost Countries": Rhys Davies's Wales', in Meic Stephens (ed.), *Rhys Davies: Decoding the Hare* (Cardiff: University of Wales Press, 2001), pp. 71–86.
11   Rhys Davies, *The Withered Root* (London: Robert Holden and Co., 1927), pp. 100, 27.
12   Ibid., p. 3.
13   Idem, *The Black Venus* (London: William Heinemann, 1944), pp. 1, 65. For a detailed analysis of the novel see Kirsti Bohata, *Postcolonialism Revisited*

(Cardiff: University of Wales Press, 2004), pp. 40–50. On 'courting in bed' see Catrin Stevens, *Welsh Courting Customs* (Llandysul: Gomer, 1993). On strategies of surveillance in industrial Wales see Andy Croll, *Civilizing the Urban: Popular Culture and Public Space in Merthyr, c.1870–1914* (Cardiff: University of Wales Press, 2000), pp. 62–103.

14 Davies, *The Black Venus*, p. 65.

15 Idem, *My Wales*, p. 21.

16 Ibid., pp. 21–2.

17 Brown, 'The Memory of Lost Countries', p. 74.

18 Quoted in David N. Livingstone, *The Geographical Tradition* (Oxford: Blackwells, 1992), p. 287. For accounts of Fleure in a Welsh context see Pyrs Gruffudd, 'Back to the Land: Historiography, Rurality and the Nation in Interwar Wales', *Transactions of the Institute of British Geographers*, 19 (1994), 61–77. Also, idem, 'Yr Iaith Gymraeg a'r Dychymyg Daearyddol 1918–1950', in Geraint Jenkins and Mari Williams (eds), *'Eu Hiaith a Gadwant'? Y Gymraeg yn yr Ugeinfed Ganrif* (Caerdydd: University of Wales Press, 2000), pp. 107–32.

19 Davies, *Print*, p. 141.

20 D. H. Lawrence, *St Mawr*, in *The Complete Short Novels* (London: Penguin, 1982), p. 291.

21 Ibid., p. 296.

22 Ibid., p. 374.

23 Murray G. H. Pittock, *Celtic Identity and the British Image* (Manchester: Manchester University Press, 1999).

24 Matthew Arnold, *On the Study of Celtic Literature* (1867), in idem, *The Complete Prose Works of Matthew Arnold*, ed. R. H. Super, 11 vols (Ann Arbor: University of Michigan Press, 1960–77), vol. III, pp. 294–5. This will be abbreviated from now on as *CPW*, followed by volume number. See my extended discussion in Daniel G. Williams, *Ethnicity and Cultural Authority: From Arnold to Du Bois* (Edinburgh: Edinburgh University Press, 2006).

25 *CPW*, III, pp. 295–6.

26 Ibid., p. 291.

27 Ibid., p. 346.

28 Ibid., p. 311.

29 Ibid., pp. 344, 345, 347.

30 Raymond Williams, *Culture and Society: Coleridge to Orwell* (1958; London: Hogarth Press, 1990), p. xviii.

31 See, for instance, Williams's *Politics and Letters: Interviews with New Left Review* (London: Verso, 1979), pp. 118, 119.

32 *CPW*, III, p. 291.

33 Lawrence, *St Mawr*, p. 337.

34 Ibid., pp. 346–7.

35 Davies, 'Blodwen', in *Collected Stories Volume 1*, pp. 81, 86.

36 Idem, *The Withered Root*, pp. 43, 53.

37 Ibid., p. 229.

38 Ibid., p. 27.

39 Arnold, *Culture and Anarchy* (1869), in *CPW*, V, p. 105.

[40] *CPW*, III, pp. 296–7.

[41] *CPW*, V, p. 113.

[42] Arnold, 'A French Critic on Goethe' (1878) in *CPW*, VIII, p. 256.

[43] *CPW*, III, pp. 296–7; D. H. Lawrence, *The Letters of D. H. Lawrence: Vol III: October 1916–June 1921*, ed. James T. Boulton and Andrew Robertson (Cambridge: Cambridge University Press, 1984), p. 719.

[44] Lawrence, *St Mawr*, p. 365.

[45] Ibid., pp. 404, 406.

[46] Ibid., p. 322.

[47] Ibid., p. 285.

[48] Ibid., p. 360.

[49] Davies, *The Withered Root*, p. 280.

[50] Reuben's 'frigidity' and the primitive's inability to procreate may be linked to Rhys Davies's homosexuality, discussed illuminatingly by Huw Edwin Osborne in *Rhys Davies* (Cardiff: University of Wales Press, 2009), pp. 15–25. In his study of 'arrested development' in colonial fictions, Jed Esty suggests that just as colonies never achieve full independent nationhood, the protagonists in colonial narratives never achieve full heterosexual maturity. 'Novels of colonial adolescence ... resist or forestall the traditional plot of libidinal closure in the bildungsroman (heterosexual coupling and reproduction) and feature instead story lines driven by homoerotic investment, sexual indifference, homosexual panic and same-sex desire.' Esty suggests that 'sexually dissident protagonists' such as Lord Jim (Conrad), Rachel Vinrace (Woolf) and Stephen Dedalus (Joyce) 'suggest a deep epochal link between the queer/adolescent and the colonial/native as twin subjects of arrested-development discourse'. His analysis strikes me as being highly applicable to the writings of Rhys Davies and to many other Welsh authors. Jed Esty, *Unseasonable Youth: Modernism, Colonialism and the Fiction of Development* (Oxford: Oxford University Press, 2012), p. 22. I hope to return to this theme in the forthcoming final volume of the *Oxford Literary History of Wales*.

[51] D. H. Lawrence, 'On Being a Man', in idem, *Reflections on the Death of a Porcupine and Other Essays*, ed. Michael Herbert (Cambridge: Cambridge University Press, 1988), pp. 215–16.

[52] Rhys Davies, 'Fear', idem in *Collected Stories Volume 2*, ed. Meic Stephens (Llandysul: Gomer, 1996), p. 124.

[53] Ibid.

[54] Idem, *Print*, p. 139.

[55] Idem, *My Wales*, p. 70.

[56] Idem, *The Withered Root*, p. 111; idem, *My Wales*, p. 81.

[57] Idem, 'From My Notebook', *Wales*, 2 (October 1943), 11.

[58] Ibid., 10, 11, 12.

[59] Ibid., 10.

[60] D. H. Lawrence, *Studies in Classic American Literature*, ed. Ezra Greenspan, Lindeth Vasey and John Worthen (1923; Cambridge: Cambridge University Press, 2002), pp. 65, 67.

[61] Ibid., p. 146.

[62] Ibid., p. 18.
[63] Davies, 'From My Notebook', 10.
[64] Lawrence, *Studies*, p. 78.
[65] Ibid., p. 65.
[66] Idem, *St Mawr*, p. 389.
[67] Davies, 'From My Notebook', 10.
[68] Idem, *My Wales*, p. 220; idem, 'From My Notebook', 12.

Notes to Chapter 2

[1]   Owen Martell, *Dyn yr Eiliad* (Llandysul: Gomer, 2003), p. 165.
[2]   It is reproduced in Peter Stead and Gareth Williams (eds), *Wales and its Boxers: The Fighting Tradition* (Cardiff: University of Wales Press, 2008), p. 118.
[3]   Kasia Boddy, *Boxing: A Cultural History* (London: Reaktion Books, 2008).
[4]   Ralph Ellison, *Invisible Man* (1952; New York: Vintage, 1995), p. 8.
[5]   Gerald Early, *The Culture of Bruising: Essays on Prizefighting, Literature and Modern American Culture* (Hopewell, NJ: The Ecco Press, 1994), pp. 11–12.
[6]   On the transformation of Ali's reputation see Mike Marqusee, *Redemption Song: Muhammad Ali and the Spirit of the Sixties* (London: Verso, 1999), pp. 3–6.
[7]   David Reynolds, *Rich Relations: The American Occupation of Britain 1942–1945* (London: Harper Collins, 1995), pp. 174–5.
[8]   See the *Daily Telegraph*'s obituary for Jack Matthews who died aged ninety-two on 18 July 2012, *http://www.telegraph.co.uk/news/obituaries/sport-obituaries/9641521/Dr-Jack-Matthews.html* (accessed 1 August 2013).
[9]   Ralph Ellison, 'In a Strange Country', in idem, *Flying Home and Other Stories* (1996; London: Penguin, 1998), pp. 138–9.
[10] Ibid., p. 140.
[11] Idem, 'A Storm of Blizzard Proportions', Several Drafts. The Ralph Ellison Papers. Library of Congress, Washington DC. Box 165. File 7. On Ellison and boxing see Boddy, *Boxing*, pp. 309–15.
[12] Graeme Kent, *A Welshman in the Bronx: Tommy Farr vs Joe Louis* (Llandysul: Gomer, 2009), p. 33.
[13] Ralph Ellison, 'Interview with Robert B. Stepto and Michael S. Harper', in Michael S. Harper and Robert B. Stepto (eds), *Chant of Saints: A Gathering of Afro-American Literature, Art and Scholarship* (Urbana: University of Illinois Press, 1979), p. 460.
[14] Dai Smith, 'Call me Tommy: Tommy Farr and the Tonypandy Kid', in Stead and Williams (eds), *Wales and its Boxers*, pp. 87–100.
[15] In Lowri Roberts (ed.), *Canu Clod y Campau: Detholiad o Farddoniaeth y Maes Chwarae* (Llanrwst: Gwasg Carreg Gwalch, 2009), p. 33. Thanks to Cyril Jones for drawing my attention to this poem.
[16] T. Gwynn Jones, *The Culture and Civilization of Wales* (Wrecsam: Hughes a'i Fab, 1927), p. 22.
[17] Raymond Williams, *Border Country* (1960; Cardigan: Parthian, 2005), pp. 270–1.
[18] See the discussion of Fleure in chapter 1.

[19] Geraint Goodwin, *The Heyday in the Blood* (1936; Cardigan: Parthian, 2009), p. 187.
[20] W. J. Gruffydd, 'Hen Atgofion', *Y Llenor*, XVII (1938), 8–9. Translated by D. Myrddin Lloyd as W. J. Gruffydd, *The Years of the Locust* (Llandysul: Gomer, 1976), p. 175. The passage reads as follows in the original:

> Yr wyf yn cofio adegau yn hanes y genedl pan oedd y pulpud a'r eisteddfod yn llwyfannau i'r ysbryd [cystadleuol] hwn, – pwy oedd y pregethwr gorau, pwy oedd wedi ennill y gadair, pa gôr a gurodd, pa un o ddau dwrne a oedd yn mynd i ennill yr etholiad. Gwelaf heddiw – ym Morgannwg o leiaf – mai'r hyn sy'n anfeidrol bwysig i ni fel cenedl o Gymry ydyw siawns Jac Petersen neu Tommy Farr neu ryw Sais arall a aned yng Nghymru i roi cweir â dyrnau i Sais a aned yn Lloegr neu i ddyn du o America.

[21] Tommy Farr, *Thus Farr* (London: Optomen Press, 1989), pp. 69, 81.
[22] Daniel Owen, *Gwen Tomos* (1894; Wrecsam: Hughes a'i Fab, 1967), pp. 88–92.
[23] Caradog Pritchard, *Un Nos Ola Leuad*. Translated as *One Moonlit Night*. Bilingual edition (Harmondsworth: Penguin, 1999), pp. 144–6.
[24] On Pennar Davies and Freddie Welsh see Ivor Thomas Rees, *Saintly Enigma: A Biography of Pennar Davies* (Talybont: Y Lolfa, 2011), p. 221; D. Densil Morgan, *Pennar Davies: Dawn Dweud* (Cardiff: University of Wales Press, 2003), p. 173. On 'Fred Cymry' see Andrew Gallimore, *Occupation Prizefighter: The Freddie Welsh Story* (Bridgend: Seren, 2006), pp. 56–7.
[25] Pennar Davies, 'Pencampwr', in idem, *Llais y Durtur* (Llandysul: Gomer, 1985), pp. 85–8.
[26] Myrddin ap Dafydd, 'Newid Enw: Pan Drodd Cassius Clay i Fod yn Muhammad Ali', in Roberts (ed.), *Canu Clod y Campau*, p. 37.
[27] Selwyn Griffith, 'Arwyr', in ibid., p. 33.
[28] Jack Jones, *Black Parade* (London: Faber, 1935), pp. 72–3, 96, 280.
[29] Ibid., pp. 145–6.
[30] Randy Roberts, *Jack Dempsey: The Manassa Mauler* (London: Robson Books, 1987), pp. 213–15. I'm grateful to Gareth Williams for this reference.
[31] Paul O'Leary, *Immigration and Integration: The Irish in Wales, 1798–1922* (Cardiff: University of Wales Press, 2000), pp. 144–51, 302–4.
[32] Ellison, *Invisible Man*, p. 17.
[33] Eric Lott, *Love and Theft: Blackface Minstrelsy and the American Working Class* (Oxford: Oxford University Press, 1993), p. 52.
[34] Marshall Berman, *All That Is Solid Melts into Air: The Experience of Modernity* (1982; London: Verso, 1983), p. 15.
[35] Louise Walsh, *Fighting Pretty* (Bridgend: Seren, 2008), pp. 15–16.
[36] Gwyn A. Williams, *When Was Wales? A History of the Welsh* (London: Black Raven Press, 1985), pp. 173–81; idem, *The Welsh in their History* (London: Croom Helm, 1982), p. 177; Dai Smith, *Wales! Wales?* (London: Allen and Unwin, 1984), pp. 20–7.
[37] Susan Gubar, *Racechanges: White Skin, Black Face in American Culture* (Oxford: Oxford University Press, 1997), p. 65.

[38] Kevin K. Gaines, *Uplifting the Race: Black Leadership, Politics, and Culture in the Twentieth Century* (Chapel Hill: University of North Carolina Press, 1996), p. 70; Gubar, *Racechanges*, p. 48.

[39] Driscoll is also the subject of a Welsh-language poem by Grahame Davies, 'Peerless Jim Driscoll', in Roberts (ed.), *Canu Clod y Campau*, p. 36.

[40] Alexander Cordell, *Peerless Jim* (London: Hodder and Stoughton, 1984), p. 143.

[41] Ibid., pp. 228–9.

[42] Leslie Norris, 'The Ballad of Billy Rose', in Meic Stephens (ed.), *Poetry 1900–2000* (Cardigan: Parthian, 2007), pp. 257–60. Also collected with other Welsh boxing literature in Gareth Williams (ed.), *Sport* (Cardigan: Library of Wales, 2007), pp. 194–6.

[43] Leslie Norris, 'A Big Night' (1976), *The Collected Stories of Leslie Norris* (Bridgend: Seren, 1996), p. 51.

[44] Ibid. A 'colour' bar was in operation in British boxing from 1911 to 1947. See P. F. McDevitt, *May the Best Man Win: Sport, Masculinity, and Nationalism in Great Britain and the Empire, 1880–1935* (London: Palgrave, 2008).

[45] Norris, 'A Big Night', p. 51.

[46] Jack Jones, *The Black Welshman*, Manuscript in the Jack Jones Papers, National Library of Wales, Aberystwyth, p. 1. The novel was serialized in *The Empire News*, beginning on 23 June 1957, 6.

[47] Ibid.

[48] Ibid.

[49] Ron Berry, *So Long Hector Bebb* (1970, Cardigan: Parthian, 2005), p. 214.

[50] Ibid., pp. 106–7.

[51] Ibid., pp. 196–7.

Notes to Chapter 3

[1] Julio Cortázar, 'El perseguidor' [The Pursuer], in *Las armas secretas* (Buenos Aires: Sudamericana, 1959), pp. 149–313. Translated by Paul Blackburn in *Blow Up and Other Stories* (New York: Collier Books, 1985), pp. 161–220. Doris Sommer, 'Grammar Trouble for Cortázar', in eadem, *Proceed with Caution, When Engaged by Minority Writing in the Americas* (Cambridge, MA: Harvard University Press, 1999), p. 220.

[2] Cortázar, 'The Pursuer', p. 238.

[3] Kenneth Rexroth, 'Disengagement: The Art of the Beat Generation' (1959), in idem, *The Alternative Society* (New York: Herder and Herder, 1970), p. 1.

[4] Dylan Thomas, *Collected Letters*, ed. Paul Ferris (1985; London: J. M. Dent, 2000), p. 617.

[5] Randall Jarrell, *A Sad Heart at the Supermarket: Essays and Fables* (London: Eyre and Spottiswoode, 1965); Allen Ginsberg, *Collected Poems 1947–1980* (New York: Harper and Rowe, 1984); Lawrence Ferlinghetti, *These Are My Rivers: New and Selected Poems* (New York: New Directions, 1993). Quoted in Eric Homberger, *The Art of the Real: Poetry in England and America Since 1939* (London: Dent, 1977), p. 71.

6 Theodore Roethke, *The Collected Poems* (New York: Anchor Books, 1975), p. 56.
7 Karl Shapiro, *The Wild Card: Selected Poems, Early and Late* (Urbana: University of Illinois Press, 1998), p. 15.
8 Quoted by Carolyn Gaiser, 'Gregory Corso: A Poet, the Beat Way', in Thomas Parkinson (ed.), *A Casebook on the Beat* (New York: Thomas Y. Crowell, 1961), pp. 266–75.
9 Alan Dugan, *Poems Seven: New and Complete Poems* (New York: Seven Stories Press, 2001), p. 138.
10 Saul Bellow, *Seize the Day* (New York: Viking, 1956), p. 7.
11 J. D. Salinger, *The Catcher in the Rye* (New York: Little Brown, 1951), pp. 23, 65.
12 Norman Mailer, 'The White Negro', in Ann Charters (ed.), *The Penguin Book of the Beats* (Harmondsworth: Penguin, 1993), p. 585.
13 Karl Shapiro, 'Dylan Thomas' (1955), in E. W. Tedlock (ed.), *Dylan Thomas: The Legend and the Poet* (1960; London: Mercury Books, 1963), pp. 281, 277, 273.
14 For a wide-ranging discussion see Ernst Gombrich's posthumous volume *The Preference for the Primitive* (London: Phaidon, 2002).
15 Allen Ginsberg, *Howl*, in Charters (ed.), *The Penguin Book of the Beats*, p. 62; Jack Kerouac, *On the Road* (1957; Harmondsworth: Penguin, 2000), p. 180.
16 Mailer, 'The White Negro', p. 586.
17 Jack Kerouac, *Selected Letters 1940–1956*, ed. Ann Charters (New York: Viking, 1995), p. 204.
18 Matthew Arnold, 'Democracy' (1861), in idem, *The Complete Prose Works of Matthew Arnold*, ed. R. H. Super, 11 vols (Ann Arbor: University of Michigan Press, 1960–77), vol. II, pp. 15–16.
19 Arnold, *On the Study of Celtic Literature* (1867), in ibid., vol. III, pp. 344, 345, 347.
20 W. B. Yeats, *Uncollected Prose Volume 1*, ed. John P. Frayne (London: Macmillan, 1970), p. 268.
21 Mike Zwerin offers an analysis of this process, while contributing to it, in *The Case for the Balkanisation of Practically Everyone* (London: Wildwood House, 1976). Zwerin is an interesting figure, for he was also a trombonist on Miles Davis's seminal *Birth of the Cool* recordings of 1948.
22 See Daniel G. Williams, *Ethnicity and Cultural Authority: From Arnold to Du Bois* (Edinburgh: Edinburgh University Press, 2006), pp. 42–52.
23 Neil Leonard, *Jazz: Myth and Religion* (Oxford: Oxford University Press, 1987), pp. 122–3.
24 Ross Russell, *Bird Lives: The High Life and Hard Times of Charlie 'Yardbird' Parker* (1973; New York: Da Capo, 1996), p. 257. Quoted in Leonard, *Jazz*, p. 123.
25 Miles Davis, *Miles: The Autobiography* (London: Macmillan, 1989), pp. 55–6.
26 M. Wynn Thomas, *Corresponding Cultures: The Two Literatures of Wales* (Cardiff: University of Wales Press, 1999), p. 46. Also idem, *In the Shadow of the Pulpit: Literature and Nonconformist Wales* (Cardiff: University of Wales Press, 2010), p. 230.
27 Dylan Thomas, 'After the Funeral (In Memory of Ann Jones)', *Collected Poems 1934–1953*, ed. Walford Davies and Ralph Maud (1988; London: Everyman Library, 1989), pp. 73–4.

[28] Idem, *Collected Letters*, p. 31.

[29] John Berryman, 'After many a summer: memories of Dylan Thomas', *Times Literary Supplement* (3 September 1993), 13–14.

[30] John Malcolm Brinnin, *Dylan Thomas in America* (Boston: Little Brown, 1955), pp. 75–6.

[31] Quoted in Leonard, *Jazz*, p. 127.

[32] Cornel West, *Keeping Faith: Philosophy and Race in America* (London: Routledge, 1993), p. 11.

[33] Ibid.

[34] See Alan M. Wald, *The New York Intellectuals: The Rise and Decline of the Anti-Stalinist Left from the 1930s to the 1980s* (Chapel Hill: University of North Carolina Press, 1987); Stefan Collini, *Absent Minds: Intellectuals in Britain* (Oxford: Oxford University Press, 2006), pp. 226–32.

[35] Alfred Kazin, 'The Posthumous Life of Dylan Thomas', *Atlantic Monthly*, 200 (October 1957), 164–8. Collected in Georg Gaston (ed.), *Critical Essays on Dylan Thomas* (Boston: G. K. Hall and Co., 1989), pp. 35–42. As I noted in the introduction, Kazin had personal reasons for writing, for Thomas had been involved in an intense love affair with his sister Pearl. See Jeff Towns (ed.), *A Pearl of Great Price: The Love Letters of Dylan Thomas to Pearl Kazin* (Cardigan: Parthian, 2014).

[36] Kazin, in Gaston (ed.), *Critical Essays on Dylan Thomas*, p. 35.

[37] Ted Gioia, *The History of Jazz* (Oxford: Oxford University Press, 2011), p. 190.

[38] Ibid.

[39] Carl Woideck (ed.), *The Charlie Parker Companion: Six Decades of Commentary* (New York: Schirmer Books, 1998), p. 51; Gioia, *The History of Jazz*, p. 72.

[40] Billy Taylor, 'America's Classical Music', in Robert Walser (ed.), *Keeping Time: Readings in Jazz History* (Oxford: Oxford University Press, 1999), pp. 327–31. John Goodby discusses the ways in which Thomas's writing 'reveals the process of exchange between different cultural levels' in '"Very Profound and Very Box-Office": The Later Poems and Under Milk Wood', in John Goodby and Chris Wigginton (eds), *Dylan Thomas: New Casebook* (Basingstoke: Palgrave, 2001), p. 195. An interesting figure in this connection is the American scholar of medieval English, Marshall Stearns (1908–66). Stearns was one of the earliest critics to appreciate Dylan Thomas in America, and was also an early champion of bebop in general, and Charlie Parker in particular. Marshall Stearns, 'Unsex the Skeleton (1944)', in E. W. Tedlock, *Dylan Thomas: The Legend and the Poet* (London: Mercury Books, 1963), pp. 113–31; Marshall Stearns, 'Interview: Charlie Parker, Marshall Stearns, John Maher and Chan Parker' (1950), in Carl Woideck (ed.), *The Charlie Parker Companion* (New York: Schirmer Books, 1998), pp. 91–108. John Gennari discusses Stearns's jazz criticism in *Blowin' Hot and Cool: Jazz and its Critics* (Chicago: Chicago University Press, 2006), pp. 144–55. A more ambivalent attitude towards both Dylan Thomas and Charlie Parker is to be found in the writings of Philip Larkin. See *Required Writing: Miscellaneous Pieces 1955–1982* (London: Faber, 2002) and *All What Jazz* (London: Faber, 1985).

[41] Ross Russell, *Bird Lives: The High Life and Hard Times of Charlie (Yardbird) Parker* (1973; New York: Da Capo Press, 1996), p. 363.

[42] Max Harrison, 'A Rare Bird' (1997), in Woideck (ed.), *The Charlie Parker Companion*, p. 207.

[43] James A. Davies, 'Questions of Identity: The Movement and "Fern Hill"', in Goodby and Wigginton (eds), *Dylan Thomas*, p. 63.

[44] Claude Levi-Strauss, *The Raw and the Cooked*, trans. John and Doreen Weightman (New York: Harper and Row, 1969), p. 16.

[45] Charlie Parker, 'Now's the Time'. Savoy 2201. Master No. Take. S5851–4. 26 November 1945.

[46] Simon Frith, *Performing Rites: Evaluating Popular Music* (Oxford: Oxford University Press, 1998), p. 157.

[47] Thomas, *In the Shadow of the Pulpit*, pp. 230–1.

[48] Thomas, *Collected Letters*, p. 329.

[49] Idem, *Collected Poems*, p. 58.

[50] Ibid., pp. 110, 111.

[51] Ibid., pp. 52, 24.

[52] Idem, *Under Milk Wood*, ed. Walford Davies and Ralph Maud (1954; London: Everyman, 1995), pp. 40–1.

[53] Idem, *Collected Poems*, pp. 134–5.

[54] Vernon Watkins (ed.), *Dylan Thomas: Letters to Vernon Watkins* (London: Faber, 1957), p. 16.

[55] Thomas, *Collected Poems*, p. 201.

[56] Theodor Adorno, 'Lyric Poetry and Society' (1957), in Brian O'Connor (ed.), *The Adorno Reader* (Oxford: Blackwell, 2000), p. 218.

[57] Dylan Thomas, *Early Prose Works*, ed. Walford Davies (New York: New Directions, 1972), pp. 154–5. See J. Hillis Miller, *Poets of Reality: Six Twentieth-Century Writers* (Cambridge, MA: Harvard University Press, 1965), pp. 195–7.

[58] John Goodby, *The Poetry of Dylan Thomas: Under the Spelling Wall* (Liverpool: Liverpool University Press, 2013), p. 65.

[59] Thomas, *Collected Poems*, pp. 45–6.

[60] Ralph Maud, *Where Have the Old Words Got Me? Explications of Dylan Thomas's Collected Poems* (Cardiff: University of Wales Press, 2003), p. 192.

[61] Goodby, *The Poetry of Dylan Thomas*, p. 65.

[62] Goodby suggests that 'it is a parody of an avant-garde poem and an avant-garde poem as parody', *The Poetry of Dylan Thomas*, p. 65.

[63] Thomas, *Collected Poems*, pp. 17, 47.

[64] Goodby, *The Poetry of Dylan Thomas*, p. 206. He does not read 'Now' within this thematic context, but offers an illuminating account of the poem in a discussion of 'mannerist modernism', pp. 64–6.

[65] Maud, *Where Have the Old Words*, p. 192.

[66] William York Tindall, *A Reader's Guide to Dylan Thomas* (Syracuse: Syracuse University Press, 1962), p. 103.

[67] Frith, *Performing Rites*, p. 157.

[68] Shapiro, 'Dylan Thomas', p. 269.

[69] Kenneth Rexroth, 'Thou Shalt Not Kill', in Charters (ed.), *The Penguin Book of the Beats*, pp. 233–41.

[70] Ginsberg, *Howl*, p. 62.

[71] Jack Kerouac and Allen Ginsberg, *The Letters*, ed. Bill Morgan and David Stanford (London: Penguin, 2011), p. 406.

[72] Kerouac, '239th Chorus' from *Mexico City Blues*, in Charters (ed.), *The Penguin Book of the Beats*, pp. 53–4. Recorded on Jack Kerouac and Steve Allen, *Poetry for the Beat Generation*, Hanover LP #5000. Originally released June 1959.

[73] David Yaffe, *Fascinating Rhythm: Reading Jazz in American Writing* (Princeton: Princeton University Press, 2006), p. 143.

[74] James Baldwin, 'The Black Boy Looks at the White Boy', in idem, *Nobody Knows My Name, Collected Essays: Vol. 2* (New York: Library of America, 1998), p. 278.

[75] Eldridge Cleaver, *Soul on Ice* (New York: McGraw-Hill, 1968), p. 72.

[76] A. Robert Lee, 'Black Beats: The Signifying Poetry of LeRoi Jones/Amiri Baraka, Ted Joans and Bob Kaufman', in idem (ed.), *Beat Generation Writers* (London: Pluto Press, 1996), p. 159.

[77] Bob Kaufman, 'Afterwards they Shall Dance', in idem, *Solitudes Crowded With Loneliness* (New York: New Directions, 1965), p. 6. For a selection of Ted Joans's writings see Sascha Feinstein and Yusef Komunyakaa (eds), *The Jazz Poetry Anthology* (Bloomington: Indiana University Press, 1991), pp. 104–6.

[78] LeRoi Jones/Amiri Baraka, *Dutchman*, in Henry Louis Gates, Jr. (general ed.), *The Norton Anthology of African American Literature* (New York: Norton, 1997), pp. 1897–8.

[79] Amiri Baraka, *The Autobiography of LeRoi Jones* (Chicago: Lawrence Hill Books, 1984), pp. 187–8.

[80] Ibid., p. 187.

[81] Richard Wright, *White Man, Listen!* (1957), in idem, *Black Power: Three Books from Exile* (New York: Harper Perennial, 2008), pp. 643, 727.

[82] Ishmael Reed, personal correspondence, March 2009.

[83] Al Young, 'The Dylan Thomas I Looked Up' (2002), in Jack Foley (ed.), *The Alsop Review*, http://www.alsopreview.com/foley/jfdthomas.html (accessed 18 June 2002).

[84] Idem, 'A Poem for Dylan Thomas', *Heaven: Collected Poems 1956–1990* (New York: Creative Arts Books Company, 1992), p. 17.

[85] Igor Stravinsky, 'The Opera that Might Have Been', *Adam: International Review*, 238 (1953), 8.

[86] Brinnin, *Dylan Thomas in America*, p. 216.

[87] See, for example, Astradur Eysteinsson, *The Concept of Modernism* (Ithaca: Cornell University Press, 1990), pp. 73–6.

[88] Thomas, *Collected Poems*, p. 22.

[89] Woideck (ed.), *The Charlie Parker Companion*, p. 51; Ted Gioia, *The Imperfect Art* (Oxford: Oxford University Press, 1988), p. 72.

[90] Woideck (ed.), *The Charlie Parker Companion*, p. 68.

[91] Ibid., p. 152.

[92] Alfred Appel, Jr., *Jazz Modernism: From Ellington and Armstrong to Matisse and Joyce* (New York: Alfred A. Knopf, 2002), p. 60.

[93] Martin Williams, 'Charlie Parker: The Burden of Innovation' (1970), in Woideck (ed.), *The Charlie Parker Companion*, p. 13.

Notes to Chapter 4

[1] *Tribune*, 15 August 1958. Quoted in Michael Foot, *Aneurin Bevan 1945–1960* (London: Davis-Poyntner, 1973), p. 608.
[2] *Western Mail*, 4 August 1958, 6.
[3] *Merthyr Express*, 9 August, 1958, 6.
[4] *Western Mail*, 4 August 1958, 6.
[5] *Merthyr Express*, Saturday, 9 August 1958, 6.
[6] For a fascinating analysis of stuttering see Marc Shell, *Stutter* (Cambridge, MA: Harvard University Press, 2005).
[7] *Merthyr Express*, Saturday, 9 August 1958, 6.
[8] The Caernarfon Pavilion (demolished in 1961) was filled to capacity four times during the 1930s. In 1934 for the Robeson concert, in 1935 for the National Eisteddfod, in 1937 for a meeting to welcome Saunders Lewis, Lewis Valentine and D. J. Williams back from their period of incarceration for setting light to an RAF bombing school in Penyberth, and for a Labour Day Festival in 1938. The title of the Memorial Meeting appears on the programme held at the South Wales Miners' Library, Swansea.
[9] See Alan Llwyd, *Cymru Ddu/Black Wales: A History* (Cardiff: Hughes a'i Fab, 2005), pp. 119–20; Neil Sinclair, *The Tiger Bay Story* (Cardiff: Dragon and Tiger Enterprises, 1997), p. 42.
[10] Hywel Francis has produced a useful list of Robeson's connections with Wales, 'Paul Robeson and Wales', held in the 'Paul Robeson File' at the South Wales Miners' Library, Swansea. See my detailed discussion of Robeson in 1930s Wales in *Black Skin, Blue Books: African Americans and Wales 1845–1945* (Cardiff: University of Wales Press, 2012), pp. 142–207.
[11] Dai Smith, *Aneurin Bevan and the World of South Wales* (Cardiff: University of Wales Press, 1993), p. 10. See also idem, 'In Place of Wales: A Coda', in idem, *Wales: A Question for History* (Bridgend: Seren, 1999), pp. 191–205.
[12] T. J. Davies, *Paul Robeson* (Abertawe: Christopher Davies, 1981), pp. 194–5. My translation.
[13] Raymond Williams, 'Community', in idem, *Who Speaks for Wales? Nation, Culture, Identity*, ed. Daniel Williams (Cardiff: University of Wales Press, 2003), p. 27.
[14] Gwynfor Evans, *Aros Mae* (Abertawe: Gwasg John Penry, 1971), p. 296. My translation.
[15] Angharad Tomos, *Hiraeth am Yfory: David Thomas a Mudiad Llafur Gogledd Cymru* (Llandysul: Gomer, 2002), p. 240. See also Robert Griffiths, 'The Other Aneurin Bevan', in Janet Davies (ed.), *Compass Points: The First 100 Issues of Planet* (Cardiff: University of Wales Press, 1993), pp. 130–1.
[16] R. Merfyn Jones and Ioan Rhys Jones, 'Labour and the Nation', in D. Tanner, C. Williams a D. Hopkin (eds), *The Labour Party in Wales* (Cardiff: University of Wales Press, 2000), p. 258; Griffiths, 'The Other Aneurin Bevan', pp. 127–32.
[17] Jones and Jones, 'Labour and the Nation', p. 258.
[18] Saunders Lewis, *Cerddi*, ed. R. Geraint Gruffydd (Caerdydd: University of Wales Press, 1992), p. 10. Translated by Gwyn Thomas in Alun R. Jones and Gwyn

Thomas (eds), *Presenting Saunders Lewis* (Cardiff: University of Wales Press, 1973), p. 177. Saunders Lewis and Kate Roberts, *Annwyl Kate, Annwyl Saunders*, ed. Dafydd Ifans (Aberystwyth: National Library of Wales, 1992), p. 16.

19 There is a semantic issue here. A case might be made for thinking of the 'Cymry' ('Welsh') as 'Welsh-language speakers'. This is still a common usage, and was the dominant definition of 'Cymry' until the twentieth century. The 'Cymry' in this sense are a linguistic minority in a nation where the majority are 'Welsh'. 'Cymraeg' culture is therefore distinct from 'Welsh' culture. There are sound methodological and political reasons for thinking in this way, for Welsh-language texts will contain resonances, allusions, rhetorical tropes, and so on that are distinctive to the Welsh-language tradition. Similarly, studies of a non-Welsh-speaking author need not engage with Welsh-language culture. At this historical juncture, where it is crucial for its future that the Welsh language be made a key component in the culture underpinning Welsh citizenship, it seems incongruous to use the older, linguistically exclusionary definition of 'Cymro' and 'Cymraes'. For an account of the etymological development of 'Cymry' see Simon Brooks and Richard Glyn Roberts, 'Pwy yw'r Cymry? Hanes Enw', in idem and idem (eds), *Pa Beth yr Aethoch Allan i'w Achub?* (Llanrwst: Gwasg Carreg Gwalch, 2013), pp. 23–39.

20 Alun Ffred Jones, *Y Cyfryngau Wedi'r Cynulliad* (Talybont: Lolfa, 1999), p. 16. My translation.

21 See the series of volumes edited by Hywel Teifi Edwards, *Cyfres y Cymoedd* (Gomer).

22 Smith, *Aneurin Bevan and the World of South Wales*, p. 258.

23 Ibid., p. 189.

24 Ibid., p. 197.

25 *Merthyr Express*, Saturday, 9 August 1958, 6.

26 Aneurin Bevan, 'The Claim of Wales: A Statement'. First published in *Tribune*. Re-printed in *Wales: The National Magazine*, VII, 25 (spring 1947), 151–3.

27 Quoted by Harri Webb in 'Against Imperialism', *No Half Way House*, ed. Meic Stephens (Talybont: Y Lolfa, 1997), p. 98.

28 Ibid. Thanks to Nicholas Jones for this reference. See his article 'Supercharging the Struggle: Models of Nationalist Victory in the Poetry of Harri Webb', *Welsh Writing in English: A Yearbook of Critical Essays*, ed. Tony Brown, 9 (2004), pp. 102–22.

29 Quoted by Dai Smith, *Wales! Wales?* (London: Allen and Unwin, 1984), p. 132.

30 Karl Marx, 'The British Rule in India', in idem and Engels, *Basic Writings on Politics and Philosophy*, ed. Lewis Feuer (Garden City, NY: Anchor Books, 1959), p. 480.

31 Foot, *Aneurin Bevan 1945–1960*, pp. 394–6.

32 Gwyn Thomas interviewed by Michael Parkinson Part 2. Accessed on YouTube: *https://www.youtube.com/watch?v=EgVIIhUHnpE* (accessed 1 September 2012). This quotation starts at 3 minutes 30 seconds. First broadcast 28 November 1971.

33 Walter Benn Michaels, *The Trouble with Diversity: How We Learned to Love Identity and Ignore Inequality* (New York: Holt, 2006), p. 203.

34 Sterling Stuckey, *Slave Culture: Nationalist Theory and the Foundations of Black America* (Oxford: Oxford University Press, 1987), pp. 351–2.

[35] Martin Duberman, *Paul Robeson: A Biography* (1988; New York: New Press, 1989), p. 228.

[36] Marie Seton, *Paul Robeson* (London: Dobson, 1958), p. 121.

[37] Paul Robeson, 'The People of America are the Power' (1951), *Paul Robeson Speaks: Writings, Speeches, Interviews 1918–1974*, ed. Philip S. Foner (London: Quartet Books, 1978), p. 271.

[38] 'Robeson and Bevan Get Big Welcome', *Western Mail*, 4 August 1958, 1.

[39] Charles L. Blockson, 'Paul Robeson: A Bibliophile in Spite of Himself', in J. C. Stewart (ed.), *Paul Robeson: Artist and Citizen* (New Brunswick: Rutgers University Press, 1998), pp. 235–50.

[40] I discuss this in detail in *Black Skin, Blue Books*, pp. 151–68.

[41] Paul Robeson, *Here I Stand* (1958; Boston, Beacon Press, 1988), p. 36.

[42] Idem, 'How I Discovered Africa' (1953), in idem, *Paul Robeson Speaks: Writings, Speeches, Interviews 1918–1974*, ed. Philip S. Foner (London: Quartet Books, 1978), p. 352. Also idem, *Here I Stand*, p. 36.

[43] Programme for concert held at the Majestic Cinema, Wrexham, Sunday, 25 March 1934. Copy in the Paul Robeson Collection at the Miners Library, Swansea University Swansea. See also the programme for a concert held at the Empire Cinema, Neath in the Schomburg Library, Lawrence Brown Collection (Microfilm Reel 5). Duberman, *Paul Robeson: A Biography*, p. 178.

[44] Robeson, *Here I Stand*, p. 54.

[45] Idem, 'Robeson Spurns Music He Doesn't Understand' (1933), in *Paul Robeson Speaks*, p. 85.

[46] Idem, 'I Want to be African' (1934), in ibid., p. 90.

[47] Idem, 'Pacifica Radio Interview' (1958), in ibid., p. 453.

[48] Kate Baldwin, *Beyond the Color Line and the Iron Curtain* (Durham: Duke University Press, 2002), p. 211.

[49] Stuckey, *Slave Culture*, p. 351.

[50] Richard Wyn Jones describes the 'hysterically hostile reception' afforded Michael Hechter's *Internal Colonialism* in 'The Colonial Legacy in Welsh Politics', in Jane Aaron and Chris Williams (eds), *Postcolonial Wales* (Cardiff: University of Wales Press, 2005), p. 25. Dai Smith rejects Hechter and postcolonialism in 'Psycho-colonialism', *New Welsh Review*, 66 (winter 2004), 22–9.

[51] For example, Chris Williams's vision of a post-national Wales in 'Problematizing Wales: An Exploration in Historiography and Postcoloniality', in Aaron and Williams (eds), *Postcolonial Wales*, pp. 16–17.

[52] An indicative example of this shift in Wales are the essays collected in Charlotte Williams, Neil Evans and Paul O'Leary (eds), *A Tolerant Nation? Exploring Ethnic Diversity in Wales* (Cardiff: University of Wales Press, 2003).

[53] Nancy Fraser, 'Rethinking Recognition', *New Left Review II*, 3 (May/June 2000), 107–20.

[54] Raymond Williams, *Culture and Society: Coleridge to Orwell* (1958; London: Hogarth Press, 1990).

[55] Idem, 'Culture and Revolution: a Response', in Terry Eagleton and Brian Wicker (eds), *From Culture to Revolution* (London: Sheed and Ward, 1968), p. 308.

56 See Williams's account in *Politics and Letters: Interviews with New Left Review* (London: Verso, 1979), p. 113.

57 See Daniel Williams, 'Cymdeithas a Chenedl yng Ngwaith Raymond Williams', *Taliesin*, 97 (gwanwyn 1997), 55–76.

58 Ned Thomas, *The Welsh Extremist: A Culture in Crisis* (London: Gollancz, 1971); Williams, *Who Speaks for Wales?*, p. 4.

59 Idem, 'The Practice of Possibility' (1987), in ibid., p. 214. Also idem, *Towards 2000* (London: Chatto and Windus, 1983).

60 I am returning here to a question that I discussed with Ned Thomas and Dai Smith in 'The Exchange: Raymond Williams', *Planet: The Welsh Internationalist* (summer 2009), 45–66.

61 There is a longstanding debate in Marxist theory regarding the question of whether class is a scientific measurement (class 'in itself'), or a matter of 'consciousness' ('for itself'). Historian E. P. Thompson argued that 'if we stop history at a given point, then there are no classes, but simply a multitude of individuals with a multitude of experiences'. In his view 'class itself is not a thing, it is a happening'. G. A. Cohen objects to this view and argues for a structural definition of classes in which classes 'undergo a process of cultural and political formation'. See G. A. Cohen, *Karl Marx's Theory of History: A Defence* (Princeton: Princeton University Press, 1978), pp. 76–7; E. P. Thompson, *The Making of the English Working Class* (1963; Harmondsworth: Penguin, 1968), p. 11.

62 Benn Michaels, *The Trouble with Diversity*, pp. 10–16.

63 My thinking here is influenced by idem, 'Plots against America: Neoliberalism and Antiracism', *American Literary History*, 18, 2 (2006), 288–302.

64 Richard Wyn Jones, *Rhoi Cymru'n Gyntaf: Syniadaeth Plaid Cymru* (Caerdydd: University of Wales Press, 2007), p. 87.

65 Quoted in T. Robin Chapman, *Un Bywyd o Blith Nifer: Cofiant Saunders Lewis* (Llandysul: Gomer, 2006), p. 275. 'Mae gan y Blaid Genedlaethol Gymreig athroniaeth wleidyddol sy'n sylfaenedig ar draddodiadau hanesyddol Cymreig ac sy'n gwbl groes i athroniaeth Sosialaeth Seisnig a Sosialaeth Marx.'

66 Simon Brooks, *Yr Hawl i Oroesi: Ysgrifau Gwleidyddol a Diwylliannol* (Llanrwst: Gwasg Carreg Gwalch, 2009), p. 117.

67 Ibid., p. 118; my translation. 'Mewn gwlad iach byddai Ceidwadaeth yn gefnogol i'r Gymraeg – am ei bod o blaid cadw pethau, ac am fod rhai gwerthoedd (megis iaith neu enaid cenedl) yn ei thyb hi yn oesol ... Nid felly Sosialaeth gyda'i ragfarn yn erbyn haniaethau o'r fath.'

68 Translated by the author from the play *Buchedd Garmon* (1937), in *Dramâu Saunders Lewis*, cyfrol 1, ed. Ioan M. Williams (Caerdydd: University of Wales Press, 1996), p. 139.

69 Benn Michaels, *The Trouble with Diversity*, pp. 64–5.

70 Lewis Jones, *Cwmardy* (1937) and *We Live* (1939) reprinted as one volume in *Cwmardy and We Live*, Library of Wales (Aberteifi: Parthian, 2005). See for example Hywel Francis's introduction to the Library of Wales edition.

71 Ibid., p. 297.

72 Ibid., pp. 617–20.

73 In fact the novel leaves the possibility open that Jane is actually carrying Len's child. Consider Big Jim's ambiguous words: 'The little babby you are going to

bring in to the world belongs to no one but the people in this house. It will be ours and no one else's. There will be no wedding before it is born, and its father is not Evan the Overman's son. Do you understand my words, Jane bach?' Ibid., pp. 67–8.

74 Ibid., p. 82.
75 Marc Shell, *Children of the Earth: Literature, Politics and Nationhood* (Oxford: Oxford University Press, 1993), p. 4.
76 This is the desire that informs Williams's *Culture and Society*.
77 Martin Duberman, *The Politics of Exclusion: Essays 1964–1999* (New York: Basic Books, 1999), p. 427.
78 Roberto Mangabeira Unger, *The Left Alternative* (London: Verso, 2005), p. 51.
79 See William Julius Wilson's controversial volume, *The Declining Significance of Race* (Chicago: Chicago University Press, 1978).

Notes to Chapter 5

1 Henry Louis Gates, Jr., *Tradition and the Black Atlantic: Critical Theory in the African Diaspora* (New York: Basic Books, 2010). 'Internally' appears in Gates's book, but it is actually 'internationally' in the original. Raymond Williams, *Towards 2000* (London: Chatto and Windus, 1983), pp. 195–6.
2 John Higgins, *Raymond Williams: Literature, Marxism and Cultural Materialism* (London: Routledge, 1999), p. 170; Rajagopalan Radhakrishnan, 'Cultural Theory and the Politics of Location', in D. Dworkin and L. Roman (eds), *Views Beyond the Border Country: Raymond Williams and Cultural Politics* (London: Routledge, 1993), p. 291; Benita Parry, 'A Critique Mishandled', *Social Text*, 35 (1993), 123; Laura Chrisman, 'Imperial Space, Imperial Place: Theories of Empire and Culture in Fredric Jameson, Edward Said and Gayatri Spivak', *New Formations: A Journal of Culture/Theory/Politics*, 34 (1998), 53; Cornel West, *Prophetic Thought in Postmodern Times* (Monroe: Common Courage Press, 1993), p. 174; Houston A. Baker, Jr., Manthia Diawara and Ruth Lindeborg (eds), *Black British Cultural Studies: A Reader* (Chicago: Chicago University Press, 1996), pp. 4–5.
3 Gates, *Tradition and the Black Atlantic*, pp. 39–40.
4 Williams, *Towards 2000*, p. 193.
5 Gates, *Tradition and the Black Atlantic*, p. 40.
6 Paul Gilroy, *'There Ain't No Black in the Union Jack': The Cultural Politics of Race and Nation* (Chicago: Chicago University Press, 1987), p. 49.
7 Quoted in Robert Shepherd, *Enoch Powell* (London: Pimlico, 1996), p. 352.
8 Williams, *Towards 2000*, p. 195.
9 Gilroy, *There Ain't No Black in the Union Jack*, pp. 49–50.
10 Stuart Hall, 'Our Mongrel Selves', *Borderlands*, a supplement with *New Statesman*, 19 June 1992, 7.
11 Williams, *Towards 2000*, p. 195.
12 Ibid.
13 Gilroy, *There Ain't No Black in the Union Jack*, p. 59.

[14]   Idem, *The Black Atlantic: Modernity and Double Consciousness* (Cambridge, MA: Harvard University Press, 1993).

[15]   Gates, *Tradition and the Black Atlantic*, p. 45.

[16]   Neil Lazarus, *Nationalism and Cultural Practice in the Postcolonial World* (Cambridge: Cambridge University Press, 1999), p. 65.

[17]   Raymond Williams, *Politics and Letters: Interviews with New Left Review* (London: Verso, 1979), p. 36.

[18]   Idem, 'The Shadow of the Dragon' (1985), in idem, *Who Speaks for Wales? Nation, Culture, Identity*, ed. Daniel Williams (Cardiff: University of Wales Press, 2003), p. 67.

[19]   Gates, *Tradition and the Black Atlantic*, p. 41.

[20]   Ibid., p. 45.

[21]   Raymond Williams, *Culture and Society: Coleridge to Orwell* (1958; London: Hogarth Press, 1990); idem, *The Long Revolution* (1961; Harmondsworth: Penguin, 1971).

[22]   Idem, *The Long Revolution*, p. 252.

[23]   Ibid., p. 303.

[24]   Ibid., p. 15.

[25]   Idem, *Border Country* (1960; Cardigan: Parthian, 2006), p. 35. This is the Library of Wales edition.

[26]   Ibid., p. 177.

[27]   Ibid., pp. 240, 400.

[28]   Ibid., p. 145.

[29]   Ibid., p. 219.

[30]   Roland Barthes, *S/Z*, tr. Richard Miller (London: Farrar, Straus & Giroux Inc., 1975); Catherine Belsey, *Critical Practice* (London: Routledge, 1980); Colin MacCabe, *James Joyce and the Revolution of the Word* (London: Macmillan, 1978). The role of Welsh in *Border Country* is similar to that of Hebrew in Eliot's *Daniel Deronda* as theorized by MacCabe. '[P]erhaps most powerfully of all, the Hebrew language which rests uninvestigable at the centre of *Daniel Deronda*, question[s] and hold[s] in suspense the project of Eliot's text ... Deronda's discovery of the Jewish language and the poems of Mordecai trouble the meta-language in so far as the Jewish language constitutes an area outside its control. Deronda hears the news that Mordecai's work is in Hebrew and untranslatable with "anxiety". Such a feeling is not surprising when we recognise that the poems constitute a fatal threat to the meta-language.' MacCabe, *James Joyce and the Revolution of the Word*, p. 21.

[31]   The eisteddfod is a distinctively Welsh cultural festival which, in the novel, is part of the communal life of the border country.

[32]   Williams, *Border Country*, pp. 258–9.

[33]   Ibid., p. 250.

[34]   Idem, 'Community' (1985), in *Who Speaks for Wales?*, p. 27.

[35]   Idem, *Border Country*, p. 3.

[36]   Ibid., pp. 331–2.

[37]   Ibid., pp. 3, 12.

[38]   Ibid., p. 368.

[39] Idem, 'Who Speaks for Wales' (1971), in *Who Speaks for Wales?*, p. 3.

[40] Christopher Prendergast, 'Introduction', in idem (ed.), *Cultural Materialism: On Raymond Williams* (Minneapolis: University of Minnesota Press, 1995), p. 18.

[41] Raymond Williams, 'Dylan Thomas's Play for Voices', *Critical Quarterly*, 1 (1959), 18–26. Collected in C. B. Cox (ed.), *Dylan Thomas: A Collection of Critical Essays* (Englewood Cliffs NJ: Prentice-Hall, 196), pp. 89–98; Williams, 'All Things Betray Thee' (1986), in *Who Speaks for Wales?*, p. 161.

[42] Idem, 'Dylan Thomas's Play for Voices', in C. B. Cox (ed.), *Dylan Thomas: A Collection of Critical Essays* (Englewood Cliffs, NJ: Prentice-Hall, 1966), p. 98; Williams, 'Working-Class, Proletarian, Socialist' (1982), in *Who Speaks for Wales?*, p. 155.

[43] Williams, 'Remaking Welsh History' (1980), in *Who Speaks for Wales?*, p. 72; idem, 'West of Offa's Dyke' (1986), in *Who Speaks for Wales?*, p. 34.

[44] Idem, *The Long Revolution*, p. 308.

[45] Idem, *Border Country*, p. 8.

[46] Ibid, pp. 81–2.

[47] Ibid., p. 4.

[48] Ibid., p. 353.

[49] Ibid., p. 8.

[50] Ibid., p. 89.

[51] Ibid.

[52] Edward Said, *Orientalism: Western Conceptions of the Orient* (1978; London: Penguin, 1995), p. 240.

[53] Raymond Williams, *Loyalties* (London: Hogarth Press, 1985), p. 307.

[54] Idem, *Politics and Letters*, pp. 118–19.

[55] Idem and Edward Said, 'Media, Margins and Modernity', in Raymond Williams, *The Politics of Modernism: Against the New Conformists*, ed. Tony Pinkney (London: Verso, 1989), p. 196.

[56] Edward Said, *Culture and Imperialism* (1993; London: Vintage, 1994), pp. 98–9. Said also discusses Williams in *The World, The Text and the Critic* (Cambridge, MA: Harvard University Press, 1983), pp. 237–42.

[57] Idem, *Culture and Imperialism*, p. 98.

[58] Raymond Williams, *The Country and the City* (1973; London: Hogarth Press, 1985), p. 280.

[59] Ibid.

[60] Ibid., pp. 303–4.

[61] Dai Smith, 'Relating to Wales', in Terry Eagleton (ed.), *Raymond Williams: Critical Perspectives* (Cambridge: Polity, 1989), p. 35.

[62] Gauri Viswanathan, 'Raymond Williams and British Colonialism', in Prendergast (ed.), *Cultural Materialism*, p. 190.

[63] Gilroy, *There Ain't No Black in the Union Jack*, pp. 49–50.

[64] Williams, *Towards 2000*, p. 193.

[65] Ibid., p. 196.

[66] Idem, *Politics and Letters*, pp. 296, 26.

[67] Idem, 'The Importance of Community' (1977), in *Who Speaks for Wales*, p. 179; idem, 'Who Speaks for Wales?', p. 3.

[68]   Idem, 'Who Speaks for Wales?', p. 3.
[69]   Idem, 'Community', p. 27.
[70]   Ibid.
[71]   Ibid., p. 28.
[72]   Idem, 'Marxism, Poetry, Wales: an interview with J. P. Ward' (1977), in *Who Speaks for Wales?*, p. 87.
[73]   Idem, *Second Generation* (London: Chatto and Windus, 1964), pp. 321–2.
[74]   Patrick Parrinder, *The Failure of Theory* (Brighton: Harvester, 1987), p. 78; James A. Davies, 'Not going back but ... exile ending: Raymond Williams's Fictional Wales', in W. J. Morgan and P. Preston (eds), *Raymond Williams: Politics, Education, Letters* (London: Macmillan, 1993), p. 207.

Notes to Chapter 6

[1]   Robert Minhinnick, *To Babel and Back* (Bridgend: Seren, 2005), p. 31.
[2]   Ibid., p. 32.
[3]   Ibid., p. 33.
[4]   See also M. Wynn Thomas and Daniel Williams, 'A Sweet Union? Dylan Thomas and Post-War American Poetry', in Gilbert Bennett, Eryl Jenkins and Eurwen Price (eds), *I Sang in My Chains: Essays and Poems in Tribute to Dylan Thomas* (Swansea: The Dylan Thomas Society of Great Britain, 2003), pp. 68–79.
[5]   Matthew Arnold, 'Democracy' (1861), in idem, *The Complete Prose Works of Matthew Arnold*, ed. R. H. Super, 11 vols (Ann Arbor: University of Michigan Press, 1960–77), vol. II, pp. 15–16.
[6]   Idem, *On the Study of Celtic Literature* (1867), in idem, *The Complete Prose Works of Matthew Arnold*, vol III. This will be abbreviated from now on as *CPW*, followed by volume number. For a detailed discussion, see Ned Thomas, 'Renan, Arnold, Unamuno: Philology and the Minority Languages', *Bedford Occasional Papers: Essays in Language, Literature and Area Studies*, 6 (1984), 1–14, and Daniel G. Williams, *Ethnicity and Cultural Authority: From Arnold to Du Bois* (Edinburgh: Edinburgh University Press, 2006).
[7]   R. F. Foster, *Paddy and Mr. Punch: Connections in Irish and English History* (London: Penguin, 1993), p. 9.
[8]   W. B. Yeats, *Uncollected Prose Volume I*, ed. John P. Frayne (London: Macmillan, 1970), p. 268.
[9]   On Yeats's influence on R. S. Thomas see Neal Alexander, 'Dialogues of Self and Soul: The Autobiographies of W. B. Yeats and R. S. Thomas', *Almanac: A Yearbook of Welsh Writing in English*, 12 (2007–8), 1–31, and Damian Walford Davies, '"Yeats Said That": R. S. Thomas and W. B. Yeats', *Almanac: A Yearbook of Welsh Writing in English*, 13 (2008–9), 1–26. Also of relevance here is Tony Brown, 'The Romantic Nationalism of R. S. Thomas', in Norman Page and Peter Preston (eds), *The Literature of Place* (Basingstoke: Macmillan, 1993), pp. 156–69, and Kirsti Bohata's discussion of Thomas in *Postcolonialism Revisited* (Cardiff: University of Wales Press, 2004), pp. 51–7.

[10] Arnold, *CPW III*, p. 291; R. S. Thomas, 'Y Llwybrau Gynt 2', in idem, *R. S. Thomas: Selected Prose*, ed. Sarah Anstey (Bridgend: Poetry Wales Press, 1983), pp. 137–8.

[11] W. B. Yeats, *Autobiographies* (London: Macmillan, 1955), p. 295; Yeats quoted by Elizabeth Cullingford in *Yeats, Ireland and Fascism* (London: Macmillan, 1981), p. 11; R. S. Thomas, *Cymru or Wales?* (Llandysul: Gomer, 1992), p. 12.

[12] Quoted by R. F. Foster, *W. B. Yeats: A Life I. The Apprentice Mage* (Oxford: Oxford University Press, 1997), p. 310.

[13] Thomas, *Cymru or Wales?*, p. 8.

[14] Idem, *No Truce with the Furies* (Newcastle upon Tyne: Bloodaxe Books, 1995), p. 25.

[15] Idem, 'Review of "Bury My Heart at Wounded Knee"', in idem, *R. S. Thomas: Selected Prose*, p. 179.

[16] Ibid., p. 180.

[17] M. Wynn Thomas, 'Prints of Wales: Contemporary Welsh Poetry in English', in Lothar Fietz and Hans-Werner Ludwig (eds), *Poetry in the British Isles: Non-Metropolitan Perspectives* (Cardiff: University of Wales Press, 1995), p. 98.

[18] Ibid.

[19] Robert Minhinnick, 'Living with R. S. Thomas', *Poetry Wales*, 29, 1 (July 1993), 13.

[20] Jon Dressel, 'Looking Both Ways', *New Welsh Review*, 32 (spring 1996), 57.

[21] Idem, 'Correspondence', *The Anglo-Welsh Review*, 26, 58 (spring 1977), 227.

[22] Ibid., 229.

[23] Ibid., 230.

[24] Idem, *Hard Love and a Country* (Swansea: Christopher Davies, 1977), p. 19.

[25] Idem, *Out of Wales* (Port Talbot: Alun Books, 1985).

[26] Tony Conran, *Frontiers in Anglo-Welsh Poetry* (Cardiff: University of Wales Press, 1997), p. 262.

[27] Jon Dressel, 'Introduction' to *The Road to Shiloh* (Llandysul: Gomer, 1994), p. xiii.

[28] Ibid., p. xiii; idem, 'Looking Both Ways', 57.

[29] Idem and T. James Jones, *Cerddi Ianws* (Llandysul: Gomer, 1979). For a discussion of these poems within the context of a seminal discussion of literary translation in Wales see M. Wynn Thomas, *Corresponding Cultures: The Two Literatures of Wales* (Cardiff: University of Wales Press, 1999), pp. 143–4.

[30] Dressel, 'Introduction' to *The Road to Shiloh*, p. xvii.

[31] Ibid.

[32] Ibid., p. xxii.

[33] M. M. Bakhtin, *The Dialogic Imagination: Four Essays*, trans. Caryl Emerson and Michael Holquist (Austin: University of Texas Press, 1981), p. 275.

[34] Ibid., p. 308.

[35] David W. Blight, *Race and Reunion: The Civil War in American Memory* (Cambridge, MA: Harvard University Press, 2001), p. 2.

[36] Dressel, *Road to Shiloh*, p. 32.

[37] Ibid., p. 109.

[38] Ibid., p. xix.

[39] Ibid.
[40] Ibid.
[41] Ibid.
[42] See Will Kaufman, *The Civil War in American Culture* (Edinburgh: Edinburgh University Press, 2006), pp. 33–7.
[43] Quoted in Tony Horowitz, *Confederates in the Attic: Dispatches from the Unfinished Civil War* (New York: Vintage, 1999), p. 69. See critiques of McWhinney by Rowland Berthoff, 'Celtic Mist Over the South', *The Journal of Southern History*, 52 (1986), 523–50, and Michael Newton, *We're Indians Sure Enough: The Legacy of the Scottish Highlanders in the United States* (Chapel Hill: Saorsa Media, 2001).
[44] Horowitz, *Confederates in the Attic*, p. 69.
[45] Helen Taylor, *Circling Dixie: Contemporary Southern Culture through a Transatlantic Lens* (New Brunswick: Rutgers University Press, 2001), p. 16.
[46] Dressel, *The Road to Shiloh*, p. xviii.
[47] Ibid., p. 28.
[48] Ibid., p. 61.
[49] Ibid., p. 109.
[50] Ibid., p. 71.
[51] Ibid., pp. 69–70.
[52] Ibid., p. 74.
[53] W. E. B. Du Bois, 'Robert E. Lee' (March 1928), in idem, *Writings*, ed. Nathan I. Huggins (New York: Library of America, 1986), p. 1223.
[54] Dressel, *Road to Shiloh*, pp. 88–9.
[55] Ibid., p. 110.
[56] M. Wynn Thomas, 'Gwlad o Bosibiliadau: Golwg ar Lên Cymru ac America', *Y Traethodydd*, 157 (2002), 50.
[57] Dressel, *Road to Shiloh*, p. xx.
[58] Ishmael Reed, *Another Day at the Front: Dispatches from the Race War* (New York: Basic Books, 2003), p. 100.
[59] Dressel, *Road to Shiloh*, p. xii.
[60] Nigel Jenkins, *Footsore on the Frontier: Selected Essays and Articles* (Llandysul: Gomer, 2001), p. 207.
[61] Ibid., p. 147.
[62] Ibid., p. 61.
[63] Idem, *Acts of Union: Selected Poems 1974–1989* (Llandysul: Gomer, 1990), p. 99.
[64] Ibid.
[65] Thomas, *Corresponding Cultures*, p. 227.
[66] See Bohata's nuanced discussion of these issues in *Postcolonialism Revisited*.
[67] Jenkins, 'Circus', in *Acts of Union*, p. 57.
[68] Ibid., p. 60.
[69] Ibid., p. 51.
[70] Ibid., p. 55.
[71] Ibid., p. 62.
[72] Ibid., p. 65.

73 Ibid., p. 59.
74 Ibid., p. 64.
75 Ibid., p. 54.
76 Ibid., p. 57.
77 Ibid., p. 53.
78 Ibid., p. 51.
79 Ibid., p. 26.
80 Idem, *Footsore*, pp. 63–4.
81 Ibid., pp. 62, 65.
82 Ibid., p. 64.
83 Ibid., p. 44.
84 Ibid., p. 151; idem, *Hotel Gwales* (Llandysul: Gomer, 2006), p. 24.
85 Idem, *Footsore*, p. 150.
86 Idem, *Hotel Gwales*, p. 102.
87 Susan Sontag, 'Regarding the Torture of Others', *New York Times Magazine*, 23 May 2004, http://www.nytimes.com/2004/05/23/magazine/23PRISONS.html (accessed December 2007).
88 This is Stefan Collini's apt phrase in *Common Reading: Critics, Historians, Publics* (Oxford: Oxford University Press, 2008), p. 183.
89 Thomas, *Corresponding Cultures*, p. 228.
90 R. S. Thomas's phrase quoted by Dressel, 'Correspondence', 229.
91 Duncan Bush, 'More Thoughts from the Periphery', *Planet: The Welsh Internationalist*, 121 (February/March 1997), 73.
92 Idem, 'The Zidane Effect and Criticising the Critics', *Poetry Wales*, 34, 3 (January 1999), 43, 44.
93 Idem, *Midway* (Bridgend: Seren, 1998), p. 26.
94 Ibid., p. 39.
95 Ibid., pp. 39–40.
96 Ibid., pp. 25, 40
97 Ibid., pp. 24, 14.
98 Ibid., p. 40.
99 Idem, 'Richard Poole Interviews Duncan Bush', *Poetry Wales*, 28, 1 (July 1992), 13.
100 Idem, 'Introduction to Poems', in Meic Stephens (ed.), *The Bright Field: An Anthology of Contemporary Poetry from Wales* (Manchester: Carcanet, 1991), p. 42; idem, 'Richard Poole Interviews', 12.
101 Idem, 'Robert Minhinnick interviews Duncan Bush', *Poetry Wales*, 38, 2 (autumn 2002), 47; idem, 'Richard Poole Interviews', 12.
102 While Richard Poole formulated probing questions for an interview with Bush in 1992, Robert Minhinnick, a decade later, knew what to expect and replaced questions with single words designed to elicit the appropriate response: 'I'll say one word: "Wales". Fire away'. Bush, 'Robert Minhinnick Interviews', 48.
103 Ibid., 49; Stefan Collini, *Absent Minds: Intellectuals in Britain* (Oxford: Oxford University Press, 2006), chapter 18.
104 Bush, 'Richard Poole Interviews', 14.
105 Ibid., 19–20.

[106] Idem, *Masks* (Bridgend: Seren, 1994), p. 34.
[107] Idem, 'Richard Poole Interviews', 18.
[108] Idem, *Masks*, p. 45.
[109] Ibid., pp. 55–6.
[110] Ibid., pp. 61–2.
[111] Ibid., p. 66.
[112] Ibid., p. 69.
[113] Ibid. 'V. A. shrink' refers to a 'Veteran's Administration' counsellor.
[114] Jenkins, *Acts*, p. 65.

Notes to Chapter 7

[1] Étienne Balibar and Immanuel Wallerstein, *Race, Nation, Class: Ambiguous Identities* (London: Verso, 1995), p. 97.
[2] Ibid.
[3] Daniel Williams, 'Introduction' to Raymond Williams, *Who Speaks for Wales? Nation, Culture, Identity*, ed. Daniel Williams (Cardiff: University of Wales Press, 2003), pp. xxxvi–xxxix; Ian Gregson, *The New Poetry in Wales* (Cardiff: University of Wales Press, 2007), p. 80; Chris Wigginton, *Modernism from the Margins: The 1930s Poetry of Louis MacNiece and Dylan Thomas* (Cardiff: University of Wales Press, 2007), p. 104.
[4] Raymond Williams, 'Community' (1985), in idem, *Who Speaks for Wales?*, p. 27.
[5] Wigginton, *Modernism*, p. 104.
[6] Williams, 'Community', pp. 28, 30.
[7] Ibid., p. 30.
[8] Gregson, *The New Poetry*, pp. 38, 73, 13. The same equation between 'language' and 'race' occurs in John Goodby's *The Poetry of Dylan Thomas: Under the Spelling Wall* (Liverpool: Liverpool University Press, 2013), which appeared following completion of this chapter. In celebrating the 'inclusive and pluralist' definition of Wales embraced by Dylan Thomas, Goodby compares it with 'Welsh-Wales forms of Welshness' as manifested in a few widely quoted anti-Semitic lines by Saunders Lewis (ibid., pp. 283–7). According to Goodby, Lewis was a '*racial*' absolutist, and it is therefore not surprising that 'today's *linguistic* culturalists ... say as little about his actual political beliefs as possible' (ibid., p. 284; emphasis added). As evidence he references the five-sentence introduction to Lewis that appears in Menna Elfyn and John Rowlands, *The Bloodaxe Book of Modern Welsh Poetry* (Highgreen: Bloodaxe Books, 2003), p. 77. In fact Lewis's anti-Semitism has been widely discussed, particularly following the accusations in D. Tecwyn Lloyd, *John Saunders Lewis: Y Gyfrol Gyntaf* (Dinbych: Gwasg Gee, 1988). The ensuing debate was largely in Welsh. In his biography of Lewis, *Un Bywyd o Blith Nifer: Cofiant Saunders Lewis* (Llandysul: Gomer, 2006), T. Robin Chapman explores both Lewis's fascist leanings and his anti-Semitism. Michael Cronin has described the ways in which Irish-language criticism is ignored in contemporary Irish studies: 'There is a kind of dual silencing in operation. Firstly, the sources are not heard because they are in the wrong language and

secondly, the books on the sources are ignored because they are in the wrong language. If Irish-language scholars and writers consistently list English-language sources, it is only rarely that the compliment is returned' ('Half the Picture', *Dublin Review of Books*, *http://www.drb.ie/essays/half-the-picture* (accessed 1 August 2014). Due to the relative strength of Welsh, and the commitment to cultural pluralism informing the majority of critics contributing to the field, Welsh writing in English has remained open to voices and influences from the minority-language culture. Goodby considers this a mark of the field's 'essentialist' 'linguistic culturalism' (*The Poetry of Dylan Thomas*, p. 25). While he makes some passing references to Welsh-language writers (pp. 282–4), Goodby suggests that Saunders Lewis's 'fascist-inclined' politics was 'much revivified by the rise of Cymdeithas yr Iaith Gymreig [*sic*] (the Welsh Language Movement [*sic*]) in the 1960s' (p. 46). The students who adopted a strategy of civil disobedience from the American Civil Rights movement in their fight for Welsh names to be included on road signs, for the establishment of a Welsh television channel and for legal status for Welsh would be astonished to see themselves described as 'fascist'. Goodby's accusation is a particularly unpleasant example of a wider tendency within a section of the intelligentsia in Wales, analysed by Richard Wyn Jones in *The Fascist Party in Wales? Plaid Cymru, Welsh Nationalism and the Accusation of Fascism* (Cardiff: University of Wales Press, 2014), pp. 61–70. As I will argue in this chapter, the curious desire to portray 'Welsh-Wales' in dismissive racialist terms, as a homogeneous culture without the capacity for internal critique, threatens to silence the most genuinely hybrid, inclusive and pluralist aspects of Welsh cultural studies.

9   Simon Brooks, 'The Idioms of Race: The "Racist Nationalist" in Wales', in T. Robin Chapman (ed.), *The Idiom of Dissent: Protest and Propaganda in Wales* (Llandysul: Gomer, 2006), pp. 139–63; Patrick McGuinness, '"Racism" in Welsh Politics', *Planet: The Welsh Internationalist*, 159 (June/July 2003), 7–12. Two decades earlier Raymond Williams noted the irony of the fact that 'the requirement to speak Welsh as a qualification for a social services appointment in a Welsh-speaking area is referred to the Commission for Racial Equality, while calling [Neil] Kinnock a "Welsh windbag" is not'. The 'racist' charge proved a useful tool for attacking the Welsh-speaking minority, and by extrapolation Welsh nationalists in general, following Plaid Cymru's short-lived electoral breakthrough in 1999. 'West of Offa's Dyke' (1986), in *Who Speaks for Wales?*, p. 34.

10   R. S. Thomas, 'Welcome', in idem, *The Bread of Truth* (London: Rupert Hart-Davies, 1963), p. 24.

11   John Davies, *A History of Wales* (Welsh edn, 1990; London: Penguin, 1994), pp. 645–70.

12   On 'strategic essentialism' see Stephen Morton, *Gayatri Chakravorty Spivak* (London: Routledge, 2003), p. 75; Bart Moore-Gilbert, *Postcolonial Theory: Contexts, Practices, Politics* (London: Verso, 1997), pp. 202–3.

13   Here, I am in broad agreement with Ian Gregson, who offers a reading of the poem in *The New Poetry in Wales*, pp. 12–13. Patrick McGuinness offers a robust defence of Clarke in conversation with Gregson, Ian Gregson, 'Creative

Disturbance: The Poet and Critic Ian Gregson interviewed by Patrick McGuinness', *Planet: The Welsh Internationalist*, 190 (August/September 2008), 42–3.

[14] Gillian Clarke, 'The Water Diviner', *Selected Poems* (Manchester: Carcanet, 1985), p. 85.

[15] Christine Evans, 'Second Language', in Meic Stephens (ed.), *The Bright Field: An Anthology of Contemporary Poetry from Wales* (Manchester: Carcanet, 1991), p. 90.

[16] Ibid., p. 91.

[17] Quoted by Christopher Prendergast, 'Negotiating World Literature', *New Left Review II*, 8 (March/April 2001), 101.

[18] Dale E. Peterson, *Up From Bondage: The Literatures of Russian and African American Soul* (Durham, NC: Duke University Press, 2000), p. 81. See also, Doris Sommer, *Proceed with Caution, When Engaged by Minority Writing in the Americas* (Cambridge, MA: Harvard University Press, 1999).

[19] On the idea of 'inner culture' see Partha Chatterjee, *Nationalist Thought and the Colonial World: A Derivative Discourse* (London: Zed Books, 1986).

[20] Ned Thomas, 'Parallels and Paradigms', in M. Wynn Thomas (ed.), *Welsh Writing in English: A Guide to Welsh Literature Volume VII* (Cardiff: University of Wales Press, 2003), p. 325.

[21] For a powerful expression of this argument alongside an analysis of the current situation and suggestions of some ways ahead, see Simon Brooks and Richard Glyn Roberts (eds), *Pa Beth yr Aethoch Allan i'w Achub?* (Llanrwst: Gwasg Carreg Gwalch, 2013).

[22] This is a widespread structure of feeling. See my discussion of Nigel Jenkins's 'Yr Iaith' in chapter 6. See also Emyr Humphreys, 'Taliesin's Children', in Sam Adams (ed.), *Seeing Wales Whole: Essays on the Literature of Wales* (Cardiff: University of Wales Press, 1998), p. 24.

[23] M. Wynn Thomas, *Corresponding Cultures: The Two Literatures of Wales* (Cardiff: University of Wales Press, 1999), p. 5.

[24] Geraint Evans, 'Crossing the Border: National and Linguistic Boundaries in Twentieth-Century Welsh Writing', in *Welsh Writing in English: A Yearbook of Critical Essays*, 9 (2004), 133.

[25] Ibid., 127. Toni Bianchi offered an earlier analysis of R. S. Thomas's reception in 'R. S. Thomas and His Readers', in Tony Curtis (ed.), *Wales: The Imagined Nation* (Bridgend: Poetry Wales Press, 1986), pp. 69–96.

[26] Evans, 'Crossing', 127.

[27] Ibid.

[28] On 'interpellation' see Louis Althusser, 'Ideology and Ideological State Apparatuses: Notes Toward an Investigation', in Slavoj Žižek (ed.), *Mapping Ideology* (London: Verso, 1994), pp. 100–40.

[29] Evans, 'Crossing', 127.

[30] Ibid., 133. Jason Walford Davies has explored the extent of Thomas's engagement with Welsh-language literature. First in the seminal essay, 'Allusions to Welsh Literature in the Writing of R. S. Thomas', *Welsh Writing in English: A Yearbook*

of Critical Essays, 1 (1995), 75–127. This became the basis for the volume *Gororau'r Iaith: R. S. Thomas a'r Traddodiad Llenyddol Cymraeg* (Caerdydd: University of Wales Press, 2003).

31 M. Wynn Thomas, 'Hanes dwy chwaer: olrhain hanes *Y Tri Llais*', *Barn* (Ionawr 1989), 23–5 and *Barn* (Ebrill 1989), 23–5. See also Humphreys, 'Bilingual Murmurs', in M. Wynn Thomas (ed.), *Emyr Humphreys: Conversations and Reflections* (Cardiff: University of Wales Press, 2002), pp. 194–9.

32 Evans, *Country Dance* (1932; Cardigan: Parthian, 2006), p. 1.

33 Ibid., pp. 41–3.

34 Daniel G. Williams, *Black Skin, Blue Books: African Americans and Wales 1845–1945* (Cardiff: University of Wales Press, 2012), pp. 118–40; Kirsti Bohata, *Postcolonialism Revisited* (Cardiff: University of Wales Press, 2004), pp. 119–21.

35 See Thomas, *Corresponding Cultures*, p. 143.

36 Menna Elfyn, *Eucalyptus: Detholiad o Gerddi/Selected Poems 1978–1994* (Llandysul: Gomer, 1995).

37 Thomas, *Corresponding Cultures*, p. 145.

38 See Tudur Hallam, 'When a *Bardd* Meets a Poet: Menna Elfyn and the Displacement of Parallel Facing Texts', in Daniel G. Williams (ed.), *Slanderous Tongues: Essays on Welsh Poetry in English 1997–2005* (Bridgend: Seren, 2010), p. 89–111.

39 Menna Elfyn, 'Papurau Reis/Rice Papers', *Cusan Dyn Dall/Blind Man's Kiss* (Tarset: Bloodaxe, 2001), pp. 38–9.

40 Gwyneth Lewis, 'Mother Tongue', *Keeping Mum* (Tarset: Bloodaxe, 2003), p. 15.

41 Eadem, 'Welsh Espionage' from *Parables and Faxes* (1995). Collected in *Chaotic Angels: Poems in English* (Highgreen: Bloodaxe, 2005), pp. 41–7.

42 Ibid., p. 43.

43 Eadem, 'Preface' to *Keeping Mum*, p. 9.

44 Ibid., p. 10.

45 Eadem, *Keeping Mum*, p. 14.

46 A possible rapprochement between ecological and linguistic 'conservationism' has been attempted sporadically, with varying degrees of success. A notable example was the Plaid Cymru–Green coalition in Ceredigion which propelled Cynog Dafis from fourth place in 1987 to first place in 1992, making him the first Green Member of Parliament. See the Plaid Cymru and Green Party publication *Towards a Green Welsh Future* (Talybont: Lolfa, 1992).

47 Chana Kronfeld, *On the Margins of Modernism: Decentering Literary Dynamics* (Berkeley: University of California Press, 1996), p. 72.

48 Ibid.

49 See Hallam, 'When a *Bardd* Meets a Poet', p. 90.

50 Davies Aberpennar, 'Anti-Nationalism among the Anglo-Welsh', *The Welsh Nationalist* (February 1948), 8. This was drawn to my attention by a footnote in Tony Brown, '"The Memory of Lost Countries": Rhys Davies's Wales', in Meic Stephens (ed.), *Rhys Davies: Decoding the Hare* (Cardiff: University of Wales Press, 2001), p. 86.

51 Ibid., p. 8.

52 Rhys Davies, 'From My Notebook', *Wales*, 2 (October, 1943), 10.

[53] See Marc Shell's discussion in *Children of the Earth: Literature, Politics and Nationhood* (Oxford: Oxford University Press, 1993), pp. 176–92.

[54] Aberpennar, 'Anti-Nationalism', 8.

[55] Werner Sollors, *Beyond Ethnicity: Consent and Descent in American Culture* (New York: Oxford University Press, 1986).

[56] Peter Mandler, '"Race" and "Nation" in Mid-Victorian Thought', in Stefan Collini, Richard Whatmore and Brian Young (eds), *History, Religion and Culture: British Intellectual History 1750–1950* (Cambridge: Cambridge University Press, 2000), pp. 224–44; Peter Mandler, *The English National Character: The History of an Idea from Edmund Burke to Tony Blair* (New Haven: Yale University Press, 2006).

[57] Slavoj Žižek and Glyn Daly, *Conversations with Slavoj Žižek* (Cambridge: Polity Press, 2004), pp. 156–7.

[58] See Thomas's discussion in *Corresponding Cultures*, pp. 94–100.

[59] Raymond Williams, 'The Culture of Nations' (1983), in *Who Speaks for Wales?*, p. 197.

[60] See Daniel G. Williams, *Ethnicity and Cultural Authority: From Arnold to Du Bois* (Edinburgh: Edinburgh University Press, 2006), pp. 12–20.

[61] Raymond Williams, *Culture and Society: Coleridge to Orwell* (1958; London: Hogarth Press, 1990), p. 338.

Bibliography

Aaron, Jane, 'Finding a Voice in Two Tongues: Gender and Colonization', in Jane Aaron, Teresa Rees, Sandra Betts and Moira Vincentelli (eds), *Our Sisters' Land: The Changing Identities of Women in Wales* (1994; Cardiff: University of Wales Press, 2004), pp. 183–98.

Aaron, Jane, *Pur fel y Dur: Y Gymraes yn Llên Menywod y Bedwaredd Ganrif ar Bymtheg* (Caerdydd: University of Wales Press, 1998).

Aaron, Jane and Chris Williams (eds), *Postcolonial Wales* (Cardiff: University of Wales Press, 2005).

Aaron, Jane, *Nineteenth-Century Women's Writing in Wales: Nation, Gender and Identity* (Cardiff: University of Wales Press, 2007).

Adams, Sam (ed.), *Seeing Wales Whole: Essays on the Literature of Wales* (Cardiff: University of Wales Press, 1998).

Adorno, Theodor, 'On the Fetish Character in Music and the Regression of Listening', in Andrew Arato and Eike Gebhardt (eds), *The Frankfurt School Reader* (Oxford: Blackwell, 1978), pp. 270–99.

Adorno, Theodor, *Prisms*, trans. Samuel and Sherry Weber (Cambridge, MA: MIT Press, 1983).

Adorno, Theodor, *Aesthetic Theory* (1970), trans. C. Lenhardt, ed. Gretel Adorno and Rolf Tiedemann (London: Routledge, 1984).

Adorno, Theodor, 'On Jazz', trans. J. Owen Daniel, *Discourse*, 12, 1 (1989), 45–69.

Adorno, Theodor, 'Lyric Poetry and Society' (1957), in Brian O'Connor (ed.), *The Adorno Reader* (Oxford: Blackwell, 2000).

Adorno, Theodor, *Essays on Music*, trans. Susan Gillespie (Berkeley: University of California Press, 2002).

Ahmad, Aijaz, *In Theory: Classes, Nations, Literatures* (London: Verso, 1992).

Aitchison, John and Harold Carter, *A Geography of the Welsh Language 1961–1991* (Cardiff: University of Wales Press, 1994).

Alexander, Neal, 'Dialogues of Self and Soul: The Autobiographies of W. B. Yeats and R. S. Thomas', *Almanac: A Yearbook of Welsh Writing in English*, 12 (2007–8), 1–31.

Althusser, Louis, 'Ideology and Ideological State Apparatuses: Notes Toward an Investigation', in Slavoj Žižek (ed.), *Mapping Ideology* (London: Verso, 1994), pp. 100–40.

Anderson, Benedict, *Imagined Communities* (London: Verso, 1983).

Anderson, Perry, *English Questions* (London: Verso, 1992).

Anonymous, 'Sport: Louis v. Farr', *Time Magazine*, 6 September 1937.

ap Dafydd, Myrddin, 'Newid Enw: Pan Drodd Cassius Clay i Fod yn Muhammad Ali', in Lowri Roberts (ed.), *Canu Clod y Campau: Detholiad o Farddoniaeth y Maes Chwarae* (Llanrwst: Gwasg Carreg Gwalch, 2009), p. 37.

Appel, Jr., Alfred, *Jazz Modernism: From Ellington and Armstrong to Matisse and Joyce* (New York: Alfred A. Knopf, 2002).

Appiah, Kwame Anthony and Henry Louis Gates, Jr. (eds), *Identities* (Chicago: University of Chicago Press, 1995).

Appiah, Kwame Anthony and Henry Louis Gates, Jr. (eds), *Africana: The Encyclopaedia of the African and African American Experience* (New York: Basic Books, 1999).

Arendt, Hannah, *The Origins of Totalitarianism* (New York: Harcourt Brace, 1973).

Arnold, Matthew, *The Complete Prose Works of Matthew Arnold*, ed. R. H. Super, 11 vols (Ann Arbor: University of Michigan Press, 1960–77):

    i: *On the Classical Tradition* (1960).

    ii: *Democratic Education* (1962).

    iii: *Lectures and Essays in Criticism* (1962).

    iv: *Schools and Universities on the Continent* (1964).

    v: *Culture and Anarchy* (1965).

    vi: *Dissent and Dogma* (1968).

    vii: *God and the Bible* (1970).

    viii: *Essays Religious and Mixed* (1962).

    ix: *English Literature and Irish Politics* (1973).

    x: *Philistinism in England and America* (1974).

    xi: *The Last Word* (1977).

Baker, Jr., Houston A., *Modernism and the Harlem Renaissance* (Chicago: University of Chicago Press, 1987).

Baker, Jr., Houston A., Manthia Diawara and Ruth Lindeborg (eds), *Black British Cultural Studies: A Reader* (Chicago: Chicago University Press, 1996).

Bakhtin, Mikhail, *The Dialogic Imagination: Four Essays*, trans. Caryl Emerson and Michael Holquist (Austin: University of Texas Press, 1981).

Balakrishnan, Gopal (ed.), *Mapping the Nation* (London: Verso, 1996).

Baldwin, James, 'The Black Boy Looks at the White Boy', in idem, *Nobody Knows My Name, Collected Essays: Vol. 2* (New York: Library of America, 1998).

Baldwin, Kate, *Beyond the Color Line and the Iron Curtain* (Durham: Duke University Press, 2002).

Balibar, Étienne and Immanuel Wallerstein, *Race, Nation, Class: Ambiguous Identities* (London: Verso, 1995).

Baraka, Amiri, *The Autobiography of LeRoi Jones* (Chicago: Lawrence Hill Books, 1984).

Barthes, Roland, *S/Z*, trans. Richard Miller (London: Farrar, Straus & Giroux Inc., 1975).

Bassnett, Susan (ed.), *Studying British Cultures: An Introduction* (London: Routledge, 1997).

Beckett, Clare and Francis Beckett, *Bevan* (London: Hans Publishing, 2004).

Begam, Richard and Michael Valdez Moses (eds), *Modernism and Colonialism: British and Irish Literature 1899–1939* (Durham, NC: Duke University Press, 2007).

Bellow, Saul, *Seize the Day* (New York: Viking, 1956).

Belsey, Catherine, *Critical Practice* (London: Routledge, 1980).

Benhabib, Seyla, *The Claims of Culture: Equality and Diversity in the Global Era* (Princeton: Princeton University Press, 2002).

Bennett, Gilbert, Eryl Jenkins and Eurwen Price (eds), *I Sang in My Chains: Essays and Poems in Tribute to Dylan Thomas* (Swansea: The Dylan Thomas Society of Great Britain, 2003).

Berman, Marshall, *All That Is Solid Melts into Air: The Experience of Modernity* (1982; London: Verso, 1983).

Berry, Dave, *Wales and the Cinema: The First Hundred Years* (Cardiff: University of Wales Press, 1994).

Berryman, John, 'After many a summer: memories of Dylan Thomas', *Times Literary Supplement* (3 September 1993), 13–14.

Berthoff, Rowland, 'Celtic Mist over the South', *The Journal of Southern History*, 52 (1986), 523–50.

Bevan, Aneurin, 'The Claim of Wales: A Statement'. First published in *Tribune*. Re-printed in *Wales: The National Magazine*, VII, 25 (spring 1947), 151–3.

Bevan, Aneurin, *In Place of Fear* (London: McGibbon and Kee, 1952).

Bevan, Aneurin, *Why Not Trust the Tories?* (London: Gollancz, 1944).

Bhabha, Homi, *The Location of Culture* (London: Routledge, 1994).

Bianchi, Tony, 'R. S. Thomas and His Readers', in Tony Curtis (ed.), *Wales: The Imagined Nation* (Bridgend: Poetry Wales Press, 1986), pp. 69–96.

Bianchi, Tony, 'Aztecs in Troedrhiwgwair: Recent Fictions in Wales', in Ian A. Bell (ed.), *Peripheral Visions: Images of Nationhood in Contemporary British Fiction* (Cardiff: University of Wales Press, 1995), pp. 44–76.

Blight, David W., *Race and Reunion: The Civil War in American Memory* (Cambridge, MA: Harvard University Press, 2001).

Blockson, Charles L., 'Paul Robeson: A Bibliophile in Spite of Himself', in J. C. Stewart (ed.), *Paul Robeson: Artist and Citizen* (New Brunswick: Rutgers University Press, 1998), pp. 235–50.

Boddy, Kasia, *Boxing: A Cultural History* (London: Reaktion Books, 2008).

Bohata, Kirsti, *Postcolonialism Revisited* (Cardiff: University of Wales Press, 2004).

Bohata, Kirsti and Katie Gramich, *Rediscovering Margiad Evans: Marginality, Gender and Illness* (Cardiff: University of Wales Press, 2013).

Brinnin, John Malcolm, *Dylan Thomas in America* (Boston: Little Brown, 1955).

Brooks, Simon, 'The Idioms of Race: The "Racist Nationalist" in Wales', in T. Robin Chapman (ed.), *The Idiom of Dissent: Protest and Propaganda in Wales* (Llandysul: Gomer, 2006), pp. 139–63.

Brooks, Simon, *Yr Hawl i Oroesi: Ysgrifau Gwleidyddol a Diwylliannol* (Llanrwst: Gwasg Carreg Gwalch, 2009).

Brooks, Simon and Richard Glyn Roberts (eds), *Pa Beth yr Aethoch Allan i'w Achub?* (Llanrwst: Gwasg Carreg Gwalch, 2013).

Brown, Tony, 'The Romantic Nationalism of R. S. Thomas', in Norman Page and Peter Preston (eds), *The Literature of Place* (Basingstoke: Macmillan, 1993), pp. 156–69.

Brown, Tony, '"The Memory of Lost Countries": Rhys Davies's Wales', in Meic Stephens (ed.), *Rhys Davies: Decoding the Hare* (Cardiff: University of Wales Press, 2001), pp. 71–86.

Brown, Tony, '"Stories from Foreign Countries": The Short Stories of Kate Roberts and Margiad Evans', in Alyce Von Rothkirch and Daniel Williams (eds), *Beyond the Difference: Welsh Literature in Comparative Contexts* (Cardiff: University of Wales Press, 2004), pp. 21–37.

Brown, Tony, *R. S. Thomas* (Cardiff: University of Wales Press, 2006).

Bush, Duncan, Tony Curtis and Nigel Jenkins, *Three Young Anglo-Welsh Poets* (Cardiff: Welsh Arts Council, 1974).

Bush, Duncan, *The Genre of Silence* (Bridgend: Seren, 1988).

Bush, Duncan, 'Introduction to Poems', in Meic Stephens (ed.), *The Bright Field: An Anthology of Contemporary Poetry from Wales* (Manchester: Carcanet, 1991).

Bush, Duncan, 'Richard Poole Interviews Duncan Bush', *Poetry Wales*, 28, 1 (July 1992), 11–22.

Bush, Duncan, *Masks* (Bridgend: Seren, 1994).

Bush, Duncan, 'More Thoughts from the Periphery', *Planet: The Welsh Internationalist*, 121 (February/March 1997), 72–5.

Bush, Duncan, *Midway* (Bridgend: Seren, 1998).

Bush, Duncan, 'The Zidane Effect and Criticising the Critics', *Poetry Wales*, 34, 3 (January 1999), 42–7.

Bush, Duncan, 'Robert Minhinnick interviews Duncan Bush', *Poetry Wales*, 38, 2 (autumn 2002), 46–50.

Callahan, John F., 'Introduction' to Ralph Ellison, *Flying Home and Other Stories*, ed. John F. Callahan (1996; London: Penguin, 1998), pp. ix–xxxviii.

Callahan, John F. (ed.), *Ralph Ellison's Invisible Man: A Casebook* (Oxford: Oxford University Press, 2004).

Carey, John, *The Intellectuals and the Masses* (London: Faber, 1992).

Chapman, T. Robin (ed.), *The Idiom of Dissent: Protest and Propaganda in Wales* (Llandysul: Gomer, 2006).

Chapman, T. Robin, *Un Bywyd o Blith Nifer: Cofiant Saunders Lewis* (Llandysul: Gomer, 2006).

Chatterjee, Partha, *Nationalist Thought and the Colonial World: A Derivative Discourse* (London: Zed Books, 1986).

Cheyette, Brian (ed.), *Between 'Race' and Culture: Representations of 'the Jew' in English and American Literature* (Stanford: Stanford University Press, 1996).

Chrisman, Laura, 'Imperial Space, Imperial Place: Theories of Empire and Culture in Fredric Jameson, Edward Said and Gayatri Spivak', *New Formations: A Journal of Culture/Theory/Politics*, 34 (1998), 53–69.

Clapham, Christopher, *Third World Politics: An Introduction* (Madison: University of Wisconsin Press, 1992).

Clarke, Gillian, *Selected Poems* (Manchester: Carcanet, 1985).

Cleary, Joe, *Outrageous Fortune: Capital and Culture in Modern Ireland* (Dublin: Field Day Publications, 2006).

Cleaver, Eldridge, *Soul on Ice* (New York: McGraw-Hill, 1968).

Cohen, G. A., *Karl Marx's Theory of History: A Defence* (Princeton: Princeton University Press, 1978).

Collini, Stefan, 'On Variousness', *New Left Review II*, 27 (May/June 2004), 65–97.

Collini, Stefan, *Absent Minds: Intellectuals in Britain* (Oxford: Oxford University Press, 2006).

Collini, Stefan, *Common Reading: Critics, Historians, Publics* (Oxford: Oxford University Press, 2008).

Conran, Anthony, *The Cost of Strangeness: Essays on the English Poets of Wales* (Llandysul: Gomer Press, 1982).

Conran, Tony, *Frontiers in Anglo-Welsh Poetry* (Cardiff: University of Wales Press, 1997).

Coombes, B. L., *These Poor Hands: The Autobiography of a Miner in South Wales* (1939; Cardiff: University of Wales Press, 2002).

Cordell, Alexander, *Peerless Jim* (London: Hodder and Stoughton, 1984).

Cortázar, Julio, 'El perseguidor', in *Las armas secretas* (Buenos Aires: Sudamericana, 1959), pp. 149–313.

Crawford, Robert; *Devolving English Literature* (1992; Edinburgh: Edinburgh University Press, 2000).

Croll, Andy, *Civilizing the Urban: Popular Culture and Public Space in Merthyr, c.1870–1914* (Cardiff: University of Wales Press, 2000).

Cronin, Michael, *Translating Ireland: Translation, Languages, Cultures* (Cork: Cork University Press, 1996).

Cronin, Michael, 'Global Questions and Local Visions: A Microcosmopolitan Perspective', in Alyce von Rothkirch and Daniel Williams (eds), *Beyond the*

Difference: Welsh Literature in Comparative Contexts (Cardiff: University of Wales Press, 2004), pp. 186–202.

Cronin, Michael, 'Half the Picture', *Dublin Review of Books*, *http://www.drb.ie/essays/half-the-picture* (accessed 1 August 2014).

Cullingford, Elizabeth, *Yeats, Ireland and Fascism* (London: Macmillan, 1981).

Davies, Damian Walford, '"Yeats Said That": R. S. Thomas and W. B. Yeats', *Almanac: A Yearbook of Welsh Writing in English*, 13 (2008–9), 1–26.

Davies, D. Hywel, *The Welsh Nationalist Party 1925–1945: A Call to Arms* (Cardiff: University of Wales Press, 1983).

Davies, D. Hywel, 'South Wales history which almost excludes the Welsh', *New Welsh Review*, 26 (autumn 1994), 8–13.

Davies, Grahame, *Sefyll yn y Bwlch: R. S. Thomas, Saunders Lewis, T. S. Eliot, a Simone Weil* (Caerdydd: University of Wales Press, 1999).

Davies, Grahame, 'Peerless Jim Driscoll', in Lowri Roberts (ed.), *Canu Clod y Campau: Detholiad o Farddoniaeth y Maes Chwarae* (Llanrwst: Gwasg Carreg Gwalch, 2009), p. 36.

Davies, James A., 'Not going back but ... exile ending: Raymond Williams's Fictional Wales', in W. J. Morgan and P. Preston (eds), *Raymond Williams: Politics, Education, Letters* (London: Macmillan, 1993), pp. 189–210.

Davies, James A., '"A Mental Militarist": Dylan Thomas and the Great War', *Welsh Writing in English: A Yearbook of Critical Essays*, 2 (1996), 62–81.

Davies, James A., *A Reference Companion to Dylan Thomas* (London: Greenwood Press, 1998).

Davies, James A., 'Questions of Identity: The Movement and "Fern Hill"', in John Goodby and Chris Wigginton (eds), *Dylan Thomas: New Casebook* (Basingstoke: Palgrave, 2001), pp. 158–71.

Davies, Janet (ed.), *Compass Points: The First 100 Issues of Planet* (Cardiff: University of Wales Press, 1993).

Davies, Jason Walford, 'Allusions to Welsh Literature in the Writing of R. S. Thomas', *Welsh Writing in English: A Yearbook of Critical Essays*, 1 (1995), 75–127.

Davies, Jason Walford, *Gororau'r Iaith: R. S. Thomas a'r Traddodiad Llenyddol Cymraeg* (Caerdydd: University of Wales Press, 2003).

Davies, John, *A History of Wales* (Welsh edn, 1990; London: Penguin, 1993).

Davies, Pennar (Davies Aberpennar), 'Anti-Nationalism among the Anglo-Welsh', *The Welsh Nationalist* (February 1948), 8.

Davies, Pennar, 'Pencampwr', in idem, *Llais y Durtur* (Llandysul: Gomer, 1985), pp. 85–8.

Davies, Rhys, *The Withered Root* (London: Robert Holden and Co., 1927).

Davies, Rhys, *My Wales* (London: Jarrolds, 1937).

Davies, Rhys, 'From My Notebook', *Wales*, 2 (October 1943), 10–12.

Davies, Rhys, *The Black Venus* (London: William Heinemann, 1944).

Davies, Rhys, *Print of a Hare's Foot* (London: Heinemann, 1969).

Davies, Rhys, *Collected Stories Volume 1*, ed. Meic Stephens (Llandysul: Gomer, 1996).

Davies, Rhys, *Collected Stories Volume 2*, ed. Meic Stephens (Llandysul: Gomer, 1996).

Davies, T. J., *Paul Robeson* (Abertawe: Christopher Davies, 1981).

Davis, Alex and Lee Jenkins, *Locations of Literary Modernism: Region and Nation in American Modernist Poetry* (Cambridge: Cambridge University Press, 2000).

Davis, Miles, *Miles: The Autobiography* (with Quincy Troupe) (London: Macmillan, 1989).

Deane, Seamus, *Celtic Revivals: Essays in Modern Irish Literature, 1880–1980* (London: Faber, 1985).

Deane, Seamus (ed.), *Nationalism, Colonialism and Literature* (Minneapolis: University of Minnesota Press, 1990).

DeVeaux, Scott, *The Birth of BeBop: A Social and Musical History* (1997; London: Picador, 1999).

Dix, Hywel, *After Raymond Williams: Cultural Materialism and the Break-Up of Britain* (Cardiff: University of Wales Press, 2008).

Donahaye, Jasmine, *Whose People? Wales, Israel, Palestine* (Cardiff: University of Wales Press, 2012).

Douglas, Ann, *Terrible Honesty: Mongrel Manhattan in the 1920s* (New York: Noonday Press, 1995).

Dressel, Jon, 'Correspondence', *The Anglo-Welsh Review*, 26, 58 (spring 1977), 224–30.

Dressel, Jon, *Hard Love and a Country* (Swansea: Christopher Davies, 1977).

Dressel, Jon and T. James Jones, *Cerddi Ianws* (Llandysul: Gomer, 1979).

Dressel, Jon, *Out of Wales* (Port Talbot: Alun Books, 1985).

Dressel, Jon, *The Road to Shiloh* (Llandysul: Gomer, 1994).

Dressel, Jon, 'Looking Both Ways', *New Welsh Review*, 32 (spring 1996), 56–64.

Duberman, Martin, *Paul Robeson: A Biography* (1988; New York: New Press, 1989).

Duberman, Martin, *The Politics of Exclusion: Essays 1964–1999* (New York: Basic Books, 1999).

Du Bois, W. E. B., 'Robert E. Lee' (March 1928), in idem, *Writings*, ed. Nathan I. Huggins (New York: Library of America, 1986), p. 1223.

Dugan, Alan, *Poems Seven: New and Complete Poems* (New York: Seven Stories Press, 2001).

Dworkin D. and L. Roman (eds), *Views Beyond the Border Country: Raymond Williams and Cultural Politics* (London: Routledge, 1993).

Eagleton, Terry, *Heathcliff and the Great Hunger: Studies in Irish Culture* (London: Verso, 1995).

Eagleton, Terry, *Crazy John and the Bishop and Other Essays on Irish Culture* (Cork: Cork University Press, 1998).

Early, Gerald, *The Culture of Bruising: Essays on Prizefighting, Literature and Modern American Culture* (Hopewell, NJ: The Ecco Press, 1994).

Edwards, Brent Hayes, *The Practice of Diaspora: Literature, Translation and the Rise of Black Internationalism* (Cambridge, MA: Harvard University Press, 2003).

Edwards, Hywel Teifi, *Gŵyl Gwalia: Yr Eisteddfod yn Oes Victoria* (Llandysul: Gwasg Gomer, 1980).

Edwards, Hywel Teifi, 'Victorian Wales Seeks Reinstatement', *Planet*, 52 (August/September 1985), 12–24.

Edwards, Hywel Teifi, *Codi'r Hen Wlad yn ei Hôl* (Llandysul: Gwasg Gomer, 1990).

Edwards, Hywel Teifi, *Cyfres y Cymoedd* (Llandysul, Gomer, 1993–2003).

Edwards, Hywel Teifi, *O'r Pentre Gwyn i Gwmderi: Delwedd y Pentref yn Llenyddiaeth Cymru* (Llandysul: Gomer, 2004).

Edwards, Martha, *Paul Robeson: Honorary Welshman* (Treorchy: Paul Robeson Exhibition, 1998).

Elfyn, Menna, *Eucalyptus: Detholiad o Gerddi/Selected Poems 1978–1994* (Llandysul: Gwasg Gomer, 1995).

Elfyn, Menna, 'Beirdd y Tafodau Fforchiog', *Barddas*, 226 (1996), 10–11.

Elfyn, Menna, *Cell Angel* (Newcastle upon Tyne: Bloodaxe Books, 1996).

Elfyn, Menna, *Cusan Dyn Dall/Blind Man's Kiss* (Tarset: Bloodaxe Books, 2001).

Elfyn, Menna and John Rowlands (eds), *The Bloodaxe Book of Modern Welsh Poetry* (Highgreen: Bloodaxe Books, 2003).

Elfyn, Menna, 'Menna Elfyn interviewed by PW', *Poetry Wales*, 42, 1 (2006), 20–4.

Elfyn, Menna, *Perfect Blemish/Perffaith Nam: New and Selected Poems, 1995–2007/Dau Ddetholiad & Cherddi Newydd, 1995–2007* (Tarset: Bloodaxe Books, 2007).

Elias, Norbert, *The Civilising Process* (German edn, 1939; New York: Urizen Books, 1978).

Ellison, Ralph, 'A Storm of Blizzard Proportions', Several Drafts. The Ralph Ellison Papers. Library of Congress, Washington DC. Box 165. File 7.

Ellison, Ralph, 'The Negro and the War'. Undated Typescript. MS AM 2238. Houghton Library, Harvard University.

Ellison, Ralph, 'The Red Cross in Morriston, Swansea, S.W.' Several Drafts. The Ralph Ellison Papers. Library of Congress, Washington D.C. Box 165. Files 3 and 7.

Ellison, Ralph, 'On Initiation Rites and Power: Ralph Ellison Speaks at West Point', *Going to the Territory* (New York: Vintage, 1987), pp. 39–63.

Ellison, Ralph, *Shadow and Act* (1953; New York: Quality Paperback Book Club, 1994).

Ellison, Ralph, *Invisible Man* (1952; New York: Vintage, 1995).

Ellison, Ralph, 'In a Strange Country', in *Flying Home and Other Stories* (1996; London: Penguin, 1998), pp. 137–46.

Esty, Jed, *Unseasonable Youth: Modernism, Colonialism and the Fiction of Development* (Oxford: Oxford University Press, 2012).

Evans, Christine, 'Second Language', in Meic Stephens (ed.), *The Bright Field: An Anthology of Contemporary Poetry from Wales* (Manchester: Carcanet, 1991), p. 90.

Evans, George Ewart, 'The Valleys', *Wales*, 3 (autumn 1937), 128–9.

Evans, Geraint, 'Crossing the Border: National and Linguistic Boundaries in Twentieth-Century Welsh Writing', in *Welsh Writing in English: A Yearbook of Critical Essays*, 9 (2004), 123–35.

Evans, Gwynfor, *Aros Mae* (Abertawe: Gwasg John Penry, 1971).

Evans, Margiad, 'Review of Kate Roberts, *A Summer Day*', *Life and Letters To-Day*, 51 (November 1946), 54–8.

Evans, Margiad, *Country Dance* (1932; Cardigan: Parthian, 2006).

Evans, Neil, 'Red Summers 1917–19', *History Today*, 51, 2 (February 2001), 28–33.

Eysteinsson, Astradur, *The Concept of Modernism* (Ithaca: Cornell University Press, 1990).

Farr, Tommy, *Thus Farr* (London: Optomen Press, 1989).

Faverty, Frederic E., *Matthew Arnold, the Ethnologist* (Evanston: Northwestern University Press, 1951).

Feinstein, Sascha and Yusef Komunyakaa (eds), *The Jazz Poetry Anthology* (Bloomington: Indiana University Press, 1991).

Ferraro, Thomas J., *Ethnic Passages: Literary Immigrants in Twentieth-Century America* (Chicago: University of Chicago Press, 1993).

Ferlinghetti, Lawrence, *These Are My Rivers: New and Selected Poems* (New York: New Directions, 1993).

Ffrancon, Gwenno, *Cyfaredd y Cysgodion; Delweddu Cymru a'i Phobl ar Ffilm, 1935–1951* (Caerdydd: University of Wales Press, 2003).

Ffrancon, Gwenno, 'Affro-Americaniaid a'r Cymry ar y Sgrin Fawr', in D. G. Williams (ed.), *Canu Caeth: Y Cymry a'r Affro-Americaniaid* (Llandysul: Gomer, 2010), pp. 117–33.

Fischer, Michael M. J. and George E. Marcus, *Anthropology as Cultural Critique: An Experimental Moment in the Human Sciences* (1986; Chicago: University of Chicago Press, 1999).

Fleure, H. J., 'The Racial History of the British People', *Geographical Review*, 5 (1918), 216–31.

Fleure, H. J. (ed.), *Gyda'r Wawr: Braslun o Hanes Cymru'r Oesoedd Cyntefig* (Gwercsam: Hughes a'i Fab, 1923).

Fleure, H. J., 'Wales', in Alan G. Ogilvie (ed.), *Great Britain: Essays in Regional Geography* (Cambridge: Cambridge University Press, 1928), pp. 237–63.

Fleure, H. J., 'The Welsh People', *Wales*, 10 (October 1939), reprinted in *Wales*, 1–11 (London: Frank Cass, 1969), 265–9.

Foley, Barbara, *Spectres of 1919: Class and Nation in the Making of the New Negro* (Chicago: University of Illinois Press, 2003).

Foot, Michael, *Aneurin Bevan 1945–1960* (London: Davis-Poyntner, 1973).

Foster, R. F., *Paddy and Mr. Punch: Connections in Irish and English History* (London: Penguin, 1993).

Foster, R. F., *W. B. Yeats: A Life I. The Apprentice Mage* (Oxford: Oxford University Press, 1997).

Francis, Hywel and Dai Smith, *The Fed: A History of the South Wales Miners in the Twentieth Century* (1980; Cardiff: University of Wales Press, 1998).

Francis, Hywel, *Miners against Fascism: Wales and the Spanish Civil War* (1984; Abersychan: Warren and Pell, 2004).

Francis, Hywel, 'Paul Robeson: His Legacy For Wales', A Lecture to the Friends of the National Library of Wales, Aberystwyth, 12 July 2003, http://www. epolitix.com/EN/MPWebsites/Hywel+Francis/b8a07531-f84c-4862–92db-b59a4790da4f.htm (accessed 15 August 2005).

Francis, Hywel, 'Paul Robeson: Ei Etifeddiaeth i Gymru', in Daniel G. Williams (ed.), *Canu Caeth: Y Cymry a'r Affro-Americaniaid* (Llandysul: Gomer, 2010), pp. 64–73.

Fraser, Nancy, 'Rethinking Recognition', *New Left Review II*, 3 (May/June 2000), 107–20.

Frith, Simon, *Performing Rites: Evaluating Popular Music* (Oxford: Oxford University Press, 1998).

Gaines, Kevin K., *Uplifting the Race: Black Leadership, Politics, and Culture in the Twentieth Century* (Chapel Hill: University of North Carolina Press, 1996).

Gallimore, Andrew, *Occupation Prizefighter: The Freddie Welsh Story* (Bridgend: Seren, 2006).

Gaston, Georg (ed.), *Critical Essays on Dylan Thomas* (Boston: G. K. Hall and Co., 1989).

Gates, Jr., Henry Louis (ed.), *'Race', Writing and Difference* (Chicago: University of Chicago Press, 1986).

Gates, Jr., Henry Louis, *The Signifying Monkey: A Theory of African-American Literary Criticism* (Oxford: Oxford University Press, 1988).

Gates, Jr. Henry Louis and Cornel West, *The Future of the Race* (New York: Alfred A. Knopf, 1996).

Gates, Jr., Henry Louis (general ed.), *The Norton Anthology of African American Literature* (New York: Norton, 1997).

Gates, Jr., Henry Louis, *Tradition and the Black Atlantic: Critical Theory in the African Diaspora* (New York: Basic Books, 2010).

Gennari, John, *Blowin' Hot and Cool: Jazz and its Critics* (Chicago: Chicago University Press, 2006).

Gibbons, Luke, *Transformations in Irish Culture* (Cork: Cork University Press, 1996).

Gibbons, Luke, 'Ireland and the Colonization of Theory', *Interventions: International Journal of Postcolonial Studies*, 1, 1 (1998), 27.

Gibbons, Luke, 'Peripheral Modernities: National and Global in a Post-Colonial Frame', *Nineteenth-Century Contexts: An Interdisciplinary Journal*, 29, 2 (2007), 271–81.

Gilroy, Paul, 'Nationalism, History and Ethnic Absolutism', *History Workshop Journal*, 30, 1 (1990), 114–20.

Gilroy, Paul, *'There Ain't No Black in the Union Jack': The Cultural Politics of Race and Nation* (Chicago: Chicago University Press, 1987).

Gilroy, Paul, *The Black Atlantic: Modernity and Double Consciousness* (Cambridge, MA: Harvard University Press, 1993).

Gilroy, Paul, *Between Camps: Race, Identity and Nationalism at the End of the Colour Line* (London: Penguin, 2000).

Ginsberg, Allen, *Collected Poems 1947–1980* (New York: Harper and Rowe, 1984).

Ginsberg, Allen, 'Howl', in Ann Charters (ed.), *The Penguin Book of the Beats* (Harmondsworth: Penguin, 1993).

Gioia, Ted, *The Imperfect Art* (Oxford: Oxford University Press, 1988).

Gioia, Ted, *The History of Jazz* (Oxford: Oxford University Press, 2011).

Golightly, Victor, '"Writing with dreams and blood": Dylan Thomas, Marxism and 1930s Swansea', *Welsh Writing in English: A Yearbook of Critical Essays*, 8 (2003), 67–91.

Goodby, John and Christopher Wigginton, '"Shut, too, in a tower of words": Dylan Thomas' modernism', in Alex Davis and Lee M. Jenkins (eds), *Locations of Literary Modernism* (Cambridge: Cambridge University Press, 2000) pp. 89–112.

Goodby, John and Christopher Wigginton, *Dylan Thomas: New Casebooks* (Basingstoke: Palgrave, 2001).

Goodby, John, '"Very Profound and Very Box-Office": The Later Poems and Under Milk Wood', in John Goodby and Chris Wigginton (eds), *Dylan Thomas: New Casebook* (Basingstoke: Palgrave, 2001), pp. 192–220.

Goodby, John, *The Poetry of Dylan Thomas: Under the Spelling Wall* (Liverpool: Liverpool University Press, 2013).

Gombrich, E. H., *The Preference for the Primitive* (London: Phaidon, 2002).

Gracyk, Theodore A., 'Adorno, Jazz and the Aesthetics of Popular Music', *The Musical Quarterly*, 76, 7 (winter 1992), 526–42.

Goodwin, Geraint, *The Heyday in the Blood* (1936; Cardigan: Parthian, 2009).

Gramich, Katie, 'Cymru or Wales? Explorations in a Divided Sensibility', in Susan Bassnett (ed.), *Studying British Cultures* (London: Routledge, 1997), pp. 97–112.

Gramich, Katie, *Twentieth Century Women's Writing in Wales: Land, Gender, Belonging* (Cardiff: University of Wales Press, 2007).

Gregson, Ian, *The New Poetry in Wales* (Cardiff: University of Wales Press, 2007).

Gregson, Ian, 'Creative Disturbance: The Poet and Critic Ian Gregson inter-
  viewed by Patrick McGuinness', *Planet: The Welsh Internationalist*, 190
  (August/September 2008).
Griffith, Selwyn, 'Arwyr', in Lowri Roberts (ed.), *Canu Clod y Campau:
  Detholiad o Farddoniaeth y Maes Chwarae* (Llanrwst: Gwasg Carreg
  Gwalch, 2009), pp. 31–3.
Griffiths, Robert, 'The Other Aneurin Bevan', in Janet Davies (ed.), *Compass
  Points: The First 100 Issues of Planet* (Cardiff: University of Wales Press,
  1993), pp. 130–1.
Gruffudd, Pyrs, 'Back to the Land: Historiography, Rurality and the Nation in
  Interwar Wales', *Transactions of the Institute of British Geographers*, 19
  (1994), 61–77.
Gruffudd, Pyrs, 'Yr Iaith Gymraeg a'r Dychymyg Daearyddol 1918–1950', in
  Geraint Jenkins and Mari Williams (eds), *'Eu Hiaith a Gadwant'? Y Gymraeg
  yn yr Ugeinfed Ganrif* (Caerdydd: University of Wales Press, 2000), pp.
  107–32.
Gruffydd, W. J., 'Hen Atgofion', *Y Llenor*, XVII (1938), 8–9.
Gruffydd, W. J., *The Years of the Locust*, trans. D. Myrddin Lloyd (Llandysul:
  Gomer, 1976).
Gubar, Susan, *Racechanges: White Skin, Black Face in American Culture*
  (Oxford: Oxford University Press, 1997).
Hall, Stuart, 'New Ethnicities', in J. Donald and A. Rattansi (eds), *Race, Culture
  and Difference* (London: Sage, 1992), pp. 252–60.
Hall, Stuart, 'Our Mongrel Selves', *Borderlands*, a supplement with *New
  Statesman*, 19 June 1992, 7.
Hallam, Tudur, 'When a *Bardd* Meets a Poet: Menna Elfyn and the Displacement
  of Parallel Facing Texts', in Daniel G. Williams (ed.), *Slanderous Tongues:
  Essays on Welsh Poetry in English 1997–2005* (Bridgend: Seren, 2010), pp.
  89–111.
Hannaford, Ivan, *Race: The History of an Idea in the West* (Baltimore: Johns
  Hopkins University Press, 1996).
Harper, Michael S. and Robert B. Stepto (eds), *Chant of Saints: A Gathering of
  Afro-American Literature, Art and Scholarship* (Urbana: University of
  Illinois Press, 1979).
Harrison, Max, 'A Rare Bird' (1997), in Carl Woideck (ed.), *The Charlie Parker
  Companion: Six Decades of Commentary* (New York: Schirmer Books,
  1998), pp. 204–25.
Hechter, Michael, *Internal Colonialism: The Celtic Fringe in British National
  Development 1536–1966* (London: Routledge, 1975).
Hegeman, Susan, *Patterns for America: Modernism and the Concept of Culture*
  (Princeton: Princeton University Press, 1999).
Higgins, John, *Raymond Williams: Literature, Marxism and Cultural
  Materialism* (London: Routledge, 1999).

Homberger, Eric, *The Art of the Real: Poetry in England and America Since 1939* (London: Dent, 1977).

Hopkin, Deian, Duncan Tanner and Chris Williams (eds), *The Labour Party in Wales 1900–2000* (Cardiff: University of Wales Press, 2000).

Horowitz, Tony, *Confederates in the Attic: Dispatches from the Unfinished Civil War* (New York: Vintage, 1999).

Humphreys, Emyr, *The Taliesin Tradition: A Quest for the Welsh Identity* (1983: Bridgend: Seren Books, 1989).

Humphreys, Emyr, 'Taliesin's Children', in Sam Adams (ed.), *Seeing Wales Whole: Essays on the Literature of Wales* (Cardiff: University of Wales Press, 1998), pp. 14–24.

Humphreys, Emyr, 'Bilingual Murmurs', in M. Wynn Thomas (ed.), *Emyr Humphreys: Conversations and Reflections* (Cardiff: University of Wales Press, 2002), pp. 194–9.

Hunter, Jerry, *Llwybrau Cenhedloedd: Cyd-Destunoli'r Genhadaeth Gymreig i'r Tsalagi* (Caerdydd: University of Wales Press, 2012).

Huyssen, Andreas, *After the Great Divide: Modernism, Mass Culture and Postmodernism* (1986; London: Macmillan, 1988).

Jackson, Lawrence, *Ralph Ellison: The Emergence of Genius* (New York: John Wiley and Sons, 2002).

Jameson, Fredric, *Marxism and Form: Twentieth Century Dialectical Theories of Literature* (New Jersey: Princeton University Press, 1971).

Jameson, Frederic, *Late Marxism: Adorno, or, the Persistence of the Dialectic* (London: Verso, 1990).

Jarrell, Randall, *A Sad Heart at the Supermarket: Essays and Fables* (London: Eyre and Spottiswoode, 1965).

Jarvis, Matthew, *Welsh Environments in Contemporary Welsh Poetry* (Cardiff: University of Wales Press, 2008).

Jenkins, Geraint (ed.), *Iaith Carreg fy Aelwyd: Iaith a Chymuned yn y Bedwaredd Ganrif ar Bymtheg* (Caerdydd: University of Wales Press, 1998).

Jenkins, Geraint and Mari Williams (eds), *'Eu Hiaith a Gadwant'? Y Gymraeg yn yr Ugeinfed Ganrif* (Caerdydd: University of Wales Press, 2000).

Jenkins, Gwyn, *Prifweinidog Answyddogol Cymru: Cofiant Huw T. Edwards* (Talybont: Y Lolfa, 2007).

Jenkins, Nigel, *Acts of Union: Selected Poems 1974–1989* (Llandysul: Gomer, 1990).

Jenkins, Nigel, *Ambush* (Llandysul: Gomer, 1998).

Jenkins, Nigel, *Footsore on the Frontier: Selected Essays and Articles* (Llandysul: Gomer, 2001).

Jenkins, Nigel, *Hotel Gwales* (Llandysul: Gomer, 2006).

Jenkinson, Jacqueline, *Black 1919: Riots, Racism and Resistance in Imperial Britain* (Liverpool: Liverpool University Press, 2009).

Jones, Alun Ffred, *Y Cyfryngau Wedi'r Cynulliad* (Talybont: Lolfa, 1999).

Jones, Alun R. and Gwyn Thomas (eds), *Presenting Saunders Lewis* (Cardiff: University of Wales Press, 1973).

Jones, Gwyn, *Times Like These* (1936; London: Victor Gollabcz, 1979).

Jones, Jack, *Black Parade* (London: Faber, 1935).

Jones, Jack, 'Nofelau'r Cymry Seisnig', *Tir Newydd*, 8 (Mai 1937), 5–9.

Jones, Jack, *Unfinished Journey* (London: Hamish Hamilton, 1937).

Jones, Jack, *Rhondda Roundabout* (1934; London: Hamish Hamilton, 1949).

Jones, Jack, *The Black Welshman*, Manuscript in the Jack Jones Papers, National Library of Wales, Aberystwyth. The novel was serialized in *The Empire News*, beginning on 23 June 1957.

Jones, Jack, *Bidden to the Feast* (1938; London: Corgi Books, 1968).

Jones, Leroi, *Blues People: Negro Music in White America* (New York: William Morrow, 1963).

Jones, Lewis, *We Live: The Story of a Welsh Mining Valley* (1939; London: Lawrence and Wishart, 1978).

Jones, Lewis, *Cwmardy: The Story of a Welsh Mining Valley* (1937; London: Lawrence and Wishart, 1979).

Jones, Lewis, *Cwmardy and We Live*, Library of Wales (Aberteifi: Parthian, 2005).

Jones, Merfyn, 'Beyond Identity? The Reconstruction of the Welsh', *Journal of British Studies*, 31, 4 (October 1992), 330–57.

Jones, R. Merfyn and Ioan Rhys Jones, 'Labour and the Nation', in D. Tanner, C. Williams a D. Hopkin (eds), *The Labour Party in Wales* (Cardiff: University of Wales Press, 2000).

Jones, Nicholas, 'Supercharging the Struggle: Models of Nationalist Victory in the Poetry of Harri Webb', *Welsh Writing in English: A Yearbook of Critical Essays*, ed. Tony Brown, 9 (2004), pp. 102–22.

Jones, R. M., *Ysbryd y Cwlwm: Delwedd y Genedl yn ein Llenyddiaeth* (Caerdydd: University of Wales Press, 1998).

Jones, Richard Wyn, 'The Colonial Legacy in Welsh Politics', in Jane Aaron and Chris Williams (eds), *Postcolonial Wales* (Cardiff: University of Wales Press, 2005), pp. 23–38.

Jones, Richard Wyn, *Rhoi Cymru'n Gyntaf: Syniadaeth Plaid Cymru* (Caerdydd: University of Wales Press, 2007).

Jones, Richard Wyn, *The Fascist Party in Wales? Plaid Cymru, Welsh Nationalism and the Accusation of Fascism* (Cardiff: University of Wales Press, 2014).

Jones, Robert Owen, *Hir Oes i'r Iaith: Agweddau ar Hanes y Gymraeg a'r Gymdeithas* (Llandysul: Gomer, 1997).

Jones, T. Gwynn, *The Culture and Civilization of Wales* (Wrecsam: Hughes a'i Fab, 1927).

Jordan, Glenn, '"We Never Really Noticed You Were Coloured": Postcolonialist Reflections on Immigrants and Minorities in Wales', in J. Aaron and C.

Williams (eds), *Postcolonial Wales* (Cardiff: University of Wales Press, 2005), pp. 55–81.

Julius, Anthony, *T. S. Eliot, Anti-Semitism and Literary Form* (Cambridge: Cambridge University Press, 1995).

Karp, Jonathan, 'Performing Black-Jewish Symbiosis: The "Hassidic Chant" of Paul Robeson, *American Jewish History*, 91, 1 (March 2003), 53–81.

Kaufman, Bob, 'Afterwards they Shall Dance', in idem, *Solitudes Crowded With Loneliness* (New York: New Directions, 1965).

Kaufman, Will, *The Civil War in American Culture* (Edinburgh: Edinburgh University Press, 2006).

Kazin, Alfred, *On Native Grounds: An Interpretation of Modern American Prose Literature* (New York: Harcourt, Brace and World inc., 1942).

Kazin, Alfred, 'The Posthumous Life of Dylan Thomas', *Atlantic Monthly*, 200 (October 1957), 164–8.

Kent, Graeme, *A Welshman in the Bronx: Tommy Farr vs Joe Louis* (Llandysul: Gomer, 2009).

Kerouac, Jack, *Selected Letters 1940–1956*, ed. Ann Charters (New York: Viking, 1995).

Kerouac, Jack, *On the Road* (1957; Harmondsworth: Penguin, 2000).

Kerouac, Jack and Allen Ginsberg, *The Letters*, ed. Bill Morgan and David Stanford (London: Penguin, 2011).

Kiberd, Declan, 'White Skins, Black Masks?', *Eire/Ireland: A Journal of Irish Studies*, 31 (spring–summer 1996), 163–75.

Kiberd, Declan, 'The View from Enniskillen', *New Left Review II*, 3 (May/June 2000), 153–7.

Klein, Marcus, *Foreigners: The Making of American Literature 1900–1940* (Chicago: University of Chicago Press, 1981).

Knight, Stephen, *A Hundred Years of Fiction: Writing Wales in English* (Cardiff: University of Wales Press, 2004).

Kronfeld, Chana, *On the Margins of Modernism: Decentering Literary Dynamics* (Berkeley: University of California Press, 1996).

Kymlicka, Will (ed.), *The Rights of Minority Cultures* (Oxford: Oxford University Press, 1995).

Kymlicka, Will, 'Liberal Nationalism and Cosmopolitan Justice', in Seyla Benhabib, *Another Cosmopolitanism*, ed. Robert Post (Oxford: Oxford University Press, 2006).

Larkin, Philip, *All What Jazz* (London: Faber, 1985).

Larkin, Philip, *Required Writing: Miscellaneous Pieces 1955–1982* (London: Faber, 2002).

Lawrence, D. H., *Studies in Classic American Literature*, ed. Ezra Greenspan, Lindeth Vasey and John Worthen (1923; Cambridge: Cambridge University Press, 2002).

Lawrence, D. H., *St Mawr*, in *The Complete Short Novels* (London: Penguin, 1982).

Lawrence, D. H., *The Letters of D. H. Lawrence: Vol III: October 1916–June 1921*, ed. James T. Boulton and Andrew Robertson (Cambridge: Cambridge University Press, 1984).

Lawrence, D. H., 'On Being a Man' in idem, *Reflections on the Death of a Porcupine and Other Essays*, ed. Michael Herbert (Cambridge: Cambridge University Press, 1988), pp. 215–16.

Lazarus, Neil, *Nationalism and Cultural Practice in the Postcolonial World* (Cambridge: Cambridge University Press, 1999).

Lee, A. Robert (ed.), *Beat Generation Writers* (London: Pluto Press, 1996).

Leonard, Neil, *Jazz: Myth and Religion* (Oxford: Oxford University Press, 1987).

Let Robeson Sing! A Celebration of the Life of Paul Robeson and his Relationship with Wales (Cardiff: Paul Robeson Cymru Committee/Bevan Foundation, 2001).

Levi-Strauss, Claude, *The Raw and the Cooked*, trans. John and Doreen Weightman (New York: Harper and Row, 1969).

Lewis, David Levering, 'Paul Robeson and the U.S.S.R', in J. C. Stewart (ed.), *Paul Robeson: Artist and Citizen* (New Brunswick: Rutgers University Press, 1998), pp. 217–33.

Lewis, David Levering, *W. E. B. Du Bois: The Fight for Equality and the American Century, 1919–1963* (New York: Henry Holt and Co., 2000).

Lewis, Gwyneth, 'Whose coat is that jacket? Whose hat is that cap?', *Columbia: A Journal of Literature and Art: Crossing Borders*, 27 (1996–7), 58–68.

Lewis, Gwyneth, *Keeping Mum* (Tarset: Bloodaxe, 2003).

Lewis, Gwyneth, *Chaotic Angels: Poems in English* (Highgreen: Bloodaxe, 2005).

Lewis, Saunders, 'Safonau Beirniadaeth Lenyddol', *Y Llenor*, 1, 4 (gaeaf 1922), 245.

Lewis, Saunders, 'Tueddiadau Cymru Rhwng 1919 a 1923', *Baner ac Amserau Cymru*, 6 (Medi 1923), 5.

Lewis, Saunders, 'Is There an Anglo-Welsh Literature?' (Cardiff: Guild of Graduates of the University of Wales, 1939), pamphlet.

Lewis, Saunders, *Canlyn Arthur: Ysgrifau Gwleidyddol* (1938; Llandysul: Gomer, 1985).

Lewis, Saunders and Kate Roberts, *Annwyl Kate, Annwyl Saunders*, ed. Dafydd Ifans (Aberystwyth: National Library of Wales, 1992).

Lewis, Saunders, *Cerddi*, ed. R. Geraint Gruffydd (Caerdydd: University of Wales Press, 1992).

Lewis, Saunders, *Dramâu Saunders Lewis*, cyfrol 1, ed. Ioan M. Williams (Caerdydd: University of Wales Press, 1996).

Livingstone, David N., *The Geographical Tradition* (Oxford: Blackwells, 1992).

Llewellyn, Richard, *How Green Was My Valley* (1939; London: Penguin, 1991).

Lloyd, David, 'Arnold, Ferguson, Schiller: Aesthetic Culture and the Politics of Aesthetics', *Cultural Critique*, 2 (winter 1985–6), 139–52.

Lloyd, David, *Nationalism and Minor Literature: James Clarance Mangan and the Emergence of Irish Cultural Nationalism* (Berkeley: University of California Press, 1987).

Lloyd, D. Tecwyn, *Drych o Genedl* (Abertawe: Gwasg John Penry, 1987).

Lloyd, D. Tecwyn, *John Saunders Lewis: Y Gyfrol Gyntaf* (Dinbych: Gwasg Gee, 1988).

Lloyd-Morgan, Ceridwen, *Margiad Evans* (Bridgend: Seren, 1998).

Llwyd, Alan, *Cymru Ddu/Black Wales: A History* (Cardiff: Hughes a'i Fab, 2005).

Locke, Alain and Bernhard J. Stern (eds), *When Peoples Meet: A Study in Race and Culture Contacts* (New York: Progresive Educations Association, 1942).

Loomba, Ania, *Colonialism/Postcolonialism* (London: Routledge, 1998).

Lott, Eric, *Love and Theft: Blackface Minstrelsy and the American Working Class* (Oxford: Oxford University Press, 1993).

MacCabe, Colin, *James Joyce and the Revolution of the Word* (London: Macmillan, 1978).

McDevitt, P. F., *May the Best Man Win: Sport, Masculinity, and Nationalism in Great Britain and the Empire, 1880–1935* (London: Palgrave, 2008).

McGuinness, Patrick, '"Racism" in Welsh Politics', *Planet: The Welsh Internationalist*, 159 (June/July 2003), 7–12.

McWhiney, Grady, *Cracker Culture: Celtic Ways in the Old South* (Tuscaloosa: University of Alabama Press, 1988).

Mailer, Norman, 'The White Negro', in Ann Charters (ed.), *The Penguin Book of the Beats* (Harmondsworth: Penguin, 1993), pp. 582–605.

Mandler, Peter, '"Race" and "Nation" in Mid-Victorian Thought', in Stefan Collini, Richard Whatmore and Brian Young (eds), *History, Religion and Culture: British Intellectual History 1750–1950* (Cambridge: Cambridge University Press, 2000), pp. 224–44.

Mandler, Peter, *The English National Character: The History of an Idea from Edmund Burke to Tony Blair* (New Haven: Yale University Press, 2006).

Manning, Susan, *Fragments of Union: Making Connections in Scottish and American Writing* (London: Palgrave, 2002).

Marcuse, Herbert, 'The Affirmative Character of Culture', in *Negations: Essays in Critical Theory*, trans. Jeremy J. Shapiro (Boston: Beacon Press, 1968), pp. 88–133.

Margolick, David, *Beyond Glory: Max Schmeling vs. Joe Louis and a World on the Brink* (London: Bloomsbury, 2005).

Marqusee, Mike, *Redemption Song: Muhammad Ali and the Spirit of the Sixties* (London: Verso, 1999).

Martell, Owen, *Dyn yr Eiliad* (Llandysul: Gomer, 2003).

Marx, Karl, 'The British Rule in India', in Marx and Engels, *Basic Writings on Politics and Philosophy*, ed. Lewis Feuer (Garden City, NY: Anchor Books, 1959), pp. 511–18.

Maud, Ralph, *Where Have the Old Words Got Me? Explications of Dylan Thomas's Collected Poems* (Cardiff: University of Wales Press, 2003).

Michaels, Walter Benn, *Our America: Nativism, Modernism, and Pluralism* (Durham, NC: Duke University Press, 1995).

Michaels, Walter Benn, 'Race into Culture: A Critical Genealogy of Cultural Identity', in Henry Louis Gates, Jr. and K. Anthony Appiah (eds), *Identities* (Chicago: University of Chicago Press, 1995), pp. 32–62.

Michaels, Walter Benn, 'Plots against America: Neoliberalism and Antiracism', *American Literary History*, 18, 2 (2006), 288–302.

Michaels, Walter Benn, *The Trouble with Diversity: How We Learned to Love Identity and Ignore Inequality* (New York: Holt, 2006).

Miller, J. Hillis, *Poets of Reality: Six Twentieth-Century Writers* (Cambridge, MA: Harvard University Press, 1965).

Minhinnick, Robert, 'My·Petition to the Zoo Keeper', *Planet*, 90 (December 1991/January 1992), 13–17.

Minhinnick, Robert, 'Living with R. S. Thomas', *Poetry Wales*, 29, 1 (July 1993), 11–14.

Minhinnick, Robert, *After the Hurricane* (Manchester: Carcanet, 2002).

Minhinnick, Robert, *To Babel and Back* (Bridgend: Seren, 2005).

Moore-Gilbert, Bart, *Postcolonial Theory: Contexts, Practices, Politics* (London: Verso, 1997).

Morgan, D. Densil, *Pennar Davies: Dawn Dweud* (Cardiff: University of Wales Press, 2003).

Morgan, Prys, 'The Gwerin of Wales: Myth and Reality', in I. Hume and W. T. R. Pryce (eds), *The Welsh and their Country* (Llandysul: Gomer, 1986), pp. 134–52.

Morton, H. V., *In Search of Wales* (New York: Dodd, Mead, 1932).

Morton, Stephen, *Gayatri Chakravorty Spivak* (London: Routledge, 2003).

Moses, Wilson J., *Afrotopia: The Roots of African American Popular History* (Cambridge: Cambridge University Press, 1998).

Mulhern, Francis, *The Present Lasts a Long Time: Essays in Cultural Politics* (Cork: Cork University Press, 1998).

Mullen, Bill V. and James Smethurst, *Left of the Color Line: Race, Radicalism and the Twentieth-Century Literature of the United States* (Chapel Hill: University of North Carolina Press, 2003).

Nairn, Tom, *The Break-Up of Britain* (London: New Left Books, 1977).

Nairn, Tom, *Faces of Nationalism: Janus Revisited* (London: Verso, 1997).

Nairn, Tom (in conversation with Richard Wyn Jones), 'Ukanian Discussions and Homo Britannicus', in Gerry Hassan and Rosie Ilett (eds), *Radical Scotland: Arguments for Self-Determination* (Edinburgh: Luath Press Limited, 2011), pp. 267–81.

Nelson, Cary, *Revolutionary Memory: Recovering the Poetry of the American Left* (New York: Routledge, 2001).

Newton, Michael, *We're Indians Sure Enough: The Legacy of the Scottish Highlanders in the United States* (Chapel Hill: Saorsa Media, 2001).

Norris, Leslie, 'A Big Night' (1978), *The Collected Stories of Leslie Norris* (Bridgend: Seren, 1996), pp. 47–52.

Norris, Leslie, 'The Ballad of Billy Rose', in Meic Stephens (ed.), *Poetry 1900–2000* (Cardigan: Parthian, 2007), pp. 257–60.

North, Michael, *The Dialect of Modernism: Race, Language and Twentieth-Century Literature* (Oxford: Oxford University Press, 1994).

O'Leary, Paul, *Immigration and Integration: The Irish in Wales, 1798–1922* (Cardiff: University of Wales Press, 2000).

O'Meally, Robert G., *The Craft of Ralph Ellison* (Cambridge MA: Harvard University Press, 1980).

Osborne, Huw Edwin, *Rhys Davies* (Cardiff: University of Wales Press, 2009).

Owen, Daniel, *Gwen Tomos* (1894; Wresam: Hughes a'i Fab, 1967).

Paananen, Victor A., 'The Social Vision of Dylan Thomas', *Welsh Writing in English: A Yearbook of Critical Essays*, 8 (2003), 46–66.

Parker, Charlie, 'Now's the Time'. Savoy 2201. Master No. Take. S5851–4. 26 November 1945.

Parkinson, Thomas (ed.), *A Casebook on the Beat* (New York: Thomas Y. Crowell, 1961).

Parrinder, Patrick, *The Failure of Theory* (Brighton: Harvester, 1987).

Parry, Benita, 'A Critique Mishandled', *Social Text*, 35 (1993), 121–33.

Peterson, Dale E., *Up from Bondage: The Literatures of Russian and African American Soul* (Durham, NC: Duke University Press, 2000).

Phillips, M. and T. Phillips, *Windrush: The Irresistable Rise of Multi-racial Britain* (London: Harper Collins, 2000).

Pittock, Murray G. H., *Celtic Identity and the British Image* (Manchester: Manchester University Press, 1999).

Posgrove, Carol, *Divided Minds: American Intellectuals and the Civil Rights Movement* (New York: W. W. Norton, 2001).

Posnock, Ross, *Color and Culture: Black Writers and the Making of the Modern Intellectual* (Cambridge, MA: Harvard University Press, 1998).

Prendergast, Christopher (ed.), *Cultural Materialism: On Raymond Williams* (Minneapolis: University of Minnesota Press, 1995).

Prendergast, Christopher, 'Negotiating World Literature', *New Left Review II*, 8 (March/April 2001), 100–21.

Pritchard, Caradog, *Un Nos Ola Leuad*. Translated as *One Moonlit Night*. Bilingual edition (Harmondsworth: Penguin, 1999).

Reed, Ishmael, *Another Day at the Front: Dispatches from the Race War* (New York: Basic Books, 2003).

Rees, Ivor Thomas, *Saintly Enigma: A Biography of Pennar Davies* (Talybont: Y Lolfa, 2011).

Rexroth, Kenneth, 'Disengagement: The Art of the Beat Generation' (1959), in idem, *The Alternative Society* (New York: Herder and Herder, 1970), pp. 1–16.

Reynolds, David, *Rich Relations: The American Occupation of Britain 1942–1945* (London: Harper Collins, 1995).

Rice, Alan, *Radical Narratives of the Black Atlantic* (London: Continuum, 2003).

Roberts, Harri, *Embodying Identity: Representations of the Body in Welsh Literature* (Cardiff: University of Wales Press, 2009).

Roberts, Lowri (ed.), *Canu Clod y Campau: Detholiad o Farddoniaeth y Maes Chwarae* (Llanrwst: Gwasg Carreg Gwalch, 2009).

Roberts, Lynette, *Diaries, Letters, Recollections*, ed. Patrick McGuinness (Manchester: Carcanet Press, 2008).

Roberts, Randy, *Jack Dempsey: The Manassa Mauler* (London: Robson Books, 1987).

Roberts, Randy, *Joe Louis: Hard Times Man* (New Haven: Yale University Press, 2010).

Robeson, Paul, 'I Know the Irish People', *The Irish Democrat*, August 1949, 3.

Robeson, Paul, *Paul Robeson Speaks: Writings, Speeches, Interviews 1918–1974*, ed. Philip S. Foner (London: Quartet Books, 1978).

Robeson, Paul, *Here I Stand* (1958; Boston, Beacon Press, 1988).

Robeson, Jr., Paul, 'The Paul Robeson Files', *The Nation*, December 20 (1999), 9.

Roediger, David, *The Wages of Whiteness: Race and the Making of the American Working Class* (London: Verso, 1991).

Roethke, Theodore, *The Collected Poems* (New York: Anchor Books, 1975).

Rothkirch, Alyce Von and Daniel Williams (eds), *Beyond the Difference: Welsh Literature in Comparative Contexts* (Cardiff: University of Wales Press, 2004).

Russell, Ross, *Bird Lives: The High Life and Hard Times of Charlie (Yardbird) Parker* (1973; New York: Da Capo Press, 1996).

Said, Edward, *The World, The Text and the Critic* (Cambridge, MA: Harvard University Press, 1984).

Said, Edward, *Culture and Imperialism* (1993; London: Vintage, 1994).

Said, Edward, *Representations of the Intellectual* (New York: Pantheon Books, 1994).

Said, Edward, *Orientalism: Western Conceptions of the Orient* (1978; London: Penguin, 1995).

Saldívar, José David, *Border Matters: Remapping American Cultural Studies* (Berkeley: University of California Press, 1997).

Salinger, J. D., *The Catcher in the Rye* (New York: Little Brown, 1951).

Seton, Marie, *Paul Robeson* (London: Dobson, 1958).

Shapiro, Karl, 'Dylan Thomas (1955)', in E. W. Tedlock (ed.), *Dylan Thomas: The Legend and the Poet* (1960; London: Mercury Books, 1963), pp. 269–83.

Shapiro, Karl, *The Wild Card: Selected Poems, Early and Late* (Urbana: University of Illinois Press, 1998).

Shell, Marc, *Children of the Earth: Literature, Politics and Nationhood* (Oxford: Oxford University Press, 1993).

Shell, Marc, 'The Want of Incest in the Human Family, Or, Kin and Kind in Christian Thought', *Journal of the American Academy of Religion*, LXII, 3 (1995), 625–50.

Shell, Marc (ed.), *American Babel: Literatures of the United States from Abnaki to Zuni* (Cambridge, MA: Harvard University Press, 2002).

Shell, Marc, *Stutter* (Cambridge, MA: Harvard University Press, 2005).

Shepherd, Robert, *Enoch Powell* (London: Pimlico, 1996).

Simpson, Louis, *Studies of Dylan Thomas, Allen Ginsberg, Sylvia Plath and Robert Lowell* (London: Macmillan, 1978).

Sinclair, Neil, *The Tiger Bay Story* (Cardiff: Dragon and Tiger Enterprises, 1997).

Skvorecky, Josef, 'Red Music', Foreword to the English edition of *The Bass Saxophone* (1977; London: Vintage, 1994), pp. 9–31.

Smith, Dai (David), 'Myth and Meaning in the Literature of the South Wales Coalfield – the 1930s', *The Anglo-Welsh Review*, 25, 56 (1976), 21–42.

Smith, Dai (David), *Lewis Jones* (Cardiff: University of Wales Press, 1982).

Smith, Dai, *Wales! Wales?* (London: Allen and Unwin, 1984).

Smith, Dai, 'Relating to Wales', in Terry Eagleton (ed.), *Raymond Williams: Critical Perspectives* (Cambridge: Polity, 1989), pp. 34–53.

Smith, Dai, *Aneurin Bevan and the World of South Wales* (Cardiff: University of Wales Press, 1993).

Smith, Dai, *Wales: A Question for History* (Bridgend: Seren, 1999).

Smith, Dai, 'Psycho-colonialism', *New Welsh Review*, 66 (winter 2004), 22–9.

Smith, Dai, 'Call me Tommy: Tommy Farr the Tonypandy Kid', in Peter Stead and Gareth Williams (eds), *Wales and its Boxers: The Fighting Tradition* (Cardiff: University of Wales Press, 2008), pp. 87–100.

Snead, James A., *White Screens, Black Images: Hollywood from the Dark Side* (New York: Routledge, 1994).

Sollors, Werner, *Beyond Ethnicity: Consent and Descent in American Culture* (New York: Oxford University Press, 1986).

Sollors, Werner, 'A Critique of Pure Pluralism', in Sacvan Bercovitch (ed.), *Reconstructing American Literary History*, Harvard English Studies 13 (Cambridge, MA: Harvard University Press, 1986), pp. 250–79.

Sollors, Werner (ed.), *The Invention of Ethnicity* (Oxford: Oxford University Press, 1989).

Sollors, Werner, 'Anthropological and Sociological Tendencies in American Literature of the 1930s and 1940s: Richard Wright, Zora Neale Hurston and American Culture', in Steve Ickringill (ed.), *Looking Inward, Looking Outward: From the 1930s through the 1940s* (Amsterdam: VU University Press, 1990), pp. 22–75.

Sollors, Werner (ed.), *Theories of Ethnicity: A Classical Reader* (New York: New York University Press, 1996).

Sollors, Werner (ed.), *Multilingual America: Transnationalism, Ethnicity and the Languages of American Literature* (New York: New York University Press, 1998).

Sollors, Werner, *Ethnic Modernism* (Cambridge, MA: Harvard University Press, 2008).

Sollors, Werner, 'The Celtic Nations and the African Americas', *Comparative American Studies*, 8, 4 (2010), 316–22.

Sommer, Doris, *Proceed with Caution, When Engaged by Minority Writing in the Americas* (Cambridge, MA: Harvard University Press, 1999).

Sontag, Susan, 'Regarding the Torture of Others', *New York Times Magazine*, 23 May 2004, http://www.nytimes.com/2004/05/23/magazine/23PRISONS. html (accessed December 2007).

Spivak, Gayatri Chakravorty, 'Can the Subaltern Speak? Speculations on Widow Sacrifice', in Cary Nelson and Lawrence Grossberg (eds), *Marxism and the Interpretation of Culture* (London: Macmillan, 1988), pp. 271–313.

Stead, Peter, 'Wales in the Movies', in Tony Curtis (ed.), *Wales: The Imagined Nation* (Bridgend: Poetry Wales Press, 1986), pp. 159–79.

Stead, Peter and Gareth Williams (eds), *Wales and its Boxers: The Fighting Tradition* (Cardiff: University of Wales Press, 2008).

Stearns, Marshall, 'Unsex the Skeleton (1944)', in E. W. Tedlock, *Dylan Thomas: The Legend and the Poet* (London: Mercury Books, 1963), pp. 113–31.

Stearns, Marshall, 'Interview: Charlie Parker, Marshall Stearns, John Maher and Chan Parker' (1950), in Carl Woideck (ed.), *The Charlie Parker Companion* (New York: Schirmer Books, 1998).

Stepan, Nancy, *The Idea of Race in Science: Great Britain 1800–1960* (London: Macmillan, 1982).

Stephens, Meic (ed.), *The Bright Field: An Anthology of Contemporary Poetry from Wales* (Manchester: Carcanet, 1991).

Stephens, Meic (ed.), *Rhys Davies: Decoding the Hare* (Cardiff: University of Wales Press, 2001).

Stephens, Meic, *Rhys Davies: A Writers Life* (Cardigan: Parthian, 2013).

Stevens, Catrin, *Welsh Courting Customs* (Llandysul: Gomer, 1993).

Stocking, George, *The Ethnographer's Magic and Other Essays in the History of Anthropology* (Madison: University of Wisconsin Press, 1992).

Stradling, Robert, *Wales and the Spanish Civil War: The Dragon's Dearest Cause?* (Cardiff: University of Wales Press, 2004).

Stravinsky, Igor, 'The Opera that Might Have Been', *Adam: International Review*, 238 (1953), 8.

Stuckey, Sterling, *Slave Culture: Nationalist Theory and the Foundations of Black America* (Oxford: Oxford University Press, 1987).

Tallack, Douglas, *Twentieth-Century America: The Intellectual and Cultural Context* (London: Longman, 1991).

Tanner, Duncan, Chris Williams and Deian Hopkin (eds), *The Labour Party in Wales* (Cardiff: University of Wales Press, 2000).

Taylor, Billy, 'America's Classical Music', in Robert Walser (ed.), *Keeping Time: Readings in Jazz History* (Oxford: Oxford University Press, 1999), pp. 327–31.

Taylor, Helen, *Circling Dixie: Contemporary Southern Culture through a Transatlantic Lens* (New Brunswick: Rutgers University Press, 2001).

Thomas, David (ed.), *Dylan Remembered: Interviews by Colin Edwards, Vol. 1 1914–1934* (Bridgend: Seren, 2003).

Thomas, David (ed.), *Dylan Remembered: Interviews by Colin Edwards, Vol. 2 1935–1953* (Bridgend: Seren, 2004).

Thomas, Dylan, *Collected Poems 1934–1952*, ed. Walford Davies and Ralph Maud (1988; London: Everyman Library, 1989).

Thomas, Dylan, *Early Prose Works*, ed. Walford Davies (New York: New Directions, 1972).

Thomas, Dylan, *Under Milk Wood*, ed. Walford Davies and Ralph Maud (1954; London: Everyman, 1995).

Thomas, Dylan, *Collected Letters*, ed. Paul Ferris (1985; London: J. M. Dent, 2000).

Thomas, Dylan, *The Caedmon Collection* (Harper Audio, 2003).

Thomas, M. Wynn, 'Hanes dwy chwaer: olrhain hanes *Y Tri Llais*', *Barn* (Ionawr 1989), 23–5 and *Barn* (Ebrill 1989), 23–5.

Thomas, M. Wynn, *Internal Difference: Literature in 20th-Century Wales* (Cardiff: University of Wales Press, 1992).

Thomas, M. Wynn, 'Prints of Wales: Contemporary Welsh Poetry in English', in Lothar Fietz and Hans-Werner Ludwig (eds), *Poetry in the British Isles: Non-Metropolitan Perspectives* (Cardiff: University of Wales Press, 1995).

Thomas, M. Wynn, *Corresponding Cultures: The Two Literatures of Wales* (Cardiff: University of Wales Press, 1999).

Thomas, M. Wynn, (ed.), *Gweld Sêr: Cymru a Chanrif America* (Caerdydd: University of Wales Press, 2001).

Thomas, M. Wynn, 'Gwlad o Bosibiliadau: Golwg ar Lên Cymru ac America', *Y Traethodydd*, 157 (2002), 38–52.

Thomas, M. Wynn and Daniel Williams, '"A Sweet Union"? Dylan Thomas and Post-War American Poetry', in Gilbert Bennett, Eryl Jenkins and Eurwen Price (eds), *I Sang in My Chains: Essays and Poems in Tribute to Dylan Thomas* (Swansea: The Dylan Thomas Society of Great Britain, 2003), pp. 68–79.

Thomas, M. Wynn (ed.), *Welsh Writing in English: A Guide To Welsh Literature Volume VII* (Cardiff: University of Wales Press, 2003).

Thomas, M. Wynn, *In the Shadow of the Pulpit: Literature and Nonconformist Wales* (Cardiff: University of Wales Press, 2010).

Thomas, Ned, *The Welsh Extremist: A Culture in Crisis* (London: Gollancz, 1971).

Thomas, Ned, 'Renan, Arnold, Unamuno: Philology and the Minority Languages', *Bedford Occasional Papers: Essays in Language, Literature and Area Studies*, 6 (1984), 1–14.

Thomas, Ned, 'Images of Ourselves', in John Osmond (ed.), *The National Question Again: Welsh Political Identity in the 1980s* (Llandysul: Gomer Press, 1985), pp. 306–19.

Thomas, Ned, 'Parallels and Paradigms', in M. Wynn Thomas (ed.), *Welsh Writing in English: A Guide to Welsh Literature Volume VII* (Cardiff: University of Wales Press, 2003), pp. 310–26.

Thomas, Ned, Dai Smith and Daniel G. Williams, 'The Exchange: Raymond Williams', *Planet: The Welsh Internationalist* (summer 2009), 45–66.

Thomas, R. S., *The Bread of Truth* (London: Rupert Hart-Davies, 1963).

Thomas, R. S., *Selected Prose*, ed. Sarah Anstey (Bridgend: Poetry Wales Press, 1983).

Thomas, R. S., *Selected Poems* (Newcastle: Bloodaxe, 1986).

Thomas, R. S., *Welsh Airs* (Bridgend: Poetry Wales Press, 1987).

Thomas, R. S., *Cymru or Wales?* (Llandysul: Gomer, 1992).

Thomas, R. S., *No Truce with the Furies* (Newcastle upon Tyne: Bloodaxe Books, 1995).

Thompson, E. P., *The Making of the English Working Class* (1963; Harmondsworth: Penguin, 1968).

Thompson, Mark Christian, *Black Fascisms* (Charlottesville: University of Virginia Press, 2007).

Tindall, William York, *A Reader's Guide to Dylan Thomas* (Syracuse: Syracuse University Press, 1962).

Tomos, Angharad, *Hiraeth am Yfory: David Thomas a Mudiad Llafur Gogledd Cymru* (Llandysul: Gomer, 2002).

Toscano, Alberto, 'The Spectre of Anaolgy', *New Left Review II*, 66 (November/ December, 2010), 152–60.

Towns, Jeff (ed.), *A Pearl of Great Price: The Love Letters of Dylan Thomas to Pearl Kazin* (Cardigan: Parthian, 2014).

Trilling, Lionel, *Matthew Arnold* (1939; New York: Columbia University Press, 1949).

Trilling, Lionel, *The Liberal Imagination: Essays on Literature and Society* (1950; London: Frome and Tanner, 1951).

Unger, Roberto Mangabeira, *The Left Alternative* (London: Verso, 2005).

Viswanathan, Gauri, 'Raymond Williams and British Colonialism', in Christopher Prendergast (ed.), *Cultural Materialism: On Raymond Williams* (Minneapolis: University of Minnesota Press, 1995).

Wald, Alan M., *The New York Intellectuals: The Rise and Decline of the Anti-Stalinist Left from the 1930s to the 1980s* (Chapel Hill: University of North Carolina Press, 1987).

Wald, Alan M., 'Alfred Kazin in Retrospect', in idem, *Writing from the Left: New Essays on Radical Culture and Politics* (London: Verso, 1994), pp. 28–39.

Wald, Alan M., *Exiles from a Future Time: The Forging of the Mid-Twentieth-Century Left* (Chapel Hill: University of North Carolina Press, 2002).

Walsh, Louise, *Fighting Pretty* (Bridgend: Seren, 2008).

Watkins, Vernon (ed.), *Dylan Thomas: Letters to Vernon Watkins* (London: Faber, 1957).

Webb, Andrew, *Edward Thomas and World Literary Studies* (Cardiff: University of Wales Press, 2013).

Webb, Harri, *No Half Way House*, ed. Meic Stephens (Talybont: Y Lolfa, 1997).

West, Cornel, *The American Evasion of Philosophy: A Genealogy of Pragmatism* (Madison: University of Wisconsin Press, 1989).

West, Cornel, *Keeping Faith: Philosophy and Race in America* (London: Routledge, 1993).

West, Cornel, *Prophetic Thought in Postmodern Times* (Monroe: Common Courage Press, 1993).

Wigginton, Chris, *Modernism from the Margins: The 1930s Poetry of Louis MacNiece and Dylan Thomas* (Cardiff: University of Wales Press, 2007).

Williams, Charlotte, *Sugar and Slate* (Aberystwyth: Planet, 2002).

Williams, Charlotte, Paul O'Leary and Neil Evans, *A Tolerant Nation? Exploring Ethnic Diversity in Wales* (Cardiff: University of Wales Press, 2003).

Williams, Chris, *Democratic Rhondda: Politics and Society, 1855–1951* (Cardiff: University of Wales Press, 1996).

Williams, Chris, 'Problematizing Wales: An Exploration in Historiography and Postcoloniality', in Jane Aaron and Chris Williams (eds), *Postcolonial Wales* (Cardiff: University of Wales Press, 2005), pp. 3–17.

Williams, Daniel, 'Cymdeithas a Chenedl yng Ngwaith Raymond Williams', *Taliesin*, 97 (gwanwyn 1997), 55–76.

Williams, Daniel G., *Ethnicity and Cultural Authority: From Arnold to Du Bois* (Edinburgh: Edinburgh University Press, 2006).

Williams, Daniel G. (ed.), *Canu Caeth: Y Cymry a'r Affro-Americaniaid* (Llandysul: Gomer, 2010).

Williams, Daniel G., *Black Skin, Blue Books: African Americans and Wales 1845–1945* (Cardiff: University of Wales Press, 2012).

Williams, Gareth, *Valleys of Song: Music and Society in Wales 1840–1914* (Cardiff: University of Wales Press, 1998).

Williams, Gareth (ed.), *Sport* (Cardigan: Library of Wales, 2007).

Williams, Gwyn A., 'Mother Wales Get Off Me Back', *Marxism Today* (December 1981), 14–20.

Williams, Gwyn A., *The Welsh in their History* (London: Croom Helm, 1982).

Williams, Gwyn A., *When Was Wales? A History of the Welsh* (London: Black Raven Press, 1985).

Williams, Martin, 'Charlie Parker: The Burden of Innovation' (1970), in in Carl Woideck (ed.), *The Charlie Parker Companion: Six Decades of Commentary* (New York: Schirmer Books, 1998), pp. 10–23.

Williams, Raymond, *Second Generation* (London: Chatto and Windus, 1964).

Williams, Raymond, 'Dylan Thomas's Play for Voices', in C. B. Cox (ed.), *Dylan Thomas: A Collection of Critical Essays* (Englewood Cliffs, NJ: Prentice-Hall, 1966).

Williams, Raymond, 'Culture and Revolution: a Response', in Terry Eagleton a Brian Wicker (eds), *From Culture to Revolution* (London: Sheed and Ward, 1968), pp. 296–308.

Williams, Raymond, *The Long Revolution* (1961; Harmondsworth: Penguin, 1971).

Williams, Raymond, *Marxism and Literature* (Oxford: Oxford University Press, 1977).

Williams, Raymond, *Politics and Letters: Interviews with New Left Review* (London: Verso, 1979).

Williams, Raymond, *Culture* (London: Fontana, 1981).

Williams, Raymond, *Towards 2000* (London: Chatto and Windus, 1983).

Williams, Raymond, *The Country and the City* (1973; London: Hogarth Press, 1985).

Williams, Raymond, *Loyalties* (London: Hogarth Press, 1985).

Williams, Raymond, *Keywords: A Vocabulary of Culture and Society* (1976; London: Fontana, 1988).

Williams, Raymond, *The Politics of Modernism: Against the New Conformists*, ed. Tony Pinkney (London: Verso, 1989).

Williams, Raymond, *Culture and Society: Coleridge to Orwell* (1958; London: Hogarth Press, 1990).

Williams, Raymond, 'The Idea of Culture' (1953), in John McIlroy and Sallie Westwood (eds), *Raymond Williams in Adult Education* (Leicester: NIACE, 1993), pp. 57–77.

Williams, Raymond, *Problems in Materialism and Culture* (1980; London: Verso, 1997).

Williams, Raymond, 'All Things Betray Thee' (1986), in idem, *Who Speaks for Wales? Nation, Culture, Identity*, ed. Daniel Williams (Cardiff: Cardiff University Press, 2003), pp. 159–64.

Williams, Raymond, 'Community' (1985), in idem, *Who Speaks for Wales? Nation, Culture, Identity*, ed. Daniel Williams (Cardiff: Cardiff University Press, 2003), pp. 27–33.

Williams, Raymond, 'The Culture of Nations' (1983), in idem, *Who Speaks for Wales? Nation, Culture, Identity*, ed. Daniel Williams (Cardiff: University of Wales Press, 2003), pp. 191–203.

Williams, Raymond, 'The Importance of Community' (1977), in idem, *Who Speaks for Wales? Nation, Culture, Identity*, ed. Daniel Williams (Cardiff: Cardiff University Press, 2003), pp. 177–85.

Williams, Raymond, 'Marxism, Poetry, Wales: an interview with J. P. Ward' (1977), in idem, *Who Speaks for Wales? Nation, Culture, Identity*, ed. Daniel Williams (Cardiff: University of Wales Press, 2003), pp. 81–94.

Williams, Raymond, 'Remaking Welsh History' (1980), in idem, *Who Speaks for Wales? Nation, Culture, Identity*, ed. Daniel Williams (Cardiff: University of Wales Press, 2003), pp. 69–72.

Williams, Raymond, 'The Shadow of the Dragon' (1985), in idem, *Who Speaks for Wales? Nation, Culture, Identity*, ed. Daniel Williams (Cardiff: University of Wales Press, 2003), pp. 66–8.

Williams, Raymond, 'The Welsh Industrial Novel' (1979), in Daniel Williams (ed.), *Who Speaks for Wales? Nation, Culture, Identity* (Cardiff: University of Wales Press, 2003), pp. 95–111.

Williams, Raymond, 'West of Offa's Dyke' (1986), in idem, *Who Speaks for Wales? Nation, Culture, Identity*, ed. Daniel Williams (Cardiff: University of Wales Press, 2003), pp. 34–6.

Williams, Raymond, 'Who Speaks for Wales' (1971), in idem, *Who Speaks for Wales? Nation, Culture, Identity*, ed. Daniel Williams (Cardiff: University of Wales Press, 2003), pp. 3–4.

Williams, Raymond, *Who Speaks for Wales? Nation, Culture, Identity*, ed. Daniel Williams (Cardiff: University of Wales Press, 2003).

Williams, Raymond, 'Working-Class, Proletarian, Socialist' (1982), in idem, *Who Speaks for Wales? Nation, Culture, Identity*, ed. Daniel Williams (Cardiff: University of Wales Press, 2003), pp. 147–58.

Williams, Raymond, *Border Country* (1960; Cardigan: Parthian, 2006).

Wilson, William Julius, *The Declining Significance of Race: Blacks and changing American institutions* (Chicago: Chicago University Press, 1978).

Woideck, Carl (ed.), *The Charlie Parker Companion: Six Decades of Commentary* (New York: Schirmer Books, 1998).

Wright, Richard, *White Man, Listen!* (1957), in idem, *Black Power: Three Books from Exile* (New York: Harper Perennial, 2008).

X, Malcolm, *The Autobiography of Malcolm X* (as told to Alex Haley) (New York: Ballantine Books, 1964).

Yaffe, David, *Fascinating Rhythm: Reading Jazz in American Writing* (Princeton: Princeton University Press, 2006).

Yeats, W. B., *Autobiographies* (London: Macmillan, 1955).

Yeats, W. B., *Uncollected Prose Volume I*, ed. John P. Frayne (London: Macmillan, 1970).

Yeats, W. B., *Uncollected Prose Volume II*, ed. John P. Frayne and Colton Johnson (London: Macmillan, 1975).

Yeats, W. B., *The Collected Poems*, ed. R. Finneran (New York: Collier, 1989).

Young, Al, 'A Poem for Dylan Thomas', *Heaven: Collected Poems 1956–1990* (New York: Creative Arts Books Company, 1992).

Young, Al, 'The Dylan Thomas I Looked Up' (2002), in Jack Foley (ed.), *The Alsop Review*, http://www.alsopreview.com/foley/jfdthomas.html (accessed 18 June 2002).

Young, Robert J. C., *White Mythologies: Writing History and the West* (London: Routledge, 1990).

Young, Robert J. C., *Colonial Desire: Hybridity in Theory Culture and Race* (London: Routledge, 1995).

Young, Robert J. C., *Postcolonialism: An Historical Introduction* (Oxford: Blackwell, 2001).

Zinn, Howard, *A People's History of the United States 1492–Present* (1980; New York: Harper Collins, 1995).

Žižek, Slavoj, *Did Somebody Say Totalitarianism?* (London: Verso, 2001).

Žižek, Slavoj and Glyn Daly, *Conversations with Slavoj Žižek* (Cambridge: Polity Press, 2004).

Žižek, Slavoj, 'Notes towards a politics of Bartleby: the ignorance of chicken', *Comparative American Studies*, 4, 4 (December 2006), 375–94.

Žižek, Slavoj, *In Defense of Lost Causes* (London: Verso, 2008).

Zwerin, Michael, *The Case for the Balkanization of Practically Everyone* (London: Wildwood House, 1976).

Index